INVITATION TO POSSIBILITY-LAND

AF695158

INVITATION TO POSSIBILITY-LAND

An Intensive Teaching Seminar with Bill O'Hanlon

Bob Bertolino
and
Bill O'Hanlon

Routledge
Taylor & Francis Group
LONDON AND NEW YORK

INVITATION TO POSSIBILITY-LAND: An Intensive Teaching Seminar with Bill O'Hanlon

First published 1999 by
BRUNNER/MAZEL

Published 2014 by Routledge
2 Park Square, Milton Park, Abingdon, Oxfordshire, OX14 4RN
711 Third Avenue, New York, NY 10017

First issued in paperback 2014

Routledge is an imprint of the Taylor & Francis Group, an informa business

Copyright © 1999 Taylor & Francis. All rights reserved.
Except as permitted under the United States Copyright Act of 1976, no part of this publication may be reproduced or distributed in any form or by any means, or stored in a database or retrieval system, without the prior written permission of the publisher.

Edited by Edward A. Cilurso and Jean Anderson.

CIP catalog record for this book is available from the British Library.

Library of Congress Cataloging-in-Publication Data
Bertolino, Bob, 1965–
Invitation to possibility land: an intensive teaching seminar with Bill O'Hanlon / Bob, Bertolino, Bill O'Hanlon.
p. cm.
Includes bibliographical references and index.

1. Brief psychotherapy—Congresses. 2. Solution-focused therapy—Congresses.
3. O'Hanlon, William Hudson—Congresses.
I. O'Hanlon, William Hudson. II. Title
RC488.55.B47 1999 98-20700
616.89'14—dc21 CIP

ISBN 978-0-87630-875-2 (hbk)
ISBN 978-1-13800-506-8 (pbk)

Acknowledgments

Thanks and acknowledgment to Steffanie O'Hanlon for the original idea and for work on the project, corrections, and encouragement; to Mark Tracten at Brunner/Mazel for taking a chance on us; to the folks at Family Works and Brief Therapy Associates in Portland, Maine (Marilyn Bronzi, Robin McCarthy, Lynn Bromley, and associates) for providing the space and support for the seminar; to the participants and clients who made the week what it was, thank you for your openness and trust. Thanks also to Jennifer Neidner and Sara Wright for their comments on the manuscript.

A very special thank you to Kevin Thompson for his exhaustive assistance with the transcriptions used in this book. You fill up our diskettes.

Dedication

To Bob, for being detail oriented and for being the easiest and hardest-working coauthor imaginable. Let's do a few more books together, okay? And to my wife, Steffanie, for the permission and the possibilities.—B.O'H

To Bill, for helping me to open doorways and for friendship. And to my mother, Helen: The first and best teacher I ever had.—B. B.

Invitation to Possibility-Land
An Intensive Teaching Seminar with Bill O'Hanlon

Preface

For more than ten years Bill O'Hanlon has conducted small, intensive trainings with mental health professionals from all over the world. When I first met him in 1993, the wait to get into one of these groups was nearly a year. I wondered, what was so compelling that people would travel hundreds and sometimes thousands of miles, pay a significant group fee, travel expenses, and then spend a week with people they didn't know? I soon found out.

I was able to get into a group in the early summer of 1995, in Omaha, Nebraska. What I experienced during that week has remained with me since. I was captivated by a process that to this day I have found very difficult to describe. Despite this, what remains clear is that the experience was transformative. What I experienced has enriched my life and those of many others with whom I have talked.

Bill has a reputation as a clear and engaging presenter. Thousands have attended his one-, two-, and three-day workshops and have found them to be both educational and entertaining. However, his week-long and weekend intensives offer a different process. The small group format allows him to meet people at a more intimate and personal level. Thus what became clear is that this process should be shared with a larger audience. Bill and Steffanie agreed with this, and we talked for many months about how to go about such an endeavor. This book is a result of those conversations.

The content of this book is from a week-long training that was held at Brief Therapy Associates, Inc. in Portland, Maine during 1996 (Bertolino, 1998). Although it has been edited, the process has been preserved. Many areas that concern mental health professionals in the 1990s are included as well as actual sessions with clients and individual consultations. In addition, the book is lined with footnotes to provide the reader with further information on various topics and people mentioned throughout the training.

We hope you find this book to be an engaging and perhaps, transforming experience. It is the next best thing to "being there." Welcome to Possibility-Land!

Bob Bertolino
October 1997

Meet Bill O'Hanlon

Bill O'Hanlon, M.S., has authored or coauthored fourteen books and twenty-eight articles or book chapters. He has produced or coproduced six audiotapes, two computer programs, and several videotapes about therapy. His books have been translated into French, Spanish, Portuguese, Swedish, Finish, German, Chinese, and Japanese. Since 1977, Bill has taught over 600 therapy seminars around the world. Bill has been a top-rated presenter at several national conferences, including the Family Therapy Networker Symposium, The American Association for Marriage and Family Therapy Conference, two major Ericksonian conferences, and the Annual Cape Cod Symposium. He was a developer of brief solution-oriented therapy and is a contributor to Ericksonian therapy and collaborative/constructivist approaches. He is on the advisory board of *The Journal of Collaborative Therapies* and the International Association of Marriage and Family Counselors. Bill is a licensed mental health professional, certified professional counselor, and a licensed marriage and family therapist. He lives in Santa Fe, New Mexico.

INVITATION TO POSSIBILITY-LAND

Chapter 1

Welcome to Possibility-Land

This chapter includes the opening of the teaching seminar. Many of the participants have some background in Bill's work or with similar methods and ideas, but in Bill's introduction and in themselves the tone for the week is set. Many of the themes and concerns expressed this first day by participants are subsequently woven into the fabric of the seminar.

Introduction by Bill O'Hanlon

Hi. I'm Bill O'Hanlon. I've done these intensive trainings a lot before, and I stopped doing them. I got too busy in my life, but I actually love to do them. They're intense. They're a bit like those language immersion courses where you go and you speak this language and think this way for a while. In a workshop or a book I have to tie things in little neat packages and make it sequential and organized. In this setting we can put in a lot of the messy, wonderfully human, don't fit in the box aspects of the model, so you hopefully get the spirit of it rather than the methodology or the dogma. I also get to know people at a different level than I do at workshops, and you get to know each other. I used to call these things supervision groups but they're really not exactly supervision. I don't know, maybe advanced training, intensive training, consultation. It's a combination of a lot of things, and it's somewhat what you want to make it. I used to have more of an agenda of exactly what I would do and what I would cover, and the people in the groups just bent me in some way so that I stopped doing that. I started to trust that whatever needed to would emerge, would work, and it has. I think there's a particular way I have of thinking about therapy and doing therapy. Sometimes I do hypnotic things, sometimes I do nonhypnotic things, and sometimes I do brief therapy things and sometimes I don't do brief therapy things. So, it's going to be a mixture. I tell a lot of stories and that's partly how I do my teaching. I hope that's okay. It will be woven in.

The structure I generally have for the week, although I'm flexible about this and we can make whatever arrangements we want to, is that I'll do this little introduction that I'm doing now, and then I'll want everyone to meet each other. Just introduce yourselves, say what brings you here, what you're interested in, how come you gave up a week of your time. Some of you made extremely great efforts and financial sacrifices to be here. From that I'll find out what you want for the week and that will somewhat shape what we do. In addition, the week will be a combination of talking about therapy, practicing particular skills that anybody wants to know or all of you want to know, and observing sessions. There'll also be clients. I think four are scheduled right now. I used to schedule a lot more clients, but then people complained that while it's really valuable, it takes away from other activities. So, four is the maximum. We can also talk about some of your cases. In addition, every once in a while I'll check in with all of you and find out what's coming across and what you still need to know. Near the end of the week what I'd like to do is make individual consultation time available for all of you.

Opening Doors

I play guitar, and I went to a master seminar with a great guitar player. And he said, "What I want to know is: What's the door for you? Where do you come to and there's a closed door? You see the door and you know there's something beyond the door, but you haven't gotten it open yet." During this seminar, we'll at least open the door and probably get you through. Hopefully that's what the whole week is about, but we can focus more specifically on it during individual times, and/or you can have a personal experience. We'll be doing some hypnosis during the week, and some of you will choose to have that experience. For some people that turns out to be the thing that brings the whole week together in a very profound experience, but some people choose not to do anything personal. When you're having that individual consultation time, other people will be observing, but they won't be participating in the dialogue until afterward and then we'll have them comment or ask questions. Usually that turns out to be a pretty profound aspect of the week. So, that's what I have planned. If you don't want to participate in that, that's okay too. You can always opt out. That's what I have on the agenda.

Mission Statement: Respectful and Effective

I'll say a little more about what this work is about, because every time I say it it's a bit different. I think it's good to set the thinking and the basic sensibility for the week. Some of you may have heard me say this, but I wrote a mission statement for my work a couple years ago. I was extremely surprised, because earlier in my career I went through various phases, of really being excited about a particular kind of therapy, and I went through lots. But for a while, when I first started teaching and writing, I was identified as an *Ericksonian*[1] therapist because I studied with Milton Erickson.[2] Then I was identified as a brief therapist or *solution-oriented*[3] therapist. When I wrote my mission statement it had nothing to do with any of those things. I've been identified as transpersonal and humanistic and other stuff in the past. The mission statement is, I'm interested in promoting effective and respectful approaches to therapy and really standing against and opposing disrespectful and ineffective approaches . . . so that means that if someone does an approach to therapy (that is disrespectful or ineffective), even in the name of brief therapy or solution-oriented . . . things that I've been identified with . . or Ericksonian therapy, then I would really be upset by that.

I was at the *Therapeutic Conversations*[4] conference in Denver, and there was a cleaning up at the end of the day at this "Co-Creating a Conference."[5] This woman spoke up and said, "You know, in my small group I was talking about how I do long-term therapy, and I got a very negative reaction from people because most people here do brief therapy. They were really critical of what I was doing. Now I just feel like maybe this isn't the place for me and I need to leave." I was so upset hearing that that I got up and told about how I had been seeing one of my clients for twelve years and I'm a brief therapist, and I've written all these books on brief therapy. It just pisses me off that someone would do that. (I said to her) "Tell them to come and talk to me and I'll set them straight." I spent so many years trying to get respect for brief therapy and I was often attacked by people who thought it was shallow and disrespectful to do brief therapy, so I don't want to see it go the other way. I think there are times when brief therapy is appropriate and not used because someone hasn't updated their beliefs yet, and times when it's disrespectful to do that. Both. So that's what I hope happens this week. This sense of flexibility comes across. The other thing is that the kind of approaches that I've been writing about and talking about are very directive in some ways. They're leading, they're change oriented, so it's important to balance that with acknowledgment and validation of people and really staying with people. The *MRI*[6] people that do brief therapy used to

[1] see O'Hanlon, B., & Bertolino, B. (in press).

[2] Milton Erickson (1901–1980) was a psychiatrist who was renown for his success with extremely difficult cases. His methods were often considered unorthodox and unconventional, thus subjecting him to both acclaim and criticism. One of Erickson's most significant contributions to the field of mental health was his creative and innovative use of clinical hypnosis. Dozens of books have been written about Dr. Erickson and his work, many of which were by his former students, such as Bill O'Hanlon. For a biographical sketch of Erickson's life see, Rossi, E. L., Ryan, M. O., & Sharp, F. A. (Eds.) (1983a).

[3] Bill (along with Michele Weiner-Davis) is considered the codeveloper of *solution-oriented* therapy.

[4] *Therapeutic Conversations III* was held June 27–30, 1996, in Denver, Colorado.

[5] The "Co-Creating a Conference" sessions at *Therapeutic Conversations III* took place at the end of each day. The idea was to break the distinction between "expert" faculty and "nonexpert" attendees. During these sessions faculty and attendees became involved in dialogues around their experiences at the conference.

[6] The Mental Research Institute (MRI) is located in Palo Alto, California.

say, "If you want to do brief therapy, you've got to remember the first principle of brief therapy; go slowly." It's a weird thing to say, but you have to be, I think, much better at developing relationships if you do briefer therapies. You really have to be in there with people or they're going to feel dismissed, unheard, and invalidated, or maybe they will go along with you but probably not. They may actually be pretty uncooperative or just leave, assuming that you can't get it. It's really important to balance those two aspects, the acknowledgment and validation with the possibilities for change. Both. At *Therapeutic Conversations*, sometimes the dogma is, "The client is always the expert, and you've got to tap into their expertise." Yes, and the therapist is also the expert. We know a lot of stuff. We have studied. So, we're going to be talking about how to bring your personal expertise, your life expertise, as well as your professional expertise in a way that doesn't impose on clients, and in a way that tends to make therapy brief and *solution-oriented, possibility-oriented*, or *inclusive*.

I've done these groups before, and I really have learned to trust the process. In my workshops I have a one, two, three, four, five process, and my handouts are very much like that. I like to teach in a very sequential, structured way, and I've absolutely given that up for these groups. Trust me that it will unfold as it does. There's something that's going to get into your bones here. So that's a general introduction. I would like to meet people and find out some basics: What is your name? Where do you work? Where are you from? What kind of work do you do? and, What brought you to this particular room for this particular week? Well go around the North American way, clockwise (*points to his left*). (*laughter*) We'll go around the South American way sometimes! (*more laughter*)

Group Member Introductions[7]

Lisa: My name is Lisa. I work in children's services as a family therapist for a home-based family preservation program. I got introduced to solution-oriented work through Steffanie.[8] She was coming in to do seminars and we really liked it a lot, and started to use it about two years ago with the families that we work with. So that's how I came to be here. I heard wonderful things about you; they were saying, "You have to go!" (*laughter*) I just had a baby four months ago. (*congratulations are extended from around the room*) So I'm having a hard time not thinking about him because this is the longest I have been away from him. Forgive me if sometimes I'm wanting to call to see if he's rolling over or doing something! (*laughter*) I'm trying to get into being myself, and rediscovering "Me," as opposed to "Mom," that role that I've been focusing on for almost

[7] Over the years people from around the world have attended intensive supervision/training weeks and weekends with Bill. These intensives have included participants from Australia, Canada, England, France, Japan, Russia, and the United States. The Portland, Maine, group was composed of Americans including nine women and one man from seven different states.

[8] Steffanie O'Hanlon is Bill's wife and a talented clinician, teacher, author, and editor.

a year now. This is a new thing to take time for myself, my career, and my own interests.

Bill: Thanks for making that sacrifice. I have to tell you a story. A guy came up to me at a presentation that I did some years ago. It was the first ever on solution-oriented therapy and it was called, "A Megatrend in Psychotherapy."[9] It was at the Erickson conference in 1986, and he was a psychodynamic therapist who had an interest in Erickson, so he was going that direction. He heard the presentation in which I laid out the ideas of, "Focus much more on what people are good at, and their resources, and their abilities, and you create that kind of sense with people when you do that." He came up afterward and said, "You know, I've just got to tell you I listened to your talk and I'm very disturbed." And I said, "Why?" He said, "Well, I have a sense that what you're saying is right, and if it's right, what I know is wrong. The way I've been trained is wrong and I have to make a big change. That's really upsetting!" I said, "Well, I don't think you have to make that big a change!" I was kind of minimizing it. And he said, "No, no, it's really a big change and I have a sense that this is the direction I've got to go, but I'm really upset." Through the years I kept in touch with him and he really did convert. He went to Milwaukee and spent some weeks in a supervision group with Steve de Shazer and Insoo Berg.[10] He came back and said, "That stuff is really great, but the problem is I've got this private practice, it's in the suburbs of Cleveland and it's kind of yuppie, middle class. They want analytic and psychodynamic stuff. And here, I'm moving in this direction and they're not going with it. I just don't think this stuff works with that population. It works great with that population that de Shazer and Insoo Berg work with, the homeless, the Title 19 folks, the family preservation folks. It doesn't work well with the folks I see." And I said, "Do you know where I work? I work in an upper middle class clinic in which people come in voluntarily, most of the time. It's a private practice." He said, "This stuff works with them?" I said, "Yeah." I love to hear that story from people, because what I typically hear is the other side of the story. It's like, "Oh yeah, this is fine with the yuppies, but I work with the really chronic, difficult families!" (*laughter*) If you work with that population you need to use this stuff because people are typically not so cooperative in going back to their childhoods and examining everything. Occasionally they are, but I think they really do appreciate this focus, and it becomes much more of a partnership. It's really taken off in family preservation.

[9] Bill's presentation, *Solution-Oriented Therapy: A Megatrend in Psychotherapy* took place at the Third International Congress on Ericksonian Approaches to Hypnosis and Psychotherapy held in Phoenix, Arizona, December 3–7, 1986. See O'Hanlon (1988).

[10] Steve de Shazer is considered the developer of *solution-focused* therapy. He has written numerous books and articles on the approach. Insoo Kim Berg has written on the use of solution-focused therapy with alcohol abuse and in home, family-based services. Both are located at the Brief Family Therapy Center (BFTC) in Milwaukee, Wisconsin.

Lisa: I do find that it works well with most of the families I work with.

Bill: Most. And that's the key. We're going to be talking about that this week. Good. (*looks toward Debbie*)

Debbie: My name is Debbie, and this is my sister's office. I work with kids and adults . . . low income population. I graduated from Simmons, which is a psychodynamic-oriented program. Laurie (another participant) was also there. So, I've just been practicing a couple of years. Before I went into social work, I was an outdoor leader for fifteen years, and ran a program doing outdoor trips for women. I'm finding myself trying to get back there. I'm not sure how solution-oriented fits into that, but I'll be interested to see if there is some kind of match.

Bill: I had someone come to the group who did that, mostly in management . . . outward bound, team-building kind of things. He videotaped one of the sessions he did and brought it. We found lots of places where he could move in a more solution-oriented direction.

Debbie: That's good to know. (*Debbie looks to Megan, who is on her left*)

Megan: I'm Megan. I won't be graduating with my master's degree until next month. I'm working two populations: private practice and court mandated. We call them HRS, which is like family preservation, so I get to see both sides. A professor at my university has been teaching us quite a lot of your stuff. I started playing on the Internet a couple of months ago (looks to Bill) and found all of your information. I just said, "I've got to go there!"

Bill: That's great!

Megan: And I also feel like I just kind of need to get thrown into it. Especially now, since my supervisor has been strategic. I'm kind of really fighting with the opposite stuff that I've been seeing and hearing and that I'm disturbed by.

Bill: I'll just tell you a quick story about that. I did supervision for some years with a guy who was trained by Haley and Madanes,[11] very strategic. Then he had another supervisor who was also trained by them, so he was really into that philosophy. He asked me for supervision to learn solution-oriented therapy. We did phone supervision for a couple of years. And in almost every case that he talked about, the parents had some problem that the kid's symptom was a reflection of. It was a metaphor. This is a typical strategic idea: that kids' problems

[11] Jay Haley (along with Don Jackson, John Weakland, and Willian Fry) was part of the Gregory Bateson research project on communication and is considered the developer of *strategic* family therapy. In addition to authoring and coauthoring numerous books on this approach, he has written about the work of Milton H. Erickson, M.D., and the training and supervision of therapists. Haley is the former codirector of the Family Therapy Institute of Washington, D.C. Cloé Madanes has been an innovator of the strategic approach to therapy. She has written on the subject including its application to abusive relationships. She is the current director of the Family Therapy Institute of Washington, D.C.

are always benevolently protective and they are metaphors for one or both of the parents' problems or concerns. For example, the kid wasn't finishing his homework and Dad wasn't finishing projects that he needed to finish at work and was about to get fired. I said, "It's uncanny that with every case you could find this issue of the child's problem being a metaphor for the parents, because it's not in every case of mine." He would then of course go about treating it in the strategic therapy way. I told him that if I had this idea about the situation (which I typically wouldn't), I might say, "You know, Dad, it seems to me that you have some expertise in helping your son get over this problem, because there must be times when even though you haven't finished a lot of your projects, you've finished a project. How have you done that? I'm really interested because that's one of the things it seems you need to model for your son right now who's not finishing his homework. Can you articulate what that is? Can you see if you can show it to him a little more? Can you articulate it to your son or even to us while we're all sitting here?" After many times of refocusing the supervisee like that, he said, "I get it. It's the metaphorical solution, not the metaphorical problem that we're going to work on." That's right. You go for the metaphorical resources. I think a lot of things that go on in strategic therapy are similar to what we'll be talking about here. There's something that's bothered me about the interactional, brief therapy approach at the MRI and about strategic therapy. It's this idea that the therapist has to maneuver the client in a particular direction because they don't want to change and are resistant. So you have to trick them into it. I don't think that trickiness is a necessity in those approaches, but they have that tradition and flavor. It reminds me of when I first learned Erickson's work and the people who studied with him. They would almost always say, "Do hypnosis, but once you do hypnosis, do not tell the person what you did in hypnosis. Give them amnesia . . . because if you tell them they're going to be resistant. Their conscious minds are where their resistance is, so don't let their conscious minds in on it." That always seemed creepy to me. You would put a person in trance, do something to them, and then bring them out and not let them know what it was . . . if they didn't remember themselves. I would say, "How was that?" And they would say, "Why did you ask that?" or, "What was this about . . . I had this experience?" And I would talk to them about it and explain what I knew and what made sense to me. It didn't seem to mess up the change process. I think there's a little bit of mistrust of the clients or the patients in these kinds of therapies that I don't think is warranted. I think it came out of this other paradigm that therapists sometimes have to be in opposition with client's resistance. So those are the parts that I don't love about those other approaches; otherwise, there's a lot of compatibility. There's not that much difference in the basic maneuvers, just a slightly different emphasis and a different assumption about the nature of client's resistance.

The other thing is a story about Jay Haley, a person whose work I greatly admire and have been influenced by. I was teaching the same week he was in Cape Cod and we went to dinner. I had read an interview and I asked him about it. He had said in the interview that he hasn't seen clients or patients for something like fifteen or twenty years. He's only done supervision through the one-way mirror, and he's great at it. That revelation really disturbed me, because I go out and teach workshops and I find that actually sitting in the room with people is crucial to me. Because when I go teach a workshop, it sounds great, but then sitting in the therapy room, it isn't quite so easy. It isn't quite so black and white and all put together neatly. It's in your face and doesn't always go well. I learned the most from that. So I was thinking, "Gosh, how does he learn from just supervision? Supervision is a lot easier." (*laughter*) Of course it's hard to do therapy, but that's what I like about it because that's how I get challenged and grow. In supervision, you get to stand behind the one-way mirror and make these wonderful pronouncements and usually they work. They don't always work, but it's much easier to be behind the one-way mirror than to actually be right on the front line. It's a little disturbing to me to have a theory that starts to drift away from the actual experience of the therapist. I worry about that trend. I know Cloé Madanes still sees clients occasionally. I think that's important. She's started to change her description of what she does, I think in part because she still sees people. (*looks to Katy*)

Katy: I'm Katy. I went to the University of New England and I got my master's in social work about a year ago. Then I moved back home and worked for a community mental health center. Where I live we have a lot of people from community mental health in the schools. Primarily I'm in one school. It's been a challenge for me. I'm running my program. It's the first year in the program and the school just purchased this contract, so it's sort of like I'm on my own.

Bill: Thrown into the deep end!

Katy: Yeah! Which is okay. I really love to be able to decide what I'm going to do and how I'm going to do it. But I'm trying to accommodate all of the kids, so I've never had a waiting list. It's different with kids. The clients I had in school (college) were voluntary and they knew why they were coming in. Now, I work K–12 so I have a big age range. They usually have some idea why they're there, but it's not always their idea. Sometimes the child is not the client—it may be a teacher or a whole system. I'm trying to do family work too, but it's not happening as much as I would like it to. I've been working real hard this year to do the things that I know are right. I haven't found people in my agency who think the way I do, so it's nice to be here with people who are thinking similarly. So there's a lot of things I could talk about and that will come out during the week. I think I start off really well, but I'm finding that I'm not letting kids go. There've been issues around Medicaid and having enough kids to see so that the contract will fly—that it can still be there for another year and the school can have the services. I think that's been an ethical dilemma for me.

Bill: Sure.

Katy: I needed to have the numbers and they said, "This ten kids isn't going to cut it." I have enough now. I have about thirty-five kids that I see—that's a lot actually, but it doesn't leave me a lot of time. Sometimes I just have kids in and out, in and out. I've tried to leave ten minutes for paperwork, but I think the piece about "where does it end?" is getting to be a problem with me! (*laughter*)

Bill: Yeah! That's the door.

Katy: The other piece is that the child can do so much and then I can't, without working with the family, have an effect on their living environment. They're still in the same situation and maybe it's the same as when they were referred. The child is maybe doing a little bit better with it, but the whole picture hasn't really changed a lot. That's where I'm at.

Bill: Great. I have some ideas about that. And the program you went to really gave a good background for this too.

Katy: Yeah. I feel like I have a good base. It's helpful for me to have some sort of ongoing maintenance for my ideas and development. I'm not around that very much.

Bill: Yeah. Recharge those batteries and get some new ideas.

Alice: My name is Alice. I feel like the old-timer so far. . . I've been in private practice for 15 years . . . and I'm the general practice, eclectic, wishy-washy . . .

Bill: . . . We'll fix that!

Alice: And, I'm here as part of a total life transition. Actually, I probably shouldn't be here because so much is going on, but I may as well take advantage and do everything! I'm in the midst of negotiating a divorce, selling my house myself, having a house built, refinancing the office condo and business, dissolving the business partnership, and switching over from full-time practice which is sort of (*makes a whistling noise and points downward*) because of managed care, to part-time practice and part-time teaching. I saw Bill at a workshop last October, and then again last spring and I was thinking, "I need something clinical. I need a shot in the arm!" And I said, "This is going to be it. This is going to be what I need." So, I don't have any problem opening doors, it's closing them! (*laughter*)

Bill: That's your door! That's the eclectic wishy-washy. It sounds like you're closing a few doors! (*laughter*) And, getting some new ones built.

Alice: I recently asked myself the *miracle question.*[12] I said, "Okay, what do I really want? If everything could be the way I want it, what do I really want?" And I'm in the process of doing it.

[12] *The miracle question* was developed at the BFTC. It is often used in the first session, and there are several variations. The general version is, "Suppose that one night, while you were asleep, there was a miracle and this problem was solved. How would you know? What would be different?" (p. 5). See de Shazer, S. (1988).

Bill: Making that vision happen. That's great. We'll hopefully make this week a part of the contribution to that process . . . that starts to settle things or unsettle things in a way that you want to and close the doors that you want to close. I actually have noticed this and I don't usually say it, but a fair amount of people come to the supervision group and do make major life shifts afterwards . . . and some don't! (*laughter throughout the room*) I guess I explain it in part because many of you have come all this way and spent some money to be here and in part because you are in an entirely different place. When I go overseas, I get a bird's eye view on my life. It's like you get caught up in the "everyday," and all of the sudden you get lifted out of your everyday life into a totally different environment. It's very supportive, very fun, very nice, and things become highlighted sometimes and you may realize, "Wait a minute, something's not right here. I need to make some changes." Sometimes people are seeking it because there are other things going on, and they feel the need for that. I've just noticed that people start to make significant shifts . . . out of public agencies into private practice; out of relationship stuff they're going through into something else; out of full-time practice into "I want to teach workshops" or teach at a university or write or whatever it may be. They start to make these shifts or it's part and parcel of making these shifts. It's great. Bring any of that stuff you want in during the week. I have ideas about that stuff.

I'll just tell you a quick story. Michael Hoyt,[13] whom I saw in Denver just before I came here, was in Cape Cod about five years ago now and came to the workshop I did on marital therapy. He said, "Can I take you to lunch?" I knew who he was; we had corresponded. So we went out to lunch and he said, "I want to do what you do. I want to travel internationally. I want to do workshops." I said, "Fine." He said, "How do I do it?" I said, "Well, you do this, this, this, this, this, and this. Here's how I would do it if I were you, and here's how I did it. I made a lot of mistakes and I learned something from them." About three years later somebody came up to me at a conference in Minneapolis and said, "I want to go to lunch with you!" (*laughter*) (I said) "Why?" He said, "Michael Hoyt said he went to lunch with you and now he's an international workshop leader. I want to do that!" (I said) "I'm busy. I don't have time for lunch this time, but you can call me on the phone." So I have some ideas about writing, career changes, and other things.

Alice: Well, plant some seeds. I'm fertile ground! (*laughter*)

Bill: It's change time. That's great! I've written nine books and have three more in progress. When somebody tells me about an idea they have, I'll say, "Ah, there's a book in that," and they'll look at me like I'm crazy. "What do you mean, there's a book in that for me?" Writing a book is a hard thing to do in

[13] Michael Hoyt, Ph.D., is the Director of Adult Psychiatric Services at the Kaiser Permanente Medical Center, Hayward, California. He is widely published on brief therapy and related topics.

some ways, but it's a fairly easy thing to do too, it's just intimidating for some people, so I have ideas about how to make it easier and less intimidating.

Paul: My name is Paul. I work at an agency in New York doing school intervention. I go into schools and work with children who are having difficulties that are identified by their school administration or a teacher. Then I usually end up working with the family. I was trained in the systems approach and family-of-origin, and that was two years of training, but I always felt a little unsure about that. I didn't feel comfortable with that. About two years ago, after the training, I went to see Insoo Berg at a workshop and that got me so excited about this I went to Milwaukee and spent a week there with Steve de Shazer and Insoo Berg. I came out of there thinking brief *solution-focused* therapy was the only therapy that was worthwhile. They warned me that fellow employees wouldn't be open to it. But I talked it up anyhow, and there was a great response. Since then, though, initial response has dwindled away and I'm back into the family-of-origin kind of thing. I do use *solution-focused* quite a bit, but I want to learn how to do it better. I've been to a lot of your workshops in Syracuse and various places. So I'm here to go the next step. I'm thinking about private practice and I'm trying to set up a network around brief therapy. I've also made a lot of changes in my life. Up until six years ago I wasn't doing this kind of work at all. I was in administration in a nursing home. Before that I was a clergyman. I feel like in my mid-50s, I'm still moving around and looking for change. I've done a lot of reading. I'm sort of "in my head." I read all kinds of stuff. My wife and I sit in our living room behind our stacks of books. I love that, but I want to move on to committing myself to this because I think there's a part of me that hasn't really.

Bill: We'll get it in the bones and in the guts.

Laurie: My name is Laurie. About five months ago I took what I consider to be a "flying leap," which was leaving the security of a mental health center and went out on my own in private practice. I have a private practice and I'm affiliated with a group practice on an as-needed basis. I do a lot of guardian ad liedum work in the probate courts, well in all courts. I've also been working at a psychiatric hospital every other weekend. That would describe my wings, how it was possible for me to take off and do this. I'm really enjoying my journey. I find it very exciting, the learning piece. I'm trying to fit a theoretical frame and yet be responsive to me and my style. I think that's why I was drawn to this. I went to a seminar with Bill this spring, which was a nice, "Ah-hah" for me. It dove-tailed an academic year I spent at *Cambridge Family Institute.*[14] And there's something for me that hooks into a more creative side . . . flexible. It's like I'm building my little bag of tricks, well they aren't really tricks, and my practice is eclectic much like Alice's. I see all ages, couples, and families, so I

[14]The Family Institute of Cambridge is located in Watertown, Massachusetts.

feel that all of these things are building in my little resource bag, so that when I'm sitting with somebody I can draw on these different things, so it isn't a specific theoretical thing but I'm building something through which I can be the vehicle to use these things and then hook into what I see as the creative process within the individual whom I'm with. I oftentimes think about people as if they have a funnel and they've got the broad end on their face (*puts her hands near her face and expands them to demonstrate wideness*) and narrowed down to this little (*moves her hands to show the narrowing of a funnel*). That's how they're seeing the world—through a little hole. And I like to have them turn it around and see the opportunities and the possibilities. It's interesting because I sort of carry my notes from Cambridge Family on couples around with me. They're sort of like my little "suckie." (*laughter*) There's a certain security because I can go back and refresh and remember all the different ways that we were able to connect because not everybody is going to be responsive to "one-way." So it's important to be sensitive to what you get from the client and try to use what you're learning. So I'm here to learn more. Also, the language and questioning and to be able to draw people out, what are their strengths, how you are you going do it? That's where I'm at.

Bill: I really do like to raise consciousness about language. And one of the consciousnesses I like to raise is about metaphors. Before I left home I was listening to a tape that an acquaintance of mine whom I saw in Denver gave me and it was all about metaphorical frames. (*looks to Laurie*) You had four metaphorical frames that you were using at the same time . . . eclectic, very eclectic metaphorical frames . . . just to raise your awareness of listening to people in terms of the metaphors that they use. You said you were *building* something . . . to put in a *bag* . . . it's a little bit of a mixed metaphor . . . because you wanted to *hook* into that creativity . . . "hook" is like a different metaphor and . . . is a *vehicle* for going someplace. (*laughter*) Wow! That's a lot of metaphors at once! They're all different metaphors and they can lead in different directions. So you have a lot of metaphors. We're going to give you a meta-metaphor! (*laughter*) When there's all those metaphors, to be able to find a way to have a coherence to the metaphorical frames. That's going to be one of the language awareness for the whole week for everybody. What are you saying and what are the implications of what you're saying and could you say it in a way that really reflects what you intend? And also listen to the clients and what they're saying and use that. Language is very important.

Beth: My name is Beth. I know Laurie. We worked in the same mental health center for a while. I have been gone from there for about a year now. I was there for a couple of years working in children family services there. Prior to that I worked in a school for emotionally handicapped kids. Currently I have my private practice and I also do some per diem work at a psychiatric hospital. I feel like I'm in a transitional phase in terms of the work that I do. I'm looking for a place to hang my hat, a place to go, a place that feels comfortable. I think one of the things that attracted me to this seminar was I attended that thing that you did in the spring and I was just finishing up a year at the Cambridge Family Institute, in their narrative therapy program. Prior to that, I had done a year long training at . . . I can't even remember the name of the place . . . but it's the existential, phenomenological, dialectic institute in Newton, Massachusetts. Anyway, that turned me onto the soul of an existential, possibilities kind of thing. I hadn't really found a place to put that or a way to use that and then here you are with your possibilities and also using some of the narrative language framework, and it felt very cohesive to me, and so I wanted more of that.

Bill: Good. All right.

Denise: I'm Denise. I work at a medical university in the department of psychiatry which is a very traditional, biologically oriented place. My job is pretty multidimensional. I work primarily on an inpatient unit for adults, most of whom are chronically mentally ill. I work with the families and I work with medical students and residents in teaching them about family therapy and family dynamics. I have an advantage of being able to do pretty much as little or as much outpatient work as I want to do. I've been asked in the past couple of years to work with psychiatry residents teaching them about brief therapy, which has been real interesting. It seems that everybody has really gotten it. Managed care is just beginning to breathe down our necks. It's been everywhere else, but it's just becoming a reality where I live. Also, I did some training with Michele Weiner-Davis[15] and because of having gone out and sought training in brief therapy I've become known as sort of the brief therapy expert in the institute, which is a little frightening! *(laughter)* But it was only because I'd had the only exposure for a long time and continue to have the most training of anybody around. Because of that people take me more seriously now that everybody's getting on board with it. Teaching has become something that I really enjoy doing and I'm doing some supervision with residents. Generally, residents seek out their supervisors and they usually do it based on a particular patient that they get, so they come to me with somebody that they think this will really work for. I'm in the category of, "It's a whole lot easier to teach it and to supervise it than it is to do it!" Which is one of the reasons why I'm here. I've actually been trying for years to get to one of your workshops or trainings. Michele said that you were like, "The funniest person in the world!" *(laughter)*

Bill: I'll make you laugh while you learn. Thank you, Michele, that's great!

Karen: I'm Karen. I work at the same department at the medical university. What we do is a little different. I do a lot of research there and I'm able to see outpatients too. The folks I've been seeing are adults, a lot of geriatrics. I went

[15] Michele Weiner-Davis was coauthor of Bill's. See O'Hanlon and Weiner-Davis (1989). She has published extensively on brief therapy and working with couples. Michele resides in Woodstock, Illinois.

to a workshop with Michele Weiner-Davis, one with Insoo Berg and one with Michael White[16] too. I got interested in brief therapy. I've been doing mostly individual type stuff and would like to know more about couples and family work and that kind of thing. I guess I just want to learn more about it, and I think as the week goes on I'll figure out what I want to learn more about too.

Bill: That's great. We will have one of the live sessions with a couple and we're going to see a bunch of individuals and maybe some family issues will come up in those. We'll have a chance to see couples stuff—that's what I specialized in for years. I'll see individuals, couples, families, and kids, and adults. I'll do the whole gamut, and we'll talk about the whole gamut.

Now if you don't have a transformative experience this week it's going to be very disillusioning! (*laughter*) Most people just go on, but there are a few people that go through very transformative experiences both theoretically and personally. It's been a little surprising to me and I think it's just the nature . . . you spend a week in something that's totally different from your everyday life. It can facilitate something that's already about to happen or happening. All right. So does anybody think of anything they want to amend or add or subtract from what they said? (*laughter*)

Katy: I picked up on something that Paul had said. I wanted to be able to take some things back to my agency because our agency is adopting a managed care system. So it's really scary for some people who have been in the agency for a while. We've had some cut backs and things like that, and so there's a lot of shakeup and pressure around billable hours and I think those who have been in community mental health or even private practice for a number of years have been doing things a certain way and this managed care thing hits . . . it's real scary. I think people are needing help with that, so I would really like to take some things back. We're at a point of transition, but I don't think there's enough happening to help people through that.

Bill: I think that's right. I think it's a great opportunity in some ways. I've heard people say that they went out to Milwaukee and were warned, "Don't try to bring this back . . . you'll be too much of an evangelist." I disagree. I recommend, not in a righteous way, that you bring these seeds into your workplace. That's partly why I do this work, partly why I go out and teach workshops. I want to change the field. Now is an especially crucial time because it's coming down to one of two things that's going to happen. Either we're really going to get a sense of accountability for results and taking a look at our work and really being respectful and effective, or we're going to a time-limited therapy model much more than brief therapy, saying, "You've got six sessions or three sessions or three days in the hospital, or this much money to do the treatment and that's it." And you have to do it whether this person's chronic and really in severe crisis or

[16]Michael White (along with David Epston) is considered the cocreators of *narrative* therapy. He is associated with the Dulwich Centre in Adelaide, South Australia.

just the walking well kind of person. I think that it's a critical time to be able to influence the managed care implementation so that it becomes respectful and effective and it actually does save money in the long run and contributes to the field as a whole. I've said this and some of you have heard me say this, but I don't understand why every psychotherapy organization in the world from the social workers to the psychologists to the psychiatrists to the marriage and family therapists to professional counselors do not take out big full page ads in the *New York Times* and the *Washington Post* and say, "The research is in. It's very clear. If you give brief courses of psychotherapy to people you can reduce the medical utilization and cost in this country by millions (perhaps billions) of dollars. It's very, very clear." The research is called *medical offset research.* It's here, it's been here for years.

Observation and Conversational Teams

Karen: How does it work with observed sessions? Are they in here with us?

Bill: I think that's the way we'll go. We'll just clear a space and I'll talk to them. At the end of the time there will be a chance for you to talk to them and me and usually that's a continuation of the session.

Laurie: Is it like a *reflecting team*?[17]

Bill: It's a little different from how they do it in reflecting teams. I've done this for years before I ever heard of reflecting teams. I'd say that it's nice to have it open and if you have questions for me or that person or the person we're seeing, just ask those questions whether they're technical questions or personal questions. It's like a reflecting team but it's not so formal. It's more like we're saying to the client, "We're just going to have a discussion after you leave. So let's have the discussion while you're here because some of it may be of benefit to you . . . and you just may be curious of how we're going to talk about you." Often I find that something's said in that discussion afterward that is at least as valuable as something during the session—occasionally more valuable. Somebody says something that really clicks for the person or it highlights something that didn't get highlighted. It's quite a valuable process. It's a little intimidating for people to walk in here with all of us at first, but usually after a few minutes of conversation it gets less intimidating and much more friendly. I was doing an interview session in front of a group some time ago and they said, "You didn't ask the miracle question!" I think I've only asked it once in my life, after I read about it. I thought, "Oh, that's an interesting question." I really didn't study with de Shazer and colleagues and they didn't influence me that much. I

[17] Tom Andersen is a Norwegian psychiatrist who is generally credited as being the originator of *reflecting teams*. See Andersen, T. (Ed.). (1991). However, prior to the coining of the term, many clinicians, including Bill, were already exploring the possibilities of observational and conversational teams in therapeutic and training settings.

think their work is really interesting and compatible with what I'm talking about in a lot of ways. But one of the differences is that I just don't like formulaic models, where there's a certain question or certain set of questions that one should ask. I think that's a good way to learn things, but it also is worrisome in that it could close things down.

Chapter 2

Language is a Virus

This section is more didactic, including discussions of language in therapy, the importance of metaphor, modernism, postmodernism and constructivist approaches. There is also a discussion of making therapy more collaborative and transparent and avoiding becoming dogmatic.

Creating an Awareness of Language

Laurie: Sometimes in a session I'll find myself being more involved and the client less and I'm saying I'm not asking the right questions.

Bill: You're more active.

Laurie: Right. Then I'm struggling, saying to myself, "Okay, I've got to say something that's going to open up for them another way of them seeing what they're talking about." And so that's what is not tripping off my tongue.

Bill: One of the ways to do that is to pay attention to their metaphors. It's interesting to listen to how they metaphorically approach things. They say, "There's a lot of pressure building inside." That's a certain kind of metaphor. . .or to say, "I just don't see any possibilities." That's a different kind of metaphor. I remember I went to a workshop with Bandler and Grinder,[18] the guys who started NLP, *neurolinguistic programming*, years ago. I'd read a book of theirs which was about language in therapy and I loved it. It raised my awareness about language. Then I went to a workshop and they were talking

[18] Richard Bandler and John Grinder are considered the developers of *neurolinguistic programming* (NLP), and have authored numerous books on the subject. See Bandler, R., & Grinder, J. (1975a). Grinder, J., & Bandler, R. (1976). Bandler and Grinder and colleagues also studied the processes of Milton H. Erickson's work in depth. See Bandler, R., & Grinder, J. (1975b). Grinder, J., DeLozier, J., & Bandler, R. (1977).

about something entirely different from what was in the book.[19] I thought they were going to go over what was in the book and I'd just learn it a little better and get it in my bones. During the first fifteen minutes they talked about this thing which probably most of you have heard about now, but it was such a revelation to me. They said some people use visual words and some use auditory words and some use feeling or kinesthetic sort of words or tactile words. I thought, "Wow, I just never noticed it before." At the first break, I turned to my friend and said, "They're saying that people are either visual or auditory or kinesthetic and I just don't see which one I am." It was that obvious. He just laughed and said, "What do you mean you don't *see* which one you are! It's visual, obviously!" (*laughter*) My awareness of the metaphors and language was very, very minimal. I wasn't listening at that level. I learned what they called the metamodel. It was based on Noel Chomsky's linguistics.[20] So I came home from that workshop and I was absolutely turned onto this idea of raising my awareness and other people's awareness of the language we were using. My friends found me absolutely obnoxious for a couple of months because they would say something like, "I just can't quite get it in focus," and I'd say, "So you can't see it very clearly?" They would just look at me like, "What?" Then they would say, "I just don't know." I'd say, "Don't know what?" and "How don't you know it specifically?" (*laughter*) They would say, "Stop that!" I would just fill in what Bandler and Grinder called the *deletions*, *distortions*, and *generalizations* in language.[21] I started to learn a model for raising my awareness of when that was happening and when it wasn't happening and the metaphors that people were using. I was so shocked when I went to the workshop. They were the best workshop presenters I had ever seen. They were so funny and irreverent and clear. I remember sitting in this workshop—just to tell you how long ago it was, it cost $35 for three days. I was really poor at the time so that was a stretch for me. I heard the first fifteen minutes and thought, "I got my $35 worth already! I can go home." But I stayed for three days. I remember we had just done an exercise and we were all broken into small groups. We came back to the big group and we were all sitting where we were for the exercises and there's Bandler and Grinder up on bar stools and they're talking about something and someone said, "What happened for me during this exercise is that I remembered I almost drowned when I was five years old." And they just looked at this person and instantaneously, without looking at each other, without exchanging any information as far as I could tell, both said, "And you're choked up about it still." It was like an electric shock went through my body. I thought, "How did they know?" They said it simultaneously, exactly at the same time . . . and someone said, "How did you do that?" They said, "She went like this (*puts his hands around his throat to demonstrate*) and we really pay attention to nonverbal metaphors as well."

[19] See Bandler, R., & Grinder, J. (1975a).
[20] See Chomsky, N. (1957, 1965, 1968).
[21] See Bandler, R., & Grinder, J. (1975a).

How do you attend to that stuff and still do psychotherapy? I studied with Erickson a little while later and I found a way to attend at the same time that I was talking and watching. I could watch at the same time that I was communicating and that was very, very interesting. Then an interesting thing happened. I discovered that as I was communicating out and watching, there were no more bits of attention for anything else. So I went into those states like you do in the best of whatever kind of athletics you do or music or art. I went into a place where I didn't think. At first, it was only when I did hypnosis because Erickson, the way he trained with hypnosis it was, "You have to attend so carefully to the person and what they're saying and what they're doing even when you're talking you have to attend." If I'm saying, "You could really let yourself go" and the person is responding in a way that shows that "letting yourself go" is not a good idea for them at this point, I had to notice that and say, "And you don't have to let yourself go . . . there's a possibility of holding on and letting go at the same time." But if you're not noticing that response, if you're over here in your head thinking, "I've got to come up with something clever," then you're going to miss that and lose touch. So what started to happen is that during hypnosis I had no thoughts. I just had pure attention. It was like my mind was over in the other person's body and they were telling me what to say based on my responses. I was just attending to what they were saying and noticing it but not self-consciously commenting on it like, "Oh this is a good thing to say," or "I have to do this," or "I have to move them here," or "That was dumb; you really don't know psychotherapy well." None of that critical conscious was going on. Then I started to have that same no-thinking consciousness when I was just doing psychotherapy because I started to attend with the same intensity and the same level. What I call my "Howard Cosell"[22] mind went away during the therapy process. And that was really great. Then I started teaching workshops and at first I wasn't very good at it but I liked it. After a while I got so good at teaching workshops I didn't have to think while doing them. I had my outline and I rarely looked at it anymore. It just started to come through me like when I play music. There started to be a certain kind of awareness in which I was really paying attention and I wasn't getting in the way so much. I then had my attention freed up to notice metaphors, to notice language, to notice nonverbal responses. I think before that happened I was so busy noticing my models of what I was supposed to do that I was getting in my own way. You have those moments when you know it, you're there with the client, you're into it. It doesn't matter how much you talk or they talk—that's not the relevant thing. There's a flow happening and then there are moments when there's no flow and it's stuck from one side or another. It's that flow we're talking about. You need to know your models really well, to know methods and techniques. That's all really good. And then you need to get out of your way and let the art come through you.

[22] Howard Cosell was arguably the most well-known and controversial sports broadcaster in the history of the medium. He died in 1995.

You will then begin to recognize your own voice and your style. They will obviously be influenced by your teachers, by people that you've met, people you've admired, and by your own personality, but it will come out seamlessly.

Paul: After that happens are you able to identify what went on?

Bill: I'm able to identify a lot of what went on. I think it's like meditation. You can't make yourself get into it but you can put yourself in the way of it and do some things to get yourself in that place. I think I can identify some of those things, as well as go back and recreate some things that happened in the session, so I can take notes on them. When that pure attention awareness is there rather than self-critical awareness it's very difficult to recall . . . it just comes through. So it's a good idea to record or take some notes during the process.

Alice: I call that working intuitively.

Bill: That's right. Years ago I went to a workshop with Steve Gilligan[23] and I thought he asked a really good question because it was in an Ericksonian context. Erickson was big on, "the unconscious mind is really benevolent and wise." The title of his workshop was, "If The Unconscious Is So Smart and Wise, How Come We Have Symptoms?" I thought it was a really good question because the unconscious is smart and wise except when it's not. So I started to think about, "When do you trust your intuition and when do you not?" If you learn tennis and you're really good at tennis, and you practice, and play a lot, probably the best thing to do is trust your unconscious because you really know tennis. If you don't know tennis, don't go out there and trust your unconscious. I play guitar and I could play complicated things on the guitar while I'm talking to you and it wouldn't be a distraction for me. It would probably be distracting for you to listen, but my fingers would be playing it for me and that would be in the background for me. My unconscious is playing guitar. I shouldn't try and play mandolin while I'm talking, because it would get in the way. I don't have the resources and knowledge to go intuitive in that area. So if in psychotherapy you've learned your methods and techniques and theories, get out of your way and let that intuition come. Let yourself get into that space. If you don't, then it's a good idea to use methods, techniques and theories and something that guides you until you get to the place where you say, "I know guitar well enough, I know tennis well enough, I know psychotherapy well enough to just let it come through me." It still doesn't always come through you, but you can put yourself in the wave of the intuitive experience much more. So my path for getting there was that attention . . . a certain kind of attention.

[23] Steve Gilligan, Ph.D., is a former student of Richard Bandler and John Grinder as well as Milton H. Erickson. He is the author, coauthor, and coeditor of numerous books and articles. He has published on Ericksonian approaches to hypnosis and psychotherapy, as well as the *self-relations* approach, of which he is considered the developer.

Ernie Rossi,[24] a Jungian analyst who studied with Erickson like I did, told me a story as we were sitting around at one of the conferences over drinks. We were talking about meeting Erickson and what influence he had on our lives and what the experience was like. He said, "I tried to be purely an objective observer, trying to understand what Erickson did, not adding anything of my own." (*laughter*) And of course he didn't do that. He said he'd sit with Erickson, and here was Erickson in this chair (*points to his left*) and here was Rossi in this chair (*points to his right*) and Erickson would start to work with a patient and Rossi was trying to get what he was doing, analyze it, and figure it all out. He wanted to pay attention, but Erickson was so poetic. If you've ever heard tapes of him, you'll know it's hard to listen to Erickson without going into trance. He's very poetic and vague and Rossi would all of the sudden find himself, five minutes or ten minutes later, drifting away. He'd think, "What Erickson is doing is taking apart the psychic DNA and putting it back together in new ways. Or, He's tapping into a Jungian archetype. I wonder if he ever really studied Jungian stuff. I'll have to remember to ask him that after this session. You know, I wonder if the way Erickson does hypnosis is that he schedules long sessions and then he just waits until people go into their natural rest cycles, those *ultradian* rhythms I was reading about the other day. He's just using whatever they're doing naturally." Then Erickson would look over and see Rossi and notice that he was gone (*stares toward the ceiling to imitate Rossi*) (*laughter*). Here Erickson was trying to teach Rossi about psychotherapy and Rossi said Erickson would have to literally or figuratively jab him with his elbow and say, "Dr. Rossi, there's no patient on the ceiling. The patient is over there." (*laughter*) He said Erickson would have to continue to reorient him toward the patient because Rossi was up there in theory-land and in explanation in his head. And I laughed so hard when he told me that story. I said, "Boy that was me!" But family therapy was my preferred theory. I was Mr. Systems and Erickson was one of the first systems therapists. He was seeing whole families in his office in the late 1940s when very few people were, especially psychiatrists. Erickson was very pragmatic. He'd decide, "Let's get the whole family in. Let's see what's happening." I thought, "Go see this guy. It's in the 70s now and he's been doing this for a lot of years. I love family therapy. I want to know what he has to teach." [When I got there] he wasn't doing any family therapy. He was doing hypnosis and I was totally discombobulated. Because I was up in family therapy-land and he was saying, "Pay attention. Observe and listen to the people whom you're working with and they'll teach you everything you need to know. Whether you need to do family therapy or whether you don't, they'll tell you. Every clue is there." As I started to attend more and more, that's how

[24] Ernest Rossi, Ph.D., is a former student and colleague of Milton H. Erickson, M.D. He has edited and coedited eight volumes of Erickson's work including manuscripts, seminars, workshops, and lectures. See Rossi (1980) and Rossi, Ryan, and Sharp (1983b) In addition, he has authored or coauthored numerous books on hypnosis and mind/body healing. Dr. Rossi resides in Malibu, California.

solution-oriented therapy came about. Because I started to pay attention when clients talked about what worked. I missed it before because my training was, "Let's find out what's not working and let's focus on that." And I started to listen to everything, and part of what they were saying was, "Well last week was better." I'd say, "Last week was better? Tell me about that." Erickson would attend to things that were significant to him and one of those things was what resources and skills people had. So it naturally came out of that orientation to start to listen to words, how people did things well . . . and sometimes he would listen in a weird negative way like, "So how come you didn't have a hallucination that day?" It's like Sherlock Holmes says in the middle of a case to Watson, "And then there's the strange matter of the dog barking in the night." Watson says, "The dog didn't bark in the night." Holmes says, "That's the strange matter. It's a watchdog and he didn't bark in the night." So it must have been somebody the dog knew. Erickson would attend to the negative that you would think would be there but wasn't there and would see that as a positive. It started to occur to me to listen to and pay attention to people in a different way. And also metaphors. I found it was really important to listen to the metaphors that people use.

Beth: Can I ask you a question about the metaphors? How does the way you use metaphors fit into the context of the general use of language? I guess I sort of think of phrases of language. Is that like a metaphor? Is that what you're talking about?

Bill: There are various aspects of metaphor we can talk about. There's when the therapist is using metaphors, when the client is using metaphors. When you actually use a phrase like, "Being in this marriage was like being in a concentration camp." That's a simile. Then you can have a nonobvious metaphor like, "I just want to hook into the creativity." (*looks to Laurie*) You were using a metaphor but it wasn't so clear that it was a metaphor. I'm typically listening for a metaphorical frame and the particular expressions of those metaphorical frames. Like the hook one could be fishing, we don't know without hearing more about that. But then there was a vehicle, it becomes a vehicle for me. You say, "I'm on this journey." Well, that's the journey metaphor, that's the traveling metaphor. I listen to metaphorical frames. I think there are often metaphorical frames that people are using to make sense. And in that frame you can't solve the problem. So I often suggest another frame or I use that frame and expand it. A person says, "Life's been like a merry-go-round lately." I could expand it to, "Life is like a carnival. There are lots of rides besides the merry-go-round." That's a possibility. As people talk I want to highlight the metaphors. Metaphor is only one part of language. Another part is how people speak in visual, auditory, or kinesthetic, or other kinds of phrases. If you're saying, "I can't see my way out of this," maybe you can't see your way out of this, but you can feel your way out of it or listen your way out of it. So you can move into a different mode. I think that's another possibility. And then this *metamodel*[25] that I learned. Bandler and Grinder basically had this idea. I haven't really talked about this or used this for years. I did my master's research on it. They had this idea that language is a map of the world and maps are never the territory.[26] If you had a map that was this room, it would have to be as big as this room to represent everything in this room. But if we made a map, it would necessarily drop things out—that's *deletion*—we would have to drop out some details. And it would have some things that weren't in the right proportion, that weren't exactly in the right place—that's *distortion*. And then *generalization*—it would have some things that would say like, "Here's the floor." But you know, there's the floor and then there's the floor. There are parts of the floor that are covered with things. It's a bit generalized. Like, "It's a square room." Well, it's not exactly a square room. It's a little bit generalized to say that. Or there are a couple of rooms off of it. Well, is that a room off it? Is that not? So there's deletion, distortion, and generalization in our language as well as our maps. And our language is a map of the world and it's never as rich as the world. To use a metaphor, *rich* as the world. It's never as detailed as the world and it's never as accurate as the world. And they were claiming in this first book which was called *The Structure of Magic*,[27] how to do psychotherapy is to recapture and reevoke the missing pieces, because that's where the problem is for people. It's not in the world, but it's in their map of the world that has become impoverished—again, to use a money metaphor. The experience is rich and language is impoverished in some area for that person. You can enrich it by asking certain questions. They had a list of questions that they would use that they called the metamodel challenges. When a person would say, "I'm sad," they would in effect say, "Sorry, what you've missed there is that in English, sentences have an actor, a person who's doing something or an object that's doing something, and then an action—a verb word, and then an object. A subject, an action, a verb, and an object. And in that sentence, the object is missing." So the person would say, "I'm sad," and the metamodel response is to ask, "About what?" Because that's the piece that's missing. When they fill that piece in they'll often say, "About everything." That's a generalization. To that you ask, "Can you say what you're sad about specifically? What specifically are you sad about right now?" You start to focus in and get the missing details and as you do that it fills in the person's map of the world and they get less impoverished and have more choices. That's one of the ideas.

Debbie: Earlier you said that people have frames of reference or metaphors, that you can't make changes in those frames.

Bill: Sometimes within those frames they've got themselves restricted or impoverished in terms of their choices. Sometimes those metaphors are working quite

[25] See Bandler, R., & Grinder, J. (1975a).
[26] See also Korzybski, A. (1933).
[27] Bandler, R., & Grinder, J. (1975a).

well for them and the language that they're using is working quite well for them. So perhaps the solution is not in that metaphor. It's going to be something else. That's one of the places to examine as a possibility. Is the way they have it put together helpful? It may make sense for them and that's the way they think about it, but it's not helpful. There are not that many choices. If life is a merry-go-round, you're either going to be up or you're going to be down. If life is a carnival you can get off that ride and go throw balls at milk bottles. There's a whole bunch of other choices that are available. So, we're talking about two things. One is about attending to the client. That has two effects. One is you hear things and see things that you didn't hear or see before, which might be hints about how to sort out the situation. It also has an effect on you, the therapist, if you're attending at that level. You usually shift into a different state of consciousness. The other thing is about attending to certain parts of the client's experience whether verbal or nonverbal. We're talking right now about some of the verbal aspects of their experience and some of the metaphorical aspects of those verbal things. But we can also talk about the nonverbal aspects as we go along.

Another one of the categories of language that Bandler and Grinder talked about is a thing called *nominalization*.[28] Nominalization is basically when you turn a verb into a noun, linguistically. So you turn a process into a thing. The *gestalt*[29] therapists used to do this quite a bit. "I'm wanting to go to lunch with you," they'd say, rather than, "I want to go to lunch with you." Because it's always a process for them. Someone says, "I have a lot of fear." That's taking some process, like being afraid of something, and turning it into a thing. "There's a lot of tension in my life," or "We don't have any communication in our marriage." Those are thing words that derive from a process. Bandler and Grinder say that nominalizations involve a more complex deletion, distortion, and generalization. To challenge it, you've got to change it back into a verb and then ask, "So who isn't communicating with who? And in what specific way?" or "About what aren't they communicating?" Just to complicate matters further as I'm introducing this idea, when I studied Bandler and Grinder's model of Erickson's work, one of the things that they said is, "Okay you've learned the metamodel to challenge these deletions, distortions, and generalizations and missing information. If you want to learn hypnosis, learn to put all those deletions, distortions, and generalizations back in." Nominalization is a really great thing to do to put people into trance. For example, "There's a lot of *learnings* that you have and a lot of *resources* you have, a lot of *understandings* inside. Those are three nominalizations, learnings, resources, and understandings. There's no such stuff, but if you talk that way a lot, people tend to go inside to make sense of it and go into trance, because there's so much information missing. It's like the best preachers when they're giving their sermons, they've got

[28] See Bandler, R., & Grinder, J. (1975a).

[29] *Gestalt* therapy is a phenomenological-existential therapy founded in the 1940s by Fritz Perls. See Perls, F. S. (1969, 1973).

to speak to a wide variety of people and when they say, "All of us have sinned." We all are supposed to think of our individual sins. Or "We all have the possibility of grace and being saved," and we're all supposed to think of what that means in our individual lives. Most politicians, most preachers, and most hypnotists learn to speak in these very vague ways in order to help people make particular experiences and not get in the way of those experiences and in order to invite them into a particular state of consciousness. As a therapist I want to both get the missing information and leave information out. When I'm gathering information, if I don't know the information and if the person seems impoverished in their model of the world, I want to challenge some of that and get the missing information for me and for them. But when I want to move them in a different direction, sometimes I'll use very impoverished words as rhetorical devices to create a certain kind of reality. So language can be used in both ways. There's nothing terrible about using generalized, distorted, or deleted terms, or metaphorical terms. The question is: Are they helpful or not at that particular moment?

Implications of Constructivism, Postmodernism, and Modernism

Bill: The other thing that informs this particular model of therapy, in addition to the model of language, is the *postmodern*[30] view. I don't like that term very much, but postmodern basically means that it's not quite so simple as one reality that's fixed and set. The best description I've heard of postmodern was, "Remember when Walter Cronkite used to do the news in the United States and he would say at the end, 'And that's the way it is for July 15, 1996.' It was very authoritative, 'That's the way it is.' But now, Dan Rather says at the end, 'And that's part of your world for July 15, 1996.'" That's postmodern. It says, "Yeah, that's one way to think about it. That's one way to view it." But clearly in the United States, CBS new's view and selection of news is not the way it is. It's *a* way it is. Postmodernism says that's *a* way it is. But when you make claims to authoritative truth, that's a *modernist*[31] perspective. The postmodernist says, "Here's a way to think about it. Here's a way to look at it." It's not total relativism, which is a slightly different thing, but it is a recognition that there are multiple views and voices and opinions and ways of thinking about it. Postmodern ideas in psychotherapy go beyond that into *constructivism*,[32] which

[30] The *postmodern* period in psychology and psychotherapy began in the 1980s and represented a trend similar to that in other fields where established truths began to be challenged and reexamined. See Gergen, K. J. (1991, 1994).

[31] The *modernist* movement in psychotherapy runs counter to the *postmodern* perspective in that with it is the belief that there are single truths which can be discovered. A postmodernist consideration is the notion of multiple realities and truths.

[32] *Constructivism* from a therapeutic viewpoint relates to the idea that the client's meaning system is elevated to a level that is beyond the therapist's theoretical orientation or personal beliefs. Therefore, the client's meaning system takes precedence in the therapeutic encounter. Thus, as von Glasersfeld stated, "the operations by means of which we can assemble our experiential world can be

says that the way we pay attention to things, the way we use metaphors about it, the way we use language about it, and the way we interact about it creates it the way it is. There's an old joke about umpires. There are three umpires in the bar after a game and they're bragging about their profession. One guy says, "I calls 'em the way they are." The other two drink up their beers, and the second guy says, "I calls 'em the way I sees 'em." And the third one says, "Until I calls 'em they ain't." (*laughter*) And that's the constructivist idea: "Until I calls 'em they ain't." So we've been trained a lot in psychotherapy to go in and discover what's going on with clients, but the postmodern idea and the constructivist idea says it isn't quite so simple because you're always around, influencing how it's showing up. If you ask certain questions, if you direct people's attention, if you use certain metaphors, that's going to influence how the person starts to feel and think about their situation and the reality of that concern that they brought in. It starts to get crystallized or reified or directed in a certain way. So language and interaction are part and parcel of the therapy process and problem, and problem definition, and also part of the solution, potentially.

How do you raise your awareness of this? One of the ways I did it was to start to use these metamodel questions and challenges outside of therapy to start to get my brain to notice these things and to start to challenge them and then figure out which ones were important. There are some that are merely obnoxious. When I was practicing, my friends thought I was extremely obnoxious. So if you challenge everything, it will get tedious and obnoxious, and people will get a sense you're not really listening to them. I just saw the movie *Phenomenon*, and there was this scene in which he (the character portrayed by John Travolta) becomes very, very intelligent after a particular experience, and the psychologist is trying to test him for intelligence and he says, "How old would a person be if they were born in 1928?" And he says, "Well, come on . . . you've got to get more specific. Is it a man or woman?" The psychologist says, "What does that matter?" He says, "Be specific." "Okay, it's a man." He says, "What month is it?" (Psychologist) "Born in October." (Travolta) "What day was he born?" (Psychologist) "Okay . . . , the 28th," and the psychologist is really frustrated . . . and the Travolta character says, "Where was he born?" He says, "What does it matter?" Again, "Where was he born?" "Okay, New York City!" Then the Travolta character says he would be this many years, this many months, and this many hours if he were born here, and he would be this old if he were born here . . . and he was very, very specific about it. And again that was useful to answer that question and also to make a point that he was extremely quick because he could figure it out just like that (*snaps his fingers*); he was being very specific but pretty obnoxious as well. You've got to be careful about being too specific. The way I learned this was I'd choose one or two patterns to pay

explored, and that awareness of this operating can help us do it differently and, perhaps, better" (p. 18). von Glasersfeld, E. (1984).

attention to. For example, one of the patterns is a generalization. A generalization could be *everybody, nobody, all, nothing, never, always.* One could generalize to time, and to place . . . *everywhere, nowhere.* It's either all or nothing . . . time, frequency . . . *all the time.* "Nobody ever cleans up around this house but me." I started to train myself to notice generalizations.

Attending to Metaphors

Bill: So you've got to figure out the times when it's important to challenge them, and when it's not . . . when there really are distortions. So when a person says, "I always fail" or "I never succeed," I'd say, "You've never succeeded at anything? I mean you got here today, didn't you?" So challenging those generalizations or just repeating it back as a question ("Never?" "Always?") became the metamodel challenge. I would pick out one of the patterns that I wanted to challenge that day or that week and I would try it with my friends and my family, and would try it with my clients. Then I started to get that one as an automatic pattern so I didn't have to think about it anymore, like playing tennis and practicing your backhand. That's one of the ways to do it—just pay attention to the left out object of the sentence, "I'm depressed," "About what?" Or the specificity, "How specifically are you depressed?" "Depressed" is the big word, the generalized word. I started to train myself very specifically by using certain questions. The metaphors I think are a harder pattern to teach so specifically. It's mostly a matter of attending to them and starting to get metaphorical frames. I was in Alaska one time and I was teaching a workshop for the general public; it was on relationships . . . and a guy came along with his wife who was a therapist, and he was a banker . . . and we went out to lunch and we were sitting together and he said, "This therapy stuff . . . it's all so soft and flaky and everything," and we were joking about the whole thing. . . and I was talking about metaphors, and I said, "Banking is absolutely filled with metaphors." He said, "No, banking is hard facts." I said, "You have a metaphorical frame for banking all the time. You *float* a loan . . . *liquid* assets, and we have *slush* funds . . . *hard* cash . . . you can *freeze* a bank account . . . there's *rising* liquidity, *lowering* the balance in your account, . . . and bank itself, like the *bank* of a river. That money is liquid, that's that metaphor." He said, "I never thought of that." I said, "There are certain things that are available within that metaphor and certain things that aren't available . . . it obscures some things and it highlights other things." And he said, "Yeah." And he started to get real excited because there was another metaphorical frame in banking. The closest we could come was . . . it was like . . . alpine climbing. . . . I don't remember what it was because I don't remember the metaphors exactly and the phrases exactly, but there were *gaps* . . . and things could fall in the gaps, and they could take advantage of the gaps, and they could get across the gaps, and they could earn money while the gaps were happening, and there were slippery slopes on the gaps, and the interest rates could *slide.* It's a really interesting thing to think about these metaphorical frames. So there are specific metaphors and larger metaphorical frames . . . money as liquid, or food as thinking . . . like, "That's a *half-baked* idea, or "I'll just have to let that *simmer* for a little while," or "*Percolate* through," or "I'll have to *digest* that idea." Those kind of frames . . . arguments as buildings or ideas as buildings. . . . "You have no *foundations* for your ideas," . . . "That's a rather shaky *structure* you have for that argument," or "That doesn't *stand* up," or "Your argument just crumbled to the ground." Lakoff and Johnson wrote a book called *Metaphors We Live By*[33] years ago, and it was all about these metaphorical frames and how we think we're thinking so logically and linearly and structurally and really how it's metaphorical frames and informal. . . .

Beth: . . . How do you give meaning to these metaphors or an understanding to them?

Bill: Typically there are a few things that one could do with it and one is . . . one could just understand it and speak back in the client's language. So when I spoke back to you I might say, "So does that help you see what I mean?" You said, "*See*," that was one of your metaphors. The other thing is one could move you into a different place say, "Well it's not really that I see the metaphors. I just sort of feel my way into that. I just want to feel my way into the client's world and get a sense of what it feels like for them to live within that metaphor." So I could move into a different area. The other thing is that it could stimulate new images for me or new ideas, new ways of thinking about it. . .so when you started talking about *hooking* into your creativity, I could talk about, "How do you throw out a line and really hook your creativity? What bait do you use for your creativity?" I could expand the metaphor a bit when it was only one small section of the metaphor . . . and I could add more to it and really follow onto that . . . because that's the person's idea . . . that's the way they're thinking about it, or one way that they're thinking about it. I could expand that way of thinking about it. That's typically what I'd use at first . . . is, I'd just start to use that person's metaphor and expand it a bit and find out whether there are other solutions or possibilities within that . . . or if they say, "I got *hooked* by that." I would say, "How would you cut the strings so that the hooks can be removed?" or "Could we carefully remove the hooks?" And I start speaking in terms of that metaphor or that image.

Beth: Sort of using their language.

Bill: Yeah . . . that's one way to do it. And the other is to introduce entirely different metaphors because that metaphor isn't leading them anyplace, perhaps. To say, "I know you've been talking about hooks, but I think of this more as a journey and a process . . . not like you've gotten hooked. And while you're on

[33] Lakoff, G., & Johnson, M. (1980).

that journey sometimes you have pulls that are happening, but generally your inertia is so strong on your journey that those pulls aren't going to hold you back.'' So we switch to another metaphor . . . the journey metaphor rather than the hook metaphor. Again, I don't usually speak about it so much, but I think it's a nice idea for a couple of reasons. One is that sometimes you can use it in those ways, the other thing is just to get you to pay attention to people and stop looking at the ceiling. All of the sudden you can discover all the information or the solutions that are there but you haven't noticed before. So, somebody role play, just for a few minutes, one of your clients and we'll do some of this kind of conversation . . . language conversation.

Laurie: I have a woman who has left a responsible job clerking in Quaker meetings . . . so she's sort of been the head of it. They had an issue of same sex marriages and they were trying to have a consensus at a meeting. . . .

Bill: . . . Quakers have to have a consensus or it doesn't go through, and they just wait until the consensus comes. . . .

Laurie: . . . Right. And this was her last meeting, and there was no consensus. She has taken a real nose dive and is in a depression.

Bill: That's great . . . okay, let's just stop there. A *nose dive* and she's in a depression . . . there are metaphors. (*laughter*)

Laurie: Okay . . . I just can't let it go. . . .

Bill: . . . Okay, let's stop there for a second. So, ''I just can't let it go.'' ''Can't'' is what's called . . . in this model, a *modal operator of impossibility*.[34] They say, ''Can't,'' and so the question is, ''What stops you? How specifically are you stopped from letting it go?''

(Bill and Laurie enter into a role play through which further dialogues are intertwined).

Laurie: ''I wake up in the morning; it's the first thing I think about. I'm just obsessing about it. Everybody that I talk with, my friends. . . . I can't get it out . . . it's in my conversation, it's right there all the time.''

Bill: ''So sometimes you're talking about other things . . . or is it all the time you're talking about this . . . have you talked about other things?''

Laurie: ''Oh yes. . . . I've talked about other things.''

Bill: Great! That was one of the challenges. She says, ''I talk about it all the time. I can't get it out of my mind. I'm always thinking about it.'' You just say, ''Always?'' Part of how I do the challenge these days, different from how I learned it initially from Bandler and Grinder, is I introduce the seed of change

[34] See Grinder, J., & Bandler, R. (1981).

or possibility by saying, "So sometimes you're thinking about other things or talking about other things, right? Or is it all the time?" (*Response to self in dialogue*) "Oh no, not all the time." And so the way she's taking the nose dive, I would suggest, is she's talking herself into it, into a depression if you will, in part, at least. She's saying, "It's always . . . it's overwhelming." Of course, what do depressed people do typically? They see things as generalized, "It's always been this way. It will always be this way. It's overwhelming and it's big." So part of how she talks herself into that is by saying phrases like, "All the time. I can't think of anything else." She loses her sense of power, "I can't." Then it's, "All the time." So just those slight challenges—it's just during the assessment process that you're going to be doing this. This is a process where asking questions gives information as well as gets information.

Paul: When she would say, "Always," the first thing I thought about is, "Are there times when you think about other things?" But then they could say, "No." Because you're giving them an out.

Bill: That's right . . . and so you're just going to check it out at first. But typically here's one of my problems with *solution-focused.*[35] When I first started teaching people this way of questioning, of asking about times when they aren't thinking about it or whatever it may be, they would come back after I taught them and they would say, "I watched you in here and it seemed so simple and so easy and people would come up with times when they weren't thinking about or obsessing about it. Then I go back and my clients say, 'No, there are no such times.' But you seem to find them all the time." And I realized there was a missing piece and it was this language piece. It's that I'm undoing the generalization and suggesting a more partial view of it first. And then I'm asking that question because if they say, "I think of it all the time and I can't think of anything else," the next thing I say is, "So tell me about a time when you didn't," or "Is there a time when you didn't think about it?" or "You thought about something else or focused on something else?" If they were paying attention they'd turn to me and say, "You aren't listening stupid! I just told you! And now you're asking me the opposite question!" So I think bridging a little by challenging some of those generalizations because it's really almost as if they have blinders on . . . this is a metaphor . . . and you're just kind of taking the blinders off and if you say, "Could you look around you to the other parts of the street?" And they say, "All I can see is what's in front of me." And you say, "Oh, well there's some stuff on your side." So I start to move the blinders back and give them a glimpse of what's to their side by using these language techniques . . . by challenging the generalizations, "I think about it all the time.

[35] As previously noted, Steve de Shazer is considered the developer of solution-*focused* therapy, and Bill is considered the codeveloper of solution-*oriented* therapy. (Although it appears that a man named Don Norum was really the originator of solution-based therapies in 1978.) These two approaches are consistently lumped together and understood to be the same. However, this is a misperception as there are distinct differences between these approaches.

I can't think about anything else. I can't talk about anything else. I wake up thinking about this.'' I'd say, ''So you've woken every day for the last week thinking about this or is there some day you've woken up and been thinking about something else, or forgotten to think about it for a little while?'' That would be one way to challenge it or, ''Always thinking about it or always talking about it?'' That's another way.

Denise: So what would your response have been if she had said, ''No, really . . . all the time!''

Bill: My response, and this is going beyond the metamodel . . . I would say, ''For the last while you've been thinking about it, as far as you can tell, all the time.''

Denise: Okay, I got you.

Bill: Do you hear how that starts to introduce a little possibility? For the last bit of time, not forever, because when she's depressed she's going to be thinking forever . . . into the future forever . . . into the past . . . and also that's all she's going to be able to notice. And so I say, ''It seems to you'' or ''It seems in the last while it's been all the time.'' And a little later in the session she may say, ''Well I did talk with my friend. . . . We had a good laugh the other night about this and this and this.'' Then I'll go back and say, ''Oh, at that moment you weren't really obsessing about it or thinking about what happened at the meeting.'' You'll find the opening later. You just want to plant the seed of a possibility. That's what I call *acknowledgment* and *possibility*[36] at the same time. You don't have to do, ''Oh, I'll just very politely listen to you.'' It's an active listening process . . . actually very similar to (Carl) Rogers. If you actually look at a transcript of Rogers, he's interrupting and doing this possibility talking a lot. He's not doing pure reflection. He's actually leading a bit. And I think that's what it is, it's a reflection and leading process at the same time . . . there's an unfolding of the conversation rather than just a pure reflection. It was cartoon imaged as pure reflection, and Rogers said, ''No, I actually don't want to do that. I want to understand the phenomenological world of people.'' But I think he was much more change oriented than he gave himself credit for. He didn't just want to understand the phenomenological world, he wanted to understand and shift the phenomenological world . . . value it and shift it at the same time. I think that's this process. (*looks to Laurie*) So talk a little more. . . . you're doing great.

Laurie: ''Look here, my journal . . . this is the worst journal. You know, I have a whole row of journals at home. This is the worst journal, just look at this (*as if looking at the journal*). Back here . . . it's right here. (*begins to pretend she is reading from the journal*) I woke up this morning; it was terrible. The day was overcast. I felt awful and it didn't get much better the whole day. Why can't I let it go?''

[36] See Figure 2.1, *Acknowledgment and Possibility.*

Acknowledgment and Possibility

Carl Rogers With a Twist: Introducing possibilities into past and present problem reports

1. Reflect back clients' problem reports into the past tense.

Client: I'm depressed.
Therapist: So you've been depressed.

2. When clients give generalities about their problems, introduce the possibility that the problem is not so general. Reflect clients' problem reports with qualifiers, usually of time (e.g., recently, in the last little while, in the past month or so, most of the time, much of the time), intensity (e.g., a bit less, somewhat more) or partiality (e.g., a lot, some, most, many)

Client: I've been really depressed.
Therapist: You've been depressed most of the time lately.

3. Translate clients' statements of the truth into statements of clients' perceptions or subjective realities.

Client: From the things she has said and done, it is obvious she doesn't care for me or our marriage.
Therapist: Some of the things she's done have given you the sense she doesn't care.

The Moving Walkway: Introducing a future with possibilities

1. Recast a problem statement into a statement about the preferred future or goal.

Client: I think I'm just too shy to find a relationship. I'm afraid of women and being rejected.
Therapist: So you'd like to be able to get into a relationship?

2. Use present or future tenses to reflect reports of past helpful attention, action, and viewpoints.

Client: I stopped myself from bingeing by calling a friend.
Therapist: So one of the things you do to stop bingeing is call friends.

3. Presuppose positive changes and progress toward goals by using words like "yet, "so far," "when," and "will."

Client: I broke up with my girlfriend and can't seem to find another relationship.
Therapist : So you haven't gotten into a relationship yet. When you get into a relationship, we'll know we've done something useful here.

Figure 2.1

Bill: "So a lot of the time you've been thinking about this stuff and really obsessing about it and some of the times you even obsess about why you can't let it go and that's part and parcel of the problem because you're thinking, 'What's wrong with me? Why can't I let it go?'"

Laurie: "And there is something wrong with me that I can't let it go."

Bill: "Yeah, you've really been stuck and you can't let it go." I just continue to work with it. Actually, what I would do at this point is move out of the pure language and I would tell a story. So, I'll tell you what I would say. "I was seeing this guy, Michael White, recently, a famous narrative guy from Australia. He has this model, *narrative* therapy.[37] He talks about how our culture is really obsessed with getting over things and letting go. He says the Aborigine culture has a different model. And he's been learning from the Aborigine culture, trying to learn something from their wisdom and what they've done well. He says they have the belief that when someone dies they never go away. We have this model in the United States, or North America, or western cultures that says, better get over this and let them go after a certain amount of time. You can grieve for a while, but then you better let them go or else you're pathological and holding on and there's something wrong with you. Michael White now thinks it's really important to hold on like the Aborigines keep every one of their ancestors present for them, and they do it through a ritual and they do it through their language. They have the sense that they're surrounded by their ancestors and anytime they get in trouble they can consult their ancestors in some way and say, 'What would you say about this? What would you do about this? I'm really stuck. I'm having trouble and what would you say about that?' My sense is that one of the things that's going on for you is you're putting a lot of pressure on yourself to let this go. But it's pretty disturbing for you and it sounds like you're really in process with it and trying to sort it out. What does it mean for you? You're upset about it, clearly . . . and you've been depressed about it . . . and there seems to be something you're figuring out about this, and of course, if you get stuck with this and this happens for the rest of your life . . . no fun . . . but I'm just wondering. It sounds like you're really processing this a lot, and right now it feels like maybe you're going round and round in the squirrel cage about it. But maybe there's something that's starting to come out of the squirrel cage and that you're actually sorting out from that. I'm just not sure about that right at the moment." And then we would check out that. So we start with that, "I'm stuck, I'm stuck," metaphor and, "I've got to let go." And in that framework she's fried. It's not good. In a different framework, there are other possibilities. And then she may say, "No, no . . . that's okay if somebody dies, but not this stuff. I need to get over this stuff. I need to let it go." And then we'd go in a different direction. (*looks to Laurie*) Does that make sense?

[37] See White, M., & Epston, D. (1990). *Narrative means to therapeutic ends*. New York: Norton. White, M. (1995).

Laurie: Uh huh.

Bill: All right . . . (*to the entire group*) so what did you hear there?

Megan: You reframed all of that to be an okay thing for her to do and, in that, at least letting her get rid of some of that worry over what she's doing.

Bill: That's exactly right. She's kind of getting down on herself. Part of my idea is that part of how people get stuck is they not only have troubles, but then they say they *are* the trouble—that there's something wrong with them at the core and they're bad. And one of the things I want to do in whatever way I do, and we'll find lots of other ways, is to *value* the person and say, "Whatever your experience is okay. Now, how you're *storying* the experience, what you're saying about it, how you're explaining it to yourself and to other people, there's trouble in that sometimes." It's a really simple model. You value the person and value all their experience and invite them to value themselves and all their experience . . . which isn't so easy. There are lots of ways to try and do it. Part of what gets in the way of that is they keep thinking about it in the same damn way over and over again, and they keep doing it in the same damn way over and over again. They keep repeating the explanations and where they're putting their attention, the viewing the problem . . . and they keep repeating the doing of the problem . . . actions and interactions and language. I just want to get in there in a very gentle and polite way because I'm not much on confrontation. Some people like that, that's their style, but it doesn't go with my personality well. I learned it early on. . . . I did Synanon groups,[38] where you go down people's throats and pull out their tonsils and get them to confront their addictive behavior. I could do it, but it's not my preferred mode. I much prefer a smoother and more friendly and cooperative and polite mode. It's just the way I was raised, and it's my personality. I prefer southern gentility to the confrontational approach. So I do it in this very gentle way to join with the current viewing and doing and invite them slightly out of it.

Paul: So that just opens up a little space for something.

Bill: A little space, and whatever shows up in that little space . . . sometimes they'll just respond like, "Nope, nope that isn't it," and they keep going on their same old, same old . . . and then every once in while there's an opening and they'll take that opening and I'll follow them through that opening . . . because I don't know which possibilities are going to show up as actualities. I've just got to follow them through that and the analogy I've used is like *curling* . . . this sport where you sweep on the ice in front of the stone or the puck that's going there and I'm just sweeping open possibilities; then I'm looking at the stone finding out, "Which path are you going to take, and as soon as I figure out which path your taking I'll sweep right in front of you and really facilitate this

[38] Synanon groups were tough groups for junkies started at a New York City rehabilitation house called Synanon.

process.'' So I'm going to be working my buns off to open up lots of possibilities because I never know which one is going to be right for the person.

Debbie: Bill, I have a question. It's sort of a devil's advocate statement. How do you know when you're interrupting in a process that needs to take place? Let's say that the person needs to grieve or needs to be depressed for a certain period of time. How do you know when you're just propping them up and interfering with that process?

Bill: Or stopping that process. I think that's what I was saying to this person, ''You're interfering with your process. . . . Maybe you need to do this a bit more.'' One of the ways that I do it is to say, ''Possibility, possibility, possibility.'' It's a smorgasbord of choices and they say, ''Ah, yeah, I need to do it more.''

Debbie: And then you just trust that they're going to go where they need to go.

Bill: Intuitively . . . once they've got more possibilities to open up and, as my friend Steve Gilligan calls it, once they're in touch with their *belly/mind*,[39] and really they've gotten all the stories out of the way and they're really going with their intuition . . . then I figure, trust their process. If your client says, ''You know I think you're right. . . . I've been getting down on myself, but I need to just kind of make this through for a while. Maybe I'm not so stuck. Maybe I just need to be here right now.'' I would trust that for a while. Then we would find out if she's going out and doing fine or if she's not. So that's one thing. The second thing is you never know until you get a response. I was doing a workshop down in Orlando. . . . I was doing it with other people who had different approaches to brief therapy: Michael Hoyt, Donald Meichenbaum,[40] and Peter Sifneos.[41] We're all showing videotapes of our work and talking about our work, and Meichenbaum, who's a friendly acquaintance of mine, says, ''Bill I just have one suggestion for you,'' because he hears me talking my talk about this, I don't think when I'm doing therapy . . . and he says, ''First, I recommend you think.'' (*laughter*) ''You're making a big mistake and I can see it in your work that you don't think.'' (*continued laughter*) He's tough. The second thing, and I found this more useful . . . he said, ''When you ask a client a question, before you answer the question for them, probably you should take a breath and count to ten and let them answer the question.'' (*laughter*) Because I often will answer the question and I will get in the way of their process. Sometimes I do that because I realize I've asked the question in a way that's closed down some possibilities and I want to rephrase it. Or, I notice their response as I ask the

[39] See Gilligan, S. (1997).

[40] Donald Meichenbaum, Ph.D., is a professor of psychology at the University of Waterloo, Canada. He has published numerous articles, mostly on *cognitive-behavioral* approaches to therapy and coping with stress.

[41] Peter Sifneos, M.D., is a Professor of Psychiatry at Harvard Medical School and is the author of numerous publications on *short-term psychodynamic* psychotherapy.

question, and I want say something else to ask a slightly different question based on their response . . . and sometimes I get in the way of their process. So I think the only way to answer that is only by ongoing noticing of the response. That's the way I do it, and it's a matter of guess work and intuition and paying attention. So is this dealing with what the person wants to deal with, or is this really interfering? Ultimately, you can only tell when they go outside and try things in the world and then come back and report, "Yes, this was helpful," or "Boy, that was really great," or "Things have really been moving," or "No, it's the same thing as I told you last week. I'm here and your clever ideas did not do a thing." (*looks to Debbie*) But about your playing "devil's advocate," I think that it's important, first of all, for you to ask those questions and be engaged in that. Second, that's what I want to get from the clients. Before they leave my office I want to say, "Okay, how might this not work?" and "What did I say that just kind of ran over you and wasn't right for you?" I want to ask that question to get it because I figure if you don't get the objections or concerns and include those and speak to those they're just going to bounce back between sessions. And then they'll look like they're resistant when actually they're not resistant, they're just being who they are, responding as they do . . . and you're saying things that aren't all that helpful or aren't contributing . . . and thinking that they're great ideas. My joke is, "It's too bad my clients don't come to my workshops because then they would know how they're supposed to respond wonderfully to all my interventions." (*laughter*) Unfortunately, they're just who they are, or fortunately they're just who they are . . . and they respond as they respond. Sometimes they know I'm this well-known person who's written all these books and teaches workshops; sometimes they don't have any idea, and I like that. Those come in and even if they know I'm well-known they go, "Oh, you've written all those books and you're still doing this shit stuff with me. . . . It's not working." Sometimes they don't know who I am, and they don't know that they're supposed to respond as if I'm this wise, great, well-known psychotherapist. I'm just doing what I'm doing and they're responding, and it's not helpful for them . . . and I really like that part. That's the part of why I was a little appalled about Jay Haley, because I thought, "How does he learn it?" You can learn it by watching other people do it to a certain extent, but I have to have my body in there. There's something about my body that learns when it doesn't work and when I'm frustrated or when they're frustrated, that I can't get from outside the room watching through the one-way mirror or on videotape or by just hearing the description of it.

Paul: How successful have you been at asking them at the end, "What worked; what didn't work?"

Bill: Very successful. Sometimes they're too nice and they won't say and sometimes they will. Often when they come back they'll have a little better perspective and I can ask them the next time, "Can you remember back," and they'll say, "I don't even remember what we did," and that tells you something . . . or

"Yeah, what really made a difference for me was this." I think probably most of you have had this experience. . . . Have you ever had a client go out and come back and tell you something you were pretty sure you didn't say but that they found profoundly helpful? (*laughter*)

Alice: It also amazes me the things they remember from two years ago.

Bill: Yeah . . . it was like an off-handed thing that you didn't put much significance in, but they said, "Wow, when you said that it transformed my entire life!" And you're like, "Yeah, I meant that!" Peggy Papp[42] said, "It's amazing the ability that clients have to take our most mundane statements or interventions and turn them into profound life transformations, and to take the most profound and amazing things we say and turn them into absolutely useless interventions." I think that's right. The only way I can know is by watching and listening to the response in the session, asking at the end or at the next session, and then noticing the reports between sessions.

Paul: I've even said, "Everything we say in here can't be helpful, so what was said that wasn't helpful?"

Bill: Sometimes I ask in a one-step removed way. Like, "What if there was another client that came in here who had a similar problem to you. What would you say are the most helpful things to get Bill to talk to them about or say to them? And what do you think are the least helpful things?"

Laurie: Do you do this at the end of every session?

Bill: I try to do it during the session as well as at the end of the session. Obviously during these sessions when we do this it's very helpful because then you can learn and I can learn and the person has a chance to speak up. And sometimes if they're gutsy people they'll say, "I thought that part was crap and it was really offensive and didn't like it . . . and that part I really liked and it was great," or "I don't know, I'll just have to think about the whole thing and find out how it is for me." They're pretty honest sometimes.

The Collaborative Approach

Denise: It's embarrassing even to tell it, but a couple who are women that I've been seeing came to me the other day and I've seen them about four times together . . . and part of my door is that I think I've become too formulaic and I can't get out of my own way . . . and they walked in and sat down and I said, "So what's been going well since I saw you last?" And they looked at each other and burst out laughing and said, "We knew you were going to ask that!"

[42]Peggy Papp is a faculty member of the Ackerman Institute for the Family, where she is the director of the Depression Project. She has authored and coauthored many books and articles on family therapy, feminist perspectives, and other related subjects.

(*laughter*) I was so embarrassed, but I appreciated their honesty! I needed to get that from them.

Bill: (to the client) "And what do you think would be a better question for me to ask you at the beginning of a session?" That's the *collaborative approach.*[43] There's this whole thing about the collaborative approach that we're going to intertwine. The collaborative approach for me is putting it on the table, and when those clients come in and they say that . . . you say, "You know that's really a great thing that you said that. I really appreciate your honesty about that because one of the things I've been trying to work on and I've been painfully aware of is that I've become kind of formulaic. I like what I do and I think it's generally good, and I hope you like it too, . . . but I think I've become a little too dependent on formula questions and formula interventions. I just wonder if you could coach me when you hear one of those, 'Oh, there's the typical things that Denise says. Gosh, she always says that;' whatever that is so I can start to identify, 'Here's where my clients are knowing that I'm going formulaic.' So if you find one of those things will you coach me and say that I'm doing this?" For a while I ran over on all my sessions and I just told my clients, "I'm terrible at this. I need your help. At like fifty minutes to the hour will you remind me that it's about time to stop?" Even the clients that I thought, "They want to run over. They really like the extra time," they'd say, "It's fifty minutes after the hour you need to think about quitting." (*laughter*)

Denise: What's great about that is that with this particular couple part of what's going on with them is they keep saying, "The communication thing." If they could do that with me, it would be a lot easier for them to do it with me than it would be with aeach other.

Bill: That's exactly right, "What would be helpful at this point?" I have an idea what's helpful at that time and I do it . . . and sometimes it's helpful and sometimes it's the exact opposite of helpful. So instead to say, "What would actually be helpful for me to ask you or say or do right at this point?" And sometimes that's part of the problem; the person says, "If you don't know right now then . . . " (*laughter*), but most of time they'll say, "Well, what you were saying a couple of minutes ago when you were saying . . . 'That must be really hard' . . . that's really good. . . . Say more of that." It's that way with clients if they're willing to do that partnership. I had a friend who was a psychiatrist who was mortally afraid of getting sued because he didn't take good notes. He was terrible with his paperwork, wouldn't have time between the sessions, and he was just too busy. And I have the same thing. I'm not very good at it . . . and we talked about this . . . and he decided that he would, at of the end of the

[43] The *collaborative approach* refers to a way of working with clients where there is shared expertise. The client brings expertise and experience to therapy about his or her life and problem concerns, while the therapist brings expertise and experience of assisting people with problem concerns. Together the therapist and client work collaboratively to resolve the complaint at hand.

session, tell his patients, "I am going to take notes the last five or ten minutes of the session. I'm going to dictate into my little dictaphone and you can be here. If you don't want me to do it you can tell me and I'll try and take other time, but I'm terrible at doing my notes and I'm afraid I'm going to have some problems if I don't do the notes in a timely matter. So you can correct me while I'm doing the case note." And people loved it. He did talk therapy it wasn't just medication . . . and he would dictate the notes in front of them. Everyone wanted to know what was going in those notes. They were totally fascinated with it, especially with a psychiatrist, and they would sometimes correct him and say, "No that's not right!" And he'd say, "Good," and he would back up the tape and say, "What wasn't right?" And they'd say, "I didn't try suicide twice. You misremembered that. I tried suicide once and thought about it another time." That was it, and he would just do it in the last five or ten minutes . . . collaborative case notes . . . the patients knew what was going on. He just said, "This is my problem; I'm putting it out on the table." Instead of having to deal with it himself . . . fix it himself, which he tried to do for years and wasn't very successful at it; so it's this, "I just went to this supervision group in Portland, Maine, and I just learned this and I want to try it. Is that okay?" You just tell the story and make it in a context in your life and include them in the context. Patients and clients are great generally when they're clued in and not left in the dark. If you came in and started doing new stuff, they'd say, "What the hell happened to you? What's going on?" If you say, "I went to this thing and I'm really changing and it's really coagulating some things that were just floating around, and here's what's going on," they may say, "Oh, okay, sure, try it."

Paul: What would you say to somebody that would say, "I would never do that with a borderline?"

Bill: Yeah. (*portraying a person with borderline personality disorder*) Don't you make me do your training! Didn't you go to school for that? Don't you get supervision?" To tell you the truth I would do it with someone who is borderline. In fact, I think those are the people you better do it with, because those are the people that if you don't clue them in they'll know you're sleazing out in some way and they will jam you badly. They will know that there is some hidden agenda going on and they will catch you . . . schizophrenics and borderlines will catch you all the time if you're jivin' them. . . . They will find your soft spot and they will get you. So you tell them where it is, you bare your belly and say, "Here it is." I have found great luck in that process.

Lisa: I've had it actually open up possibilities in the session because I do family work and not all the time everybody's there. So we talk about how we're going to do that. One of the solutions families come up with is I'll read the progress note of the session before so they can hear what went on. So sometimes it might phase them and they'll say, "Well I didn't say I was always depressed!" And I catch myself in writing my notes being very nonpossibility oriented, and they'll go, "I didn't say, 'always!' " So I'm like, "Oh, okay" . . . and you can kind of pull it out that way.

Bill: That's a good way to do it! All right. So we're off on language and metaphor and collaboration so far, and other things are going to unfold as we go along . . . to use another metaphor.

Escaping Dogma

Bill: So the question arises, "Is there stuff that goes on with people that's not constructive?" Because clearly when you talk to them you're going to be influencing what goes on with them. Clearly, when you interact with them it's not going to be just their stuff anymore; it's going to be theirs and your stuff. Gregory Bateson[44] years ago said that if you think of a man chopping down a tree . . . usually we think of ax, man, tree . . . but really it's a circuit . . . ax, man, tree . . . ax, man, tree . . . ax, man, tree . . . that there's an ongoing circuit as soon as they engage together. And as soon as you engage with a client, it's client-therapist conversation interaction . . . that's all happening . . . and that creates or gives structure to, or evokes or brings forth, certain realities or certain ways of thinking about or feeling or experiencing things. But is there something outside of language and interaction like a developmental process that unfolds? Is there not? Is there a soul that kind of moves people through their lives or not? Or is it all constructed? Is it existential or is it spiritual? Or is that a necessary dichotomy? That's the question. There was no such thing as childhood until someone made the distinction. And now it's really hard not to think that there's such a thing as childhood. We live in a world where, for us, you can't think of there not being such a thing as childhood, but it wasn't a thing until it was invented. So did we discover childhood or did we invent it? It doesn't matter now because it's already there. I remember the days before there was borderline personality. I did psychotherapy in those days. Did we discover it? Did we invent it? Now that it's here you can't just wish it away like you can't wish away childhood . . . because of the powerful distinction that's been made. Now there are many other distinctions that haven't taken in the psychotherapy or the culture. Why do some ideas stick and why do some ideas not? And, are there really "things" that we discover? Are there essences we discover? Or is it all constituted in language and interaction?

Alice: I have a client that was originally diagnosed MPD by somebody else then referred to me. And you talked about dissociative disorder. . . . She couldn't

[44] Gregory Bateson was a British anthropologist who among many things studied communication processes. He was the coordinator of the landmark project on schizophrenia which began in 1952 (to 1962) in Palo Alto, California, and included Jay Haley, Don Jackson, John Weakland, and William Fry. See Bateson, G., Jackson, D. D., Haley, J., & Weakland, J. (1956). Bateson is considered one of the founders of family therapy. He died in 1980.

quite connect with the separate personalities though. [I said to her], "This is sort of the current terminology here, and this is what it means." And she came back a while later and said, "I want to call this *associative order*. This is the order that I have things associated."

Bill: Associating to this kind of order . . . yeah. I had someone once tell me that he worked in a clinic where they were big on personality disorders and he said, "And I'll believe in those the day you show me an ordered personality." (*laughter*) Associative order. . . . I think that's nice. I'll tell you a story that's a nice complement to that . . . this is a weird story. So this woman called me and she said, "I've been in therapy for a couple of years. I'm really stuck. I was sexually abused. I have dissociative issues and I heard you speak about this and I think you could help me. Could you see me for just a consultation if I came out?" I said, "Yeah, I do that. We just have to wait for a time when I don't have a workshop." So she comes out . . . and basically what she says is that she was in therapy before and the therapist sexually abused her ("had sex with her" is what she actually said). That therapist had been working with her on multiple personality issues. She was sexually abused when she was younger and she knew that. She would sometimes come in high and drunk into the therapy, and one day she said to him, and she wasn't attracted to him at all, "Why don't we make out?" He was like, "Okay." And they made out a couple of times . . . and then the next time he encouraged her to come high and drunk to the session. . . . She smoked dope. . . . This guy was clearly a little off. It's a different person than she's seeing now. Eventually she decided, "This is kind of creepy. I'm not doing it anymore. I don't even like this guy . . . in terms of sexual attraction. What am I doing?" So she decided to come in and tell him, "We're not doing this anymore." And when she came in he opened his arms real big and basically said, "I've decided we're going to have sex." So, she's like, "Okay." So she takes off her clothes and he has sex with her. . . . That is what she calls it . . . sex. . . . I said, "Sex seems to me a mutual thing, but we'll call it sex if you want." So she tells me this story, and, basically, after a while he says, "Now . . . you like what I'm doing," and it did feel good in her body, . . . so he said, "I want this personality to come out or I'm not going to do anymore." He would get her to do more and more because of this. So there's this weird thing with multiple personality and the sexual exploitation that was going on . . . and finally she ended the therapy. Ultimately he's lost his license, but this is many years ago . . . partly in response to what she did, but partly obviously from other things. . . . This probably wasn't the only thing he was doing. So this is years ago and when she gets out of that situation . . . partly how she gets out of it is she meets a guy at work . . . she's becoming a therapist . . . and he's a guy at work who's a psychologist who's totally wild . . . totally into drugs and a wild guy who is into a very weird and wild lifestyle that she likes a lot and that she actually trusts. It's the first guy she's ever been with that she's ever trusted. He's wild and takes heroin and does crack cocaine and weird stuff, but it's like a good relationship based on what she's had before . . . better than that. And she tells him, one time when they're high, "You know, I'm multiple personality." And he just slaps her across the face and says, "You're not!" And she was like, "Yeah, you're right. . . . I'm not." And so it was like that single-session therapy. I said, "That was the quickest cure of multiple personality I've ever heard." (*laughter*) She said, "Actually it was good for me because I was sort of under the spell of this other guy. I didn't like him hitting me, but it wasn't that bad. He hit me another time and it wasn't good. . . . It was abusive. This time it was, 'Snap out of it.'" So she tells me this story and this relationship goes by the wayside eventually . . . it breaks up. Then she sees someone else for therapy, a solution-focused therapist. The therapist informs her, as she talks about her history, that he doesn't believe in multiple personality . . . that it's just made up, created by therapists. So she goes through the therapy and, actually, she fights with him through the whole therapy. After several years in therapy with this person, she feels really terrible and that's when she decides, "This is not going anywhere. . . . This guy is too frustrating. I need to go see this other guy, Bill O'Hanlon." And basically she comes to see me to "out" herself as a multiple personality . . . because I believe in the possibility of it. I see her for two days. We don't do anything about the multiple personality, we just work on the relationship with her and the therapist, trying to sort out what's going on with the whole thing. She said, "He said he doesn't believe in multiple personality and I don't know whether I'm multiple. My boyfriend said I wasn't, he slapped me and said, 'Snap out of it!'" I say to her the second day when she comes back, "I don't see any evidence of multiple personality, but different from your therapist I do believe in multiple personality. I've seen it. I've been convinced of it. I think it's pretty rare, and it's overdiagnosed at times, but I think it exists." So then we do a little trance work and immediately in the trance work out pop a bunch of personalities that say, "We believe in it! (*laughter*) She's really in denial about it and she's having a lot of trouble and she's very suicidal because one of us is extremely suicidal" . . . and that's part of her symptom, she cries all the time when she's not working, and she works like ninety hours a week to make sure she doesn't cry. . . . Her life is messed up in a lot of ways. So now her dilemma is, she's got a therapist she has to go back and deal with . . . that doesn't believe in multiple personality and trying to use a solution-focused model with her with no results. There's the dilemma. I think it's perfectly reasonable to work with people in a solution-focused way. It's generally good, except when it isn't. I think it's perfectly reasonable to be cautious about not creating multiple personality, except when it isn't. That's the concern. When we get hooked on certain ideas to the detriment of our clients and patients, that's when it becomes problematic and models become problematic. . . . That's back to my original question. . . . Does multiple personality exist for this person before we speak to her or before she sees Oprah Winfrey . . . or reads the latest book? Does it get created in a cultural context or in a therapeutic context . . . or both . . . or neither? And I think it's really an unanswerable question, but it's a good question to be living in for a little while. Like . . . what's the strongest influence? Is it the person's experiential life? Or is it the interventions from the culture or from the therapy culture? And so my answer to it is it's undecidable. You're always going to be around influencing your client in a certain direction, so how do you stop getting in the way of their process? (*looks to Debbie*) That was your question. For me, I stop getting in the way of their process by making sure I continue to work on me, so I'm not dogmatic. I still have beliefs. I'm not eclectic, wishy-washy. I still have beliefs and values . . . strongly held beliefs and values . . . and I'm still directing the therapy. I'm clear that I'm directing the therapy. I think if you think you're not directing therapy you're delusional. You are influencing people. How I stop from imposing and interfering with their process . . . and I think that's the question . . . is multiple choice options. I said, "I don't think you're multiple personality. . . . I haven't seen any evidence, . . . but it's a possibility." And given that small opening, "I think it's very rare," I said, "And probably overdiagnosed, but I do believe that it exists." And given that small opening she found a way through, . . . but with the therapist she was seeing there was no opening. He said, "There's no such thing as multiple personality" . . . a generalization . . . and there was no room for her to fit in between there. So what I do is offer a smorgasbord . . . another food metaphor . . . of possibilities, and find out which parts of the smorgasbord they get most attracted to. If you only offer one dish, you'll never find out what your client really wants. If you offer multiple dishes you still may not find out entirely, but you're more likely to . . . and you won't force something down their throat. It's that choice process . . . like, "You could do this, and you don't have to" . . . and, "I don't believe in multiple personality, except when I do." That's one part of the possibility therapy or inclusive therapy if you want to say it that way. Generally the idea of borderline isn't helpful, except when it is. Generally medications aren't the way I'd go, except for when I do. If you leave that opening your clients are always going to be able to sway you in one direction or another so that you're not so rigid and saying, "I don't believe in labels! I don't believe in medication! I don't believe in borderlines! I don't believe in multiple personality! I believe in the miracle question!" . . . for whatever it may be. As soon as you only have one way to think about it, or a generalized way to think about it, or a generalized way to do it, the clients can barely find their way in that. . . . So I'm not saying I don't have strongly held ideas and formulas and methods, . . . Those are good things to have, but do you have the flexibility to not do them when they're not appropriate? Can you pay attention to the client's responses when they're not as overt as saying, "We knew you were going to ask that question?" And that's great coaching. Your borderline client won't do that with you. They won't coach you so clearly. You have to attend at a different level. They won't come in and say, "Don't ask that damn question again! . . . It's stopping my process." They'll act it out typically . . . that it's stopping their process, and you'll have to guess about what's stopping their process. And so you better have enough flexibility so you can do this, do this, do this, do this, and then notice their response.

That's what I was talking about with the collaborative relationship and the flexibility of intervention. And if you don't think there's such a thing as borderline personality, guess what learning you're going to get to have in your career! Or else, clients are going to go away and you'll never get a chance to have that worry. They'll give you the opportunity again and again until you get it . . . like life will . . . or they'll go away and you'll miss the opportunity.

Paul: That's a difficulty for me. You have to have your voice, but how many different ways of approaching can you master?

Bill: You have the ones which are strongly held, and that are great, and you just make a little opening for the "or nots."

Paul: So you really operate from your base even then.

Bill: Generally I don't orient to the idea of multiple personality or borderline personality except when I'm going to make that opening for some people, because it's going to be absolutely the opening that they need to get through . . . for me to believe in that possibility . . . .not in the likelihood, because most of the time you're not going to orient in that way. You're not going to see that in your therapy except when it's a helpful thing to see, except when it's the case in which it isn't working. . . . Then you better develop some flexibility.

Paul: They end up teaching you because you stay pretty much where you're at.

Bill: Pretty much. And generally it works for you. It works most of the time and it's that one or five percent . . . and that's what Haley's missing . . . right there, I think. That's what Haley's missing by not being in that room, because when you're behind the mirror you can go one hundred percent, "I always do strategic. . . . It's always a metaphorical problem of the parents that's being reflected in the child's symptom." It is, except when it isn't. You're not going to know it behind the mirror because you can still believe that it works and the person in there isn't doing it well enough, and they haven't learned it quite well enough yet. . . . That's always your way out, . . . but if you're in the room, if Haley's in the room, and he knows it better than anybody . . . like I know solution-oriented better than anybody because I made it up . . . and I can clearly tell when it's not working . . . because it isn't a matter of me going back to school and learning it or going to another supervision group and learning it. When it isn't working there's the learning possibility for me . . . if I'm willing to have that learning experience. If I'm not, then I don't get it and my client doesn't get it, which is even more of a shame. They'll either have to go to somebody else or keep working with you and just find out if you're trainable. And this woman had spent so much time developing a trusting relationship with this therapist that she was even willing to put up with the pain in the ass that he was because he was so rigid and dogmatic around this to get the kind of help she wanted because she didn't want to have to spend the time to build up the trusting relationship with someone else. And it's a shame that she should have to work so hard because he's inflexible in this area.

Alice: I stumbled into working with clients who have been sexually exploited by therapists. It's a whole different ball game. You've got to go back and reestablish trust.

Bill: Absolutely. And she's saying, "I finally found this guy that I could do this with that I don't think will sexually abuse me. And I'm doing pretty good work with him, but then I have to deal with this other stuff."

Alice: I have to work with these people and then they go for therapy.

Bill: Yeah, that's right . . . get them ready to go to therapy so that they can trust enough. And she'd clearly done that work for herself and I thought she was making great strides. I actually thought the therapy was going well, but I think he had the idea that if it was a two-year therapy, he was failing in some way. I thought, "It sound like you've made progress. This symptom has diminished, this symptom has gone away. . . . You're doing great. . . . What's the stuck place?" That was my main consultation, "You're doing great! He's doing great . . . give him that comment back that I thought, based on the outside . . . the forest through the trees . . . I see it going well."

Chapter 3

"Cindy"

This chapter illustrates the way Bill does therapeutic consultations, as well as the open and collaborative nature of the consultation. The teaching seminar participants are in the room during the consultation, and their comments, contributions, and questions are included as part of both the consultation and the teaching. The combination of demonstration, storytelling, didactic material, discussion, and personal consultations for participants lead to experiential learning.

Individual Therapy Involving Hypnosis[45]

Bill: You and I had sat down like this once before if I remember. What will be helpful to do here?

Cindy: Well, I was thinking about this conflict I have that I would love for you to resolve.

Bill: I'm taking it on here! Okay . . . (*in a funny voice*) I can only consult with you to resolve it! No, I can maybe resolve it. . . . We'll see.

Cindy: I want you to find your solutions to my problems!

Bill: I'm good at that. . . . You know I'm the right person to ask. I'll take it on.

Cindy: When I was talking to Steffanie in Denver and she was talking about this new thing that you guys are . . .

Bill: . . . In the box, out of the box . . .

Cindy: . . . The box thing . . . and I've sort of changed it to suit me . . . and I don't know how much I need to say to other people to explain that . . . probably

[45] Cindy is the participant for the session. Jennifer, a colleague of Cindy's, also enters the room to observe.

not much. My thing is that I tend to go on one end or other of the spectrum. I tend to either feel like I am "less than," and I'm a piece of shit, and I'm depressed, . . . which I have a fifty-one year history with . . . a loving, hating history with depression . . . my best friend. The other side of the box is that I think I'm "better than," which is embarrassing to say.

Bill: The truth shall set you free, but first it will embarrass the hell out of you.

Cindy: I sometimes just feel like . . . this is very embarrassing . . . but like I am the best family therapist, at least in my area.

Bill: (*jokingly*) You haven't checked out the other regions quite as well as you could have. . . . It may expand . . .

Cindy: . . . it's a problem for me in that it's very hard for me to refer anyone who calls because I think, "No one else can do it."

Bill: No one else can do it, and you'll take it . . . and you tend to take on too much because of that?

Cindy: Yeah. Way too much. There are two things about that. I'm either less than or more than, better than, . . . which I don't want. I want to be in the middle where, in fact, I am.

Bill: Very confident about the things you're confident about . . . and also you could say, "Yeah but other people do things all right." (*Cindy*: Yeah.) And, "I'm not the most terrible person in the areas in which I would critique myself."

Cindy: But I don't seem to know how to stay in that middle area. It's like there's grease in there.

Bill: You tend to slide to either side.

Cindy: Yeah.

Bill: There's a metaphor for you. . . . (*refers to the group*) We were talking about metaphors and recognizing metaphors. So you want a little more, kind of that stuff they put in the bottom of bathtubs to make sure you don't slip.

Cindy: Those skid things.

Bill: Yeah, those skid things . . . to help you stay a little more . . .

Cindy: . . . Yeah, . . . so that's it. . . . Then there's always this depression stuff . . . and I think that that's how I've learned to do depression is by doing this better than less than. I'm not sure what the relationship of that is.

Bill: That's a good question because it is kind of a weird dichotomy. You'd think that the depression, in logical ways, would have stopped you, but it didn't stop you. You've gone on and excelled at some of those things.

Cindy: Well, God bless Prozac.

Bill: Yeah, God bless Prozac, but it's not just Prozac. There are a lot of people on Prozac who didn't start a practice last year and then have an overwhelming amount of referrals so that they can't keep up with it. I mean it's so full, but businesswise, very successful. Prozac doesn't make that happen. Right? And before Prozac was invented or whatever . . . before it came into your life . . . depression had been there for a long time, and you did things despite that. I guess I'm wanting to know, to switch metaphors, that sometimes that confidence is the wind in your sails that really helps you to move along . . . and sometimes it's like that overconfidence that has you take on too much or dis other people in some ways . . . whatever minor ways that you do that in your own head or in your behavior. And just remind me . . . and I know it does help how important that the love and the support that Craig's given you and the kind of containment or whatever he does . . . I'm not sure I'm articulating that right . . . but somehow, some way with depression as a constant companion or fairly constant companion, "best friend" as you say, for all those years you've done well despite that. . . . Remind me again how you do that because that may be partly how we put the skid marks in there . . . the nonslips.

Cindy: (*Thinking and asking herself aloud*) How have I done that? I'm a workaholic and I'm an achiever, but I think that that all has to do with being depressed too. The only way I feel good about myself is if I achieve something.

Bill: So if you have external evidence of it, it can sort of ameliorate this, "I'm a piece of shit. I don't deserve it. I'm terrible and they'll find me out," or whatever it may be. You have at least external evidence that, "I'm okay," and sometimes you feel pretty good about that stuff because you have achieved.

Cindy: And it's pretty literal for me. Like I really don't deserve a shower unless I've worked out. I don't deserve lunch unless I've worked out and done x, y. . . . I don't deserve dinner. . . . I have to . . .

Bill: . . . Earn everything.

Cindy: I have to earn everything. I think my self-esteem is pretty low.

Bill: Let me cast around . . . and forget all this area we've just been talking about . . . other places in your life . . . think back on this long history you've had in life . . . that you think you've been really out of balance about things before . . . come to some sort of balance . . . there must have been other areas . . .

Cindy: (*asks self*) . . . When in my past have I been out of balance . . .

Bill: . . . Out of balance in any area . . . in some area and then found some sort of balance . . . center, balance, . . . some sort of middle ground between extremes. Can you think of another area?

Cindy: Does alcoholism count?

Bill: That counts. And how did you find a middle ground so you weren't too fanatical one way or another? Was there a middle ground or was there just one extreme or the other?

Cindy: It is one extreme or another . . .

Bill: . . . Well, I mean in terms of either drinking or not drinking that's one extreme, but there's something else about it you seem to have a sense . . . you came to some sort of good place about it, a middle place . . .

Cindy: . . . Yeah. . . . First of all it took me a year and a half to even realize that I deserved to be in AA. I didn't think that I was even good enough to do that, or I was too good. . . . I didn't deserve a chair, or I needed a throne.

Bill: Fine . . . okay, but how do you get to that place? That's a slightly different question, but let's get there before we get to the balance thing, because that's a stepping stone along the way that I can tell . . . to use another metaphor, "stepping stone" . . . just doing metaphor teaching . . .

Cindy: . . . The teacher!

Bill: The teacher. How did you get through that year and a half? How did you finally get to figure out that it was okay to have a chair and a place in AA?

Cindy: I went to an ACoA (Adult Children of Alcoholics) week-long thing and realized that I was an alcoholic and it was a relief to me. And then, being in AA was helpful to me to do the AA work in my way . . . sort of a feminist way. It was helpful for me to do some of the internal shifting that needed to happen.

Bill: But you've skipped over my question . . . and that is, you went to the ACoA thing and that opened up the possibility because you recognized about being alcoholic. That still didn't get you a chair in an AA meeting.

Cindy: Yeah, it did.

Bill: How so? Because that was part of the week, or what do you mean?

Cindy: Oh, how so (*pondering this*) . . . I don't know.

Bill: You would have had to earn your way in there usually.

Cindy: You're right. . . . I don't know how.

Bill: Ah hah . . . you've skipped over this. Have you ever seen this Sydney Harris cartoon and there's this big long formula and then it says, "And then a miracle happens . . . equals," and then one scientist says to another, "I think you need to be a little more explicit in this part." And then a miracle happens. Did you have to like, jog before you got your seat in the AA meeting? Or go a week without a drink to earn your seat in an AA meeting? What? How did you get the permission or the idea? First, just recognizing that you're alcoholic and having that be a relief, but then it's like, "Can I possibly go to an AA meeting and do I deserve to be in there?"

Cindy: You're right. Something shifted and I don't know what it was.

Bill: That's fine. You don't know now. Now, I have a second question . . . and that may percolate through, another metaphor. And it may occur to you and it may not and it may be an inexplicit process and that's fine. . . . That's what hypnotic stuff might be good for. But then the second thing is (*looks around the room*), she said something interesting and this is where the heat-seeking missile for me goes. You did AA with your own feminist slant.

Cindy: Yeah.

Bill: How? Who are you to screw around with a tradition that's many years old and somehow find a balanced way for you to do it given your feminist sensibility and the AA tradition? How did you do that?

Cindy: I had to. I didn't like how the Gestapo, male . . .

Bill: . . . Yeah, okay. . . . So that was the one extreme of doing it. The other extreme was not doing it and saying, "Screw AA; it's not my kind of thing. It's this patriarchal, male, Gestapo thing." And you found some place in the middle for you.

Cindy: Yes.

Bill: How the hell did you do it? I know you had to . . . now we're asking how. You're still saying, "A miracle occurred. . . . Some transformation occurred." Can you retrace that step for me? You probably considered, "Screw this, this doesn't fit for me. I'm not going back there." And you probably considered, "I'll just do it their way and just go along with it because who am I to question this? This has worked for a bunch of other people." Both of those extremes you considered and you found someplace in the middle. I want to know how you put the snow skid, no slip marks in the middle.

Cindy: I think I saw or felt or perceived something about truth. Truth was available to me there, and it never had been in my life.

Bill: So it was worth sticking with it; that's why you didn't just say, "Screw it, I'm not coming back here." But how did you get to the place where you didn't just buy it lock, stock, and barrel . . . another metaphor . . . how come you didn't just accept it lock, stock, and barrel? You saw that there was some truth there, and that was good, but you also saw that that truth was being distorted in some way by those patriarchal, Gestapo, kind of lenses.

Cindy: I don't know about distorted, but it wouldn't work for me.

Bill: Right. But for you it wasn't just clear to see the truth or how it worked for you in that way . . . given that tradition that that was how it was started and that's the tradition at least in the meetings that you'd seen and that you'd heard about . . . somehow you find a way to not give it up. You said, "There's some truth here and I'm going to stick with it, and also not buy the whole thing." Like my mother goes to Catholic church. She's extremely liberal, extremely feminist, and she says, "Oh I just take the parts that I like, and I don't pay attention to the other parts." And she goes to church every day. (She's like) "Abortion. . . . I think it's okay." Like, she just doesn't buy the whole package and she still sees that there's a truth there for her. Somehow she found a way to do that. How she does that in her head, I don't know. But somehow she reconciles that. How do you do that? You take the pieces that are right for you; then you add your own pieces.

Cindy: I just sort through it. And find out what I want and leave the rest, which is another AA thing.

Bill: Yeah. Use what works and leave the rest. "Only use what works"; that's what they say. "Only use what works; discard the rest."

Cindy: That's solution-oriented.

Bill: Yeah, very solution-oriented. Okay.

Cindy: So is the implication here that I have the possibility of using what works about being grandiose and leaving the rest? And using what works about being less than and leaving the rest?

Bill: That is an implication, and another implication is that this sort of something you're saying, "I need to learn this and be able to do it," and, I'm saying by my conversation and what I'm asking you about, that it's not an inability that you have. It's an ability you have. And so far you haven't successfully or consistently applied it to this area. There are two ideas.

Cindy: Say it again.

Bill: That you need to kind of take this thing you did with AA and apply it to this grandiosity, inferiority kind of thing . . . overconfidence, lack of confidence thing and find that same kind of balance that you found with the AA thing. And second, that it's not a thing we have to start from and build within your experience, that it's already there as a capability.

Cindy: Because I already know how to do it.

Bill: Yeah. You already know how to do it, just haven't done it successfully and consistently in this area. Like it's when a person says to me, "Well, I can't really assert myself." Then I find out that they do assert themselves in some area. It's a lot easier to work with that than, "I can't assert myself." Then we have to teach them assertiveness training. If they already have asserted themselves, all we have to do is say, "Oh, okay, you know how to do it over here. Now we either have to remove the barriers for using it over here or get you to realize that you can do it and you just haven't been doing it here.'' It's a different model saying, ''We have to give you something that you don't have, rather than you already have it and we just have to make sure you use it in this area.''

Cindy: Okay.

Bill: So if we were to first just consciously and very deliberately . . . maybe we'll do some trance stuff with this, but very consciously and very deliberately, if you were going to use this same process and say that the grandiosity, if you will, and the overconfidence was like the Gestapo stuff in AA and nonconfidence, piece-of-shit stuff was like not going to AA, how do you think you could pick and choose and use the stuff that works and not use the stuff that works? if you could just tell me that in a very conscious way. What stuff works about the confidence and the grandiosity and what stuff, what pieces are helpful about the depresso, lack of confidence, piece-of-shit mentality . . . feelings?

Cindy: Okay. That's a rather complicated question.

Bill: It is. We'll take it a piece at a time, or I'll repeat it.

Cindy: Yeah, a piece at a time. What works about being grandiose . . . the good part is that I can function.

Bill: It gets you up and moving and out there and doing things so you can achieve . . . you do achieve.

Cindy: Yes. And I can act like a professional. I can be a professional. I can do that.

Bill: There's a difference between those two. I thought that was a good distinction.

Cindy: Well, as long as I'm being grandiose! So I can be professional, and I can be good at it. . . . I can be good at what I do. And I am good at what I do!

Bill: It gives you the confidence to get to a place where you know you're good at what you do.

Cindy: Right.

Bill: And it pulls you in that direction or pushes you or whatever metaphor you want to use. All right, that's the good news.

Cindy: That's the good news.

Bill: It also gets you to take a lot of referrals that maybe would have scared other people or freaked out other people and got you to go to graduate school and got you to take the family preservation job. Maybe got you into a lot of situations which did increase your achievement and expertise, and confidence . . . real confidence, not grandiose. And I think that may be the question we're talking about. Is it realistically based confidence where you actually say there's evidence for this confidence? Or is it just a general sense of grandiosity like, "I'm the best one that ever was?" That compensatory confidence . . . that's a little distorted, having to put other people down for you to get up or something like that?

Cindy: No. It doesn't have to do with other people. I don't need to put other people down to put me up. But it is . . . I don't know how to say it . . .

Bill: . . . Well, how do you know you're not the best therapist?

Cindy: I don't know (*laughing*), but Jennifer told me I was delusional!

Bill: She told you you were delusional . . . that's her diagnosis. How do you know you're not [the best therapist]? And really, this is a serious question and I'm not just joking about it. It's like, how do you do reality testing on this? How do you do reality testing on this area? Well, I have to tell you two things. This is countertransferential or whatever you want to say . . . two things . . . I used to have the same thing. I would take every . . .

Cindy: . . . I don't doubt it Bill! (*laughter*)

Bill: I would be afraid not that the other people weren't that good but that they would screw them up, that they disrespect them and they wouldn't be effective. Not necessarily that I could solve the case because I wasn't sure I could, but at least I wouldn't hurt them. I won't disrespect them. I won't screw them up. So I would tend to take them on whenever . . . and now I'll say "no" a little more and, "You're on your own and I hope you find somebody good and I'll try and help you find somebody good, but I'm not going to take it on for various reasons in my life." That's the first thing. The second thing is, I not so jokingly was telling somebody in Denver, two students of Steve Gilligan's, and they were talking about their different styles and one was like the 1,2,3,4,5 teaching like me . . . and one was like Gilligan. She came in and didn't want to have an outline. She wanted to have poetry. . . . And I was laughing with them, and I said, "There's a funny thing I just have to admit to you. For some years I was kind of surprised. . . . Why would anybody go to anybody else's workshops but mine? And even Steve Gilligan, whom I like and I admire, and I get a lot out of his workshops, but I go to a workshop of his and I try and take notes and I write down a joke he said, or a funny saying . . . and that's it. And I look at my notes at the end of the workshop and there's nothing there. I had an experience, but there's nothing to take notes on and I don't go back to my office and say, "Oh, I've got to use that Gilligan technique." What is the Gilligan technique? I have no idea. . . . Learn a lot of poetry; that's about it. And I'm joking with these people and they're like laughing when I'm saying this but I'm absolutely serious. But it came to me at a moment of realization a couple of years ago, "Oh, it's because people like different styles." I listen to classical music sometimes. I listen to rock music sometimes. I listen to country music sometimes, and I'm in different moods at different times and I get different things from it. So people must go to different workshops because they like different styles. I get it. I worked my ass off to be best workshop presenter because I have a mission that I want to warp the entire field. So I worked so hard to be so great at it and I've seen the other workshops. Their handouts are generally poor, they're disrespectful and patronizing to people when they ask questions, . . . they're disorganized. They're not great. I can be better. I know I can be better. I'm still critical of myself, but I'm damn good. So how do you reality test? Partly I would go to other people's workshops to do reality testing. I have some sense of that but also to respect that other people do have something to offer, even if they're not exactly the same as me and even if my preference would be to go to a different workshop. I certainly resonate with what you're saying in some ways, but the question is how do you know, and how do you do reality testing? How do you know if it's realistic confidence or overconfidence rather than grandiosity? Like I said I was going to change the field of psychotherapy ten years ago . . . and somebody wrote a review of something when I wrote that and said, "Bill O'Hanlon is kind of off putting in his grandiosity." And I thought, "You call it grandiosity. I call it a man with a mission and I'm going to do it. I'll talk to you in ten years, fifteen years, and we'll see whether it was grandiose or whether I did it." The reality testing is, if you pull it off it wasn't grandiose. If you don't pull it off, maybe it was grandiose. So I don't know. . . . That's a question I have. I don't know if there's even an answer, but to just live in that question. So, what's the best that the depresso, piece-of-shit part offers?

Cindy: Oh yeah, the other side.

Bill: You haven't told me about that part yet. What does it contribute?

Cindy: It keeps me humble. I'm not sure it has a whole lot of functions.

Bill: I would say, from what I've heard from the outside, you're not appreciating it as much as I would like to invite you to.

Cindy: (*laughing*) Invite depression? Yeah, right!

Bill: Clearly . . . I've given short thrift to that and the overconfidence you're quite friendly with.

Cindy: Well, it's pretty new.

Bill: So what I've heard so far is that it does, like overconfidence, get you up and achieving because you have to jog. . . .

Cindy: . . . Yeah. . . .

Bill: . . . It gets you doing some things that probably are good for you. If you're depressed, getting up and jogging is something that's good for you even though you have to work out to earn your shower.

Cindy: Right, that's true.

Bill: You had to finish your paperwork to do this, or have dessert, or go see a friend, or whatever it may be . . . gets you to finish your paperwork. So in that way, since you're always having to kind of earn your esteem or your goodies, it gets you to do things that are kind of hard to do that you need to make yourself do at least initially . . . and put forth the effort to do. . . . In that way that's a contribution. Any other contributions?

Cindy: Can I concur with my sister[46] and Jennifer?

Bill: Sure, yeah . . . use your consultants. (*Speaks to Debbie and Jennifer who are sitting on the floor nearby*) What do you think that depression, feeling like a piece of shit, might contribute, if it contributes anything?

Debbie: It helps moderate the workaholic.

Bill: How so? How does it do that?

Cindy: I think it motivates the workaholic.

Bill: It energizes it, she thinks, but you see that. . . .

Debbie: . . . I just think that it keeps you from overdoing it sometimes. . . . It pulls you back.

Bill: How?

Debbie: It can dampen your energy. . . .

Cindy: . . . Because I get tired . . .

Bill: . . . Right, or discouraged . . . and you want to do it perfectly in eighty-nine hours a week, and maybe you get depressed and you can't do it eighty-nine hours a week.

Cindy: Right.

Bill: Yeah . . . okay, I see that. Because if it didn't dampen you, you would really go even more compensatory and work even harder . . . but you're emotional energy is not going to support that sometimes . . . sometimes it will.

Jennifer: Well, I saw the same one only it's a little bit of a slant . . . that it slows you down and you stop and think about what you're doing and which way you'd rather go . . .

Bill: . . . Rather than just frantic activity . . .

Jennifer: . . . What's working and what's not working. It is the energy that stops you and has you go one way or another or ask other people.

Bill: Oh, ask other people and sort of check things out.

[46] Cindy's sister, Debbie, is a participant in the supervision week.

Jennifer: Absolutely.

Bill: Rather than just charge ahead and achieve and do and do and see more clients and see more families and do more activity. Every once in a while either that lack of self-confidence or lower energy gets her to slow down.

Cindy: That's useful.

Lisa: The first thought that came to my mind was that it keeps you open.

Cindy: (*surprised*) Oh.

Bill: To what?

Lisa: To other possibilities, other people, other ideas. . . . That's how I experienced it.

Bill: And all your input, other's input, saying you're working too hard, this is too much . . . take some time, or whatever it may be . . . or you don't need to do that. It keeps you open to the input from other people, and not so overconfident so you wouldn't even listen to other people . . . you would just say, "I have to do this to earn my shower or to earn my esteem" or whatever it may be. Okay, great . . . that's helpful. Yeah, very underappreciated.

Cindy: Yeah, that was interesting.

Bill: And I know you've experienced such misery from it, I understand that it's hard to appreciate it and give it any kind of compliment or praise or value, but I suspected as much. That's part of balance. (*looks at Jennifer who is laughing*) What's what Jennifer?

Jennifer: (*teasing Bill*) I suspected as much!

Bill: I suspected as much; that's right! Okay, well . . . let's do some trance work stuff with this. Anything else before we do that?

Cindy: (*laughing*) I'm getting scared now!

Bill: Uh oh! (*makes a ghost sound*) Ooh! It's the spooky stuff! What would you be scared about, or what would be scary about this?

Cindy: Just to go back into a place where I feel like a little kid and vulnerable and out of control . . . abused and all that shit . . . not the professional part of me.

Bill: So particularly visiting there. And maybe you'd do that with trance stuff. You've done that at least once before as far as I know. All right, anything else that's a concern or things that are important to say before you go into trance?

Cindy: No.

Bill: And my idea about doing that, I mean I don't particularly care to invite you into that no-fun experience that you're talking about . . . if that's where you go, that's where you go . . . but my idea is that some of this is that automatic process . . . that, "I don't know how it happened it just happened" . . . the change that happened to make you available to go to AA. There was something that happened there that was transformative or shifting for you. And that's the kind of shift, now that we've talked about it consciously, which may be making that shift already . . . make the shift altogether. I also want to enlist, as Steve Gilligan calls it, the belly mind . . . that sort of internal automatic process to find a balance and put those no slip, skid things in there as well. Find that middle and be able to stay there much of the time. All right, so you may want to keep the eyes open. You've had experience with that before. You may want to close the eyes, whatever is important for you or whatever works best for you. Get yourself as comfortable as possible . . . that's good . . .

Cindy: . . . Protected! (*laughter*)

Bill: Cross those arms.. . . . Yeah, I had a friend, I used to run encounter groups with him, and we'd run them Friday nights and Saturday nights and people would drop in . . . they were mostly growth groups . . . and you were trying to get to the most deep level of your truth and say it to other people . . . to bring them down so they were out of their heads and into their bodies and emotions. And one night, it's near the end of the group and there are pillows on the floor and we're all on pillows, and he's sliding down more and more and finally he's totally horizontal . . . and someone confronts him about not caring for the group because he's dropping out, and he says, "You have to remember the first rule of body language is gravity." So I don't always interpret this (*folds his arms*) as protection. Okay. So the first thing I'll say is, as usual, that I think it's okay for you to be where you are now. And what I think about your experience may not be relevant or may be relevant . . . it may be something you take under advisement. What I invite you to do is, as much as possible, value yourself as you are now. And I don't mean praise yourself or compliment yourself, I just mean more of that including and allowing, and not particularly try and get rid of or fix or change where you are now . . . whether that's that nervousness or fear or the apprehension about going to that child place that you talked about . . . just as much as possible to allow where you are right now . . . to allow the experience of where you are right now . . . to be there, as well as your self-conscious or critical mind . . . your figuring-out-mind, your analytical mind. What Steve Gilligan was talking about is having the belly/mind and the analytical mind both be available, as well as to be in relationship with . . . . yourself and me, the other or others out here. I was talking about earlier, if you went back into your practice after this group, that you don't just abruptly change your behavior with your clients or your patients . . . that you say, "I went to this group and I learned this stuff and I've been doing something different or thinking about something different." But if you give people the context in which to put it, rather than in isolation, it doesn't seem so dry. One of the things that I really learned about from working with Steffanie recently, and noticing her patterns, is that when she is in her difficult place that she absolutely disconnects from context . . . that she disconnects from relationships with herself, her body . . . and she disconnects from her external environment . . . both from external reality and reality checking . . . and from other people . . . she just drops out of context . . . and it's like those clients that you see that they have some behavior that evolved in a particular context . . . for example, when they were being abused . . . and now they're in a different context and not being abused anymore, but they're still acting . . . in some ways . . . as if they're in that old context and need to protect themselves in that way . . . and so they've dropped out of context . . . and sometimes what I think is we need to just make sure that the person isn't so isolated and they reconnect with the context . . . so that they can update with reality testing and have enough connection with the current context. . . . That's part of what your husband is for you from what I can understand from a few things you've told me and from what Steffanie's said . . . that he is somewhat an occurring context for you to continue to remind you that it's now and not then. . . . But that's a big reminder all the time . . . there may be more little reminders that you're in the now . . . that the people around you aren't the same as the people around you then . . . and that you can remember your resources . . . you can acknowledge the fears, and the difficulties, and the depression . . . and the grandiosity or the confidence . . . and then also include the current context and the reality checking, and also your relationship with yourself and other people . . . all that can be there . . . when it's surrounded in that context. . . . I was hearing Francine Shapiro talking about *EMDR*[47] stuff and she had a similar kind of theory about trauma! . . . it's almost like trauma gets like a puss-filled sack, it's isolated from the rest of the body . . . that neurologically she's talking about it, experientially . . . so anytime that some of the puss spills out, that's really quite infectious and it's not good for the person . . . and what the EMDR process is doing is reconnecting it with the rest of the body and taking away that sack so that it gets spread out and dissipated and dealt with by the whole body which has a much better ability than that little localized place . . . this time she's talking neurologically, experientially . . . so those encapsulated experiences that are isolated become what's difficult for the person . . . when it's connected with a rich association from the rest of their life it becomes a little less large . . . it becomes a smaller piece . . . it becomes much more integrated in the person's life experience . . . so as usual what I would suggest is to allow the depression, the low self-esteem, the lack of confidence . . . and allow the grandiosity, the overconfidence . . . and then in addition to connect with yourself and your body . . . the analytic mind, the body mind . . . and connect with other people in your context, current reality, and relationships . . . and let all that be there, and include all that . . . and find out how things

[47] Francine Shapiro is the developer of *eye movement desensitization and reprocessing* (EMDR). See Shapiro, F. (1995). She is also a Senior Research Fellow at the Mental Research Institute in Palo Alto, California.

shift when that happens . . . and I don't know if that's like what the process was for you in that ACoA week, . . . but somehow you connected to a context that maybe helped you make that shift . . . that somehow you connected with yourself about the feminist sensibilities as well as the AA sensibility . . . even though the tradition was there and that Gestapo tradition was there, and you were able to hold both of those things or maybe more things than that . . . and your relationship with those people and with the alcoholism . . . all at the same time so that one didn't obliterate the other or obscure the other . . . but they could all be there . . . that the valuable aspects of AA, your own feminist understandings, sensibilities to AA . . . and the Gestapo aspects . . . and then you could find your own balance between those . . . because you stayed in connection with it, didn't run from it, didn't try and rail against it or fight against it in a way that you would shoot yourself in the foot . . . somehow you found a way to speak the truth and stay with your truth and stay in context. . . . That's a very unusual thing for people to do. . . . They either avoid and isolate, or they want to dominate and control. . . . There's something else that you did in that context . . . and I suggest the same thing in this other context . . . not avoid and isolate, not dominate and control . . . but somehow, some way bring your own sensibility to it . . . your unique sensibility. . . . Jennifer sent us a tape of David Whyte,[48] the poet. . . . I was very moved by it . . . and I really liked the phrase that he used in there . . . a Mary Oliver poem that he was quoting and he said, "You *only* (*stretches out the word*)," and he said, "This is the 3,000 mile only" . . . it's a big only . . . so he says, "You *only* . . . *only* . . . *only* . . . have to love what the soft animal body in you loves." . . . That was the Mary Oliver line that he quoted that I was so moved by . . . "You only have to love what the soft animal body in you loves" . . . that's all . . . and follow your heart, follow your passion, follow your energy . . . and stay in context . . . you only have to include and allow . . . (*Cindy's body jerks*) . . . yeah, that's an interesting neurological response . . . when I first learned neurolinguistic programming they used to have people put one polarity in one hand (*puts his right hand out*) like the overconfidence, grandiosity . . . and the other polarity (*puts his left hand out*) like the feeling like a piece of shit, depression, lack of confidence . . . and they used to say, "Okay, now bring them together" (*moves his hands together slowly*) . . . and people used to do that kind of neurological thing (*jerks his body*) . . . it was really weird to watch . . . integration was occurring . . . neurologically you could actually see the person shift . . . very interesting . . . and I don't know if that was what it was . . . but it reminded me of that in some ways. . . . *Certs* is a breath mint (*holds out his left hand*), *Certs* is a candy mint (*holds out his right hand*), wait . . . they're two mints in one (*brings his hands together to show the joining of the two mints into one*) . . . and they disappear into one. I like that because I'm an inclusive kind of guy . . . and to tell you the truth, I think you're an

[48] David Whyte is a poet whose books and audiotapes are available through the Many Rivers Company, P.O. Box 868, Langley, Washington 98260.

inclusive type of gal. . . . As much as you talk about those dichotomies, my experience with you has been very inclusive . . . and I think that's part of that, at least what I've learned from my kind of rather shallow understandings from the things from Carol Gilligan[49] and *The Stone Center*[50] that I've come across and the applications of therapy is that idea of inclusiveness and relationality . . . very important feminist principles and values . . . like there's all this stuff about differentiation and individuation . . . which have their place as well, but it's about relationship and inclusiveness as well. . . . We have such an individual, isolated model in western culture, American culture especially . . . the individualism and how that dominates our world . . . and other cultures don't have that so much . . . they don't have the same brand. . . . They're very relational and inclusive. . . . We were hearing this morning about the Quaker tradition in which the whole congregation has to come to consensus before they'll do something . . . and I remember reading about Quaker congregations in the 1800s having long, ten-, fifteen-year long discussions . . . coming to terms with the idea of slavery . . . at first only one person in the congregation, or two people, would stand up and say, "I'm against slavery and we ought to work to abolish it and take a stand against it as a congregation" . . . and everybody would be really offended by it and shocked by it . . . and they'd keep the discussion going for ten to fifteen years until the entire congregation was in alignment and in consensus . . . as the consciousness shifted in the meeting the consciousness was shifting in the culture . . . and the dialogue became different . . . where it was a lone voice speaking up and standing for a certain value . . . staying in relationship and speaking their truth . . . it started to sway the whole meeting . . . because the truth is very, very powerful . . . and it can shift things. . . . When Candy Lightner's[51] child died from a drunk driver she stood up and spoke the truth and she changed a whole culture's laws, a whole country's laws about drunk driving . . . she made a difference for thousands and thousands of people . . . because she just stayed with the truth and stayed in relationship . . . and spoke to the context and did reality checks . . . somehow, some way she got out of relationship with the organization she started and they fired her later. . . . I don't know what happened . . . I was curious that a person with such passion somehow went out of relationship with the organization she started . . . so she stopped doing that reality check . . . she went out of relationship perhaps, she didn't include . . . so, I don't know, somehow it seems like you didn't go to that place that you went to last time that you might have been afraid of going to. . . . It's hard to tell from the outside. . . . What I'd like to do is invite you to reorient to the present time and the present

[49] Carol Gilligan is a professor at Harvard University and the author and coauthor of numerous publications on subjects such as women's issues.

[50] The Stone Center is located at Wellesley College in Wellesley, Massachusetts.

[51] Candy Lightner founded *Mothers Against Drunk Driving* (MADD) after her 12-year-old daughter, Cari, was killed by a drunk driver. She headed MADD for eight years. Today MADD has chapters in all fifty states and many international affiliates.

place . . . to you and your body . . . and I'd like to ask you about that. How was that? What stood out for you?

Cindy: I don't know. I feel like I don't know anything you said and I know everything you said. You just turned into a mouth. (*laughter*)

Bill: Yeah, a lot of people say that. (*laughter*)

Cindy: And I just felt like I could take it all in, but it didn't matter. It was very much to me like going to a museum, . . . which is an important experience to me. And I panic sometimes when I'm in a museum that I won't remember everything, and, of course, I can't remember everything, . . . but I need to know that it's okay because on some level everything I need to know is in there . . . and so it was like that, . . . which is probably a high compliment.

Bill: That's great . . . integration and balance . . . good, all right . . . sounds good to me. How come you didn't go, at least it didn't appear from the outside, to that child, regressed, abused . . .

Cindy: . . . I think because you made it an option that I didn't have to go down that road. I think when it's not an option I am a little perverse about it.

Bill: Yeah, forced into that.

Cindy: Well, two things: I either get afraid that I will go down it and so I do, or say, "Fuck you," for withholding that from me . . . saying, "You can't get depressed," because I can.

Bill: Right, "I'll show you!" (*laughter*) It was okay with me if you did and okay with me if you didn't. I didn't know whether you were going to or you weren't . . . it just seemed okay to me.

Cindy: I felt pretty safe. I know you, and my sister wouldn't let anything happen to me, and Jennifer wouldn't, and Lisa wouldn't.

Bill: They were here, on the ready!

Cindy: It was helpful. I feel like integration of those is much more of a possibility now. In fact, I think they already are integrated much more than I had realized that they are . . . and I can integrate them.

Bill: Yeah . . . I actually thought that they both served one function in common, at least, and that was to get you up and moving. Both do that in some ways . . . get you up and moving when depression might be really pulling you down and both of them kind of got you up and going. All right, typically what I like to do at the end of this, and this is a little unusual because Cindy has been in this situation and she knows about this, is to invite you all to comment or ask questions of either of us in terms of the process, the experience . . . what we were about, what I was about . . . why I did what . . . whatever it may be. It could be technical, therapeutic questions, experiential questions, or comments about what you noticed or what occurred in your experience that might be a contribution.

Group Observations, Reflections, and Feedback

Alice: I followed right along.

Bill: There's an extra charge for that! (*laughter*)

Alice: I was just thinking driving up here last night that I was getting a little grandiose in my plan. So I have that struggle too. When am I being grandiose and when am I being chicken? So I went right along for the ride. I did have a couple of glitches . . . of course I can't remember exactly what you were saying now . . . a couple of glitches when I felt like you were wandering off into something negative as opposed to positively worded . . . and I didn't want to go down that way.

Bill: Sure. I understand that. Hopefully if I were in front of you I would have phrased it differently, but I was really responding to Cindy. And I thought, obviously that choice of words seemed right. . . .You heard her say at the end, "If you want to avoid the negative, guess where I'm going!" Hopefully my intuition was picking up on that and I know Cindy a little bit too, so it wasn't a wild guess. For you it would have been different phrasing though.

Alice: The other thing is that I could kind of just skip over stuff that was particularly related to Cindy . . . and just fill in the blanks.

Bill: Good.

Denise: I'd like to ask Cindy a question. When you first started out you said you were a little scared. Were you aware of a point at which fear just went away? . . . Or how did you experience the dissipation of that? Or am I making more of it than what you had?

Cindy: I'm not sure how to answer that. I can dissociate on a dime, so all I have to do is see Bill start talking and moving his head and I'm gone.

Bill: And that was a comfortable experience . . . that wasn't so apprehensive or scary at that point? Or you don't remember . . . or as soon as I started talking or as soon as you said, "I'm afraid I'll go there" . . . anticipating or whatever.

Cindy: Yeah, I think I left my head, in a way, and just went with Bill . . . just went on this little trip with Bill.

Bill: That's nice.

Paul: The thought I had is how common that feeling of superiority/inferiority . . . if you want to call it the two extremes.

Cindy: Really?

Paul: Yeah, at least to me it seems . . . I've heard it so much . . . I mean it's something I've experienced. So it was kind of nice to be part of hearing you revealing that and working that through. A question I had is I wonder if that's the way therapists are—if that's common to this group of people as opposed to the general public, . . . because it seems to be very common.

Bill: I do think there is an occupational hazard of therapists because we are our instrument to a certain extent, that almost all therapists that I have ever got to know intimately in supervision or training go through bouts of severe self-doubt. Not all of them, but almost all of them. And when they go through personal life changes like you're going through a divorce and you're thinking, "If only this couple knew I was going through a divorce they wouldn't want to see me." That sort of self-doubt of, "If they only knew what problems I had. I'm anxious," or "I'm depressed," or whatever it may be. We critique ourselves and you have to have a certain amount of self-confidence to even do it this work. It's scary to be in a room with people with big life problems. You have to have a certain amount of self-confidence to do it.

Paul: It's a linking together of the two. They're part of a whole. So they're not really one good and one bad . . . they're sort of complementary.

Bill: They can be.

Megan: I guess I was struck in your situation with how that seemed to kind of take care of you when you do have, or it sounded like to me, when you do have more of a down time . . . that kind of acted to take care of you when you were doing too much, or maybe as you were saying, "Taking in information from others" . . . or being open to that . . . kind of like healed you or something in a way. It seemed like that to me.

Alice: Then there was the wonderful reframing . . . what the people who know you could do for you.

Cindy: It was very helpful to have.

Bill: Yeah, and you used them as consultants . . . that was great. So what did you see and hear that had anything to do with what we talked about today . . . or solution-oriented stuff or anything that we've talked about or that you've learned? What did you see and hear in this conversation?

Lisa: One thing that you did was you took it from the context she was really stuck in and then moved it to a different context . . . of AA, which had possibilities.

Bill: She made that change in that area so it was something that she could do now. It was a matter of doing it in this area. That's using the person's resources and abilities and reminding them that they have those resources and abilities. Not that it's this whole thing, they're going to have to learn and go through this long process . . . somehow it happened. That's one solution-oriented bit I'd say. Focus on the competence rather than the incompetence, or ability rather than in-ability.

Jennifer: And the competence of the incompetent.

Bill: How so?

Jennifer: What Cindy was holding was an incompetence. . . .

Bill: . . . Something that was terrible . . . can't see any good parts of the depression, low self-esteem, feeling like shit . . . I was searching for it but she was like, "Good parts? No thanks, . . . I don't think so!" You all were able to contribute a lot of that. I thought of one part, but then you added more.

Lisa: (*to Bill*) If we weren't here, would you say something like, "What would your best friend say?" or "What would your sister say?"

Bill: You might. She may be clueless though, . . . but you could ask that. It's very difficult to see it . . . it really is, I understand that. When you have those blinders it's difficult . . . so more than that I would probably be making guesses. And I'd say that, but my sense is sometimes she would answer that and get to it and sometimes she wouldn't, . . . so I would more likely be saying, "So I heard this part . . . that it could be good for you."

Jennifer: I've also been using, "What is your belly saying and what is your heart saying!" That's one of the things I learned from the Gilligan thing in Denver. Or if it's coming from the heart then I'll say, "What does your head say and what does your belly say?" And the belly is the part that people don't connect to, and it's the piece that connects the mind and the heart . . . or in some people I've found that the heart is connecting the belly and the mind. They somehow work to balance. . . . The person is not listening to one or the other . . . more.

Bill: The internal consultants.

Alice: What's really unique to what you do as opposed to NLP is the incredible amount of permissions you give.

Bill: It's very important. As you heard the importance of the permission to go to that childhood, regressed . . . if that isn't in there, boom . . . there we go. And there are two kinds of basic permission, "It's okay to" and "You don't have to."

Denise: You also did that before the hypnosis when you were trying to get the connection between going to AA, I believe, and she said, "I don't know," and you said, "Well okay, that's all right we don't need to go there." And you left it . . . which I felt, of course to my formulaic thinking, you didn't badger her into, "C'mon. . . ."

Bill: "Let's get to it; let's have a solution!" (*laughter*)

Denise: That's what I would have done . . . or "Keep looking! If you don't know, who does?" And you just very gently said, "Well, okay." But you really didn't even leave it.

Bill: What a tricky guy!

Denise: Yeah, you are. You just kind of went in the back door.

Bill: Yeah, I go another direction. I went through *rolfing* one time . . . deep tissue massage . . . and I loved it, I actually did . . . and I had read a book saying it hurt a lot and I wasn't excited about that . . . so I said I'll go to one session and see if it's okay. I went to one session and it was great. It didn't hurt at all. So I went to two sessions; it didn't hurt. I just kept going. Finally, about the seventh session, the woman who did it was really great, and she came into this place and she started pushing (*holds up his arm and shows the area*) and it was like, "Whoah that hurt!" And she said, "If it hurts I'm doing it wrong. So I'll come in a different way." And I think that same thing about therapy. If the person says, "Ah," I'll persist a little, but if it really feels like pestering and badgering and pushing, it's not right for me. Some people would do it and they may get a better answer. They may have better ways to do it, but it seems to me . . . in politic . . . it seems like not a southern gentleman thing to do. (*laughter*) I find that kind of sensibility much more. This guy up in Baltimore wrote an article, which unfortunately hasn't been published, but it's a great article, called "Brief solution-focused therapy as Miss Manners." It basically said, just follow all Miss Manners[52] and you will be a good solution-focused therapist. I thought, "Isn't that nice! I like that!" It's really Miss Manners therapy. Miss Manners is great. . . . She's firm, she's clear, and she's really respectful and polite. She doesn't let people walk all over her, and she doesn't walk all over people. I like that.

Talking Hypnosis

Debbie: How often do you use hypnosis?

Bill: I don't know. It goes in phases. I've been calling it *solution-oriented inner work*[53] because trance freaks people out. Cindy's already done trance, so I didn't think we needed to worry about that, but I think this is different from the hypnotic trance where, "You vill go into trance!" It's a very cooperative, very permissive process and it's much more experiential . . . get down to that belly mind and allow the head stuff to be there but from the heart and the belly. We're just going to move you into that experience much more, so you're not so figuring it out. (*looks to Cindy*) You did some figuring it out very consciously and then just say, "Let's go into your experience and we don't have to analyze what your experience is, we don't have to figure out where it came from, we just have to move you in your experience and have things start to move on . . . new possibilities open up or open up a smorgasbord." So it depends on what people come in

[52] Judith Martin (a.k.a. Miss Manners) is a well-known author of newspaper and magazine columns, articles, and books.

[53] See Figure 3.1, *Wordsmithing in Solution-Oriented Inner Work.*

WORDSMITHING IN SOLUTION-ORIENTED INNER WORK

1. Use possibility, permission, and empowering words and phrases.

- *"Feel free to tune out anything that I say that doesn't fit for you."*
- *"You can just let yourself respond in whatever way you do and validate that response."*

2. Use inclusive language and phrases.

- *"You can be distracted as you go into an inner state or you might be focused on just what I say or you might be concentrating in a relaxed way."*
- *"You don't have to be relaxed and you can relax."*

3. Make distinctions (Splitting).

- *"You can distinguish between the things that you did and the things that were done to you."*
- *"One part of you can be paying attention to the sounds around and another can pay attention to the sounds inside."*

4. Attribute resistance, distractions, skepticism, and analysis to the conscious mind and automatic experience and ability to the unconscious.

- *"Your conscious mind may be thinking that you can't go deeply inside and at the same time your unconscious mind is beginning the process of going deeper inside."*

5. Propose linkages and associations (Linking).

- *"As your breathing starts to change, you can find yourself drifting a little and letting your muscles relax even more."*
- *"And in the future, when you need it, your unconscious can give you access to the resources you need to solve your difficulties."*

6. Encourage desired responses and include potentially troublesome ones.

- *"You can open your eyes, as you just did, and still be internally focused. They might close or remain open. . . I don't know what will be right for you."*

7. Presuppose certain responses and then speculate as to how and when the responses will occur.

- *"I don't know how quickly that hand will lift up to your face."*
- *"I don't know exactly what you'll accomplish when you are inside. Perhaps you won't even be able to tell for sure until after you come out ."*

8. Use words that are unspecified as to person, place, time, thing, or action. Use outline words for which the client has to provide much of the specific meaning.

- *"There are lots of learnings that you have had in the past that you have consciously forgotten about."*
- *"You can draw upon experiences, wishes, hopes, dreams, skills, abilities, and anything else you need to accomplish your goals."*
- *"You can go to a certain time and certain place to get what you need; it might be a time in the past or a time in the future; it might be nearby or far away."*

Figure 3.1

for. It goes in phases in my work. Some people have no clue I do any of that inner work. I just stay focused on the outside stuff, asking the conscious, deliberate questions. Some people do. I'd say it's about a third to a half of the time depending on what their concerns are. I do have some indications of when I'll do it and when I won't.[54] First of all, Cindy's done this before, so I thought that might be a good thing to do because it seemed helpful last time . . . or to make a contribution, so that would be an indication, if it's worked before . . . may as well do some more of it. The second thing, though, is she said something during the process that made me think, "Oh, let's do some trance work on this." And what she said was, "Something happened during that ACoA thing, a shift occurred so that somehow I was open to going to AA." And I said, "What was it?" She said, "I don't really know." That to me is an indication that we have to go away from the analytic mind which figures things out . . . to something that's more of the *belly mind* or of the heart that doesn't figure things out in the same way. It's more like you have a problem, you go to sleep and you wake up in the morning and you know the solution. That's much more of the mind we need to talk to—the experiential self that somehow works things out. (*looks toward Alice*) Like, you know you need to get a divorce even though your mind is saying, "No way. I'm in practice with this person. It's a crazy thing. I'm not going to do this." It doesn't matter, somebody has got it figured out . . . that's what you need to do and they'll get your attention eventually, one way or the other. If you will, the somebody else . . . and I don't mean to make it multiple personality . . . it's really another mind in you.

Alice: The inner voice.

Bill: The inner voice . . . whatever you want to say . . . it doesn't even show up as a voice for some people. It's just a knowing that they have and it's a figuring out that they do on a different level . . . gut level, heart level, belly mind, whatever you want to say. That, "She's saying it happened and I really don't know how it happened, but these things happen for me." Well, let's go there. This is a way to deliberately invite that process to happen. So that's when I know it's time to do it. When a person says, "I know it happened, but I don't know how it happened." The other way that I know it's time to do it . . . two other ways I guess . . . one is when is when the person's really devaluing themselves and I want to invite them to value and include everything, which is part of what goes on with Cindy. And, the third thing is when they have symptoms that are the involuntary, automatic kind, like if their limbs were shaking and they couldn't find any medical reason for it. That would be a great time to do that inner, hypnotic work. If they were having migraine headaches, . . . they'd gone through all the medical interventions and nothing had worked, . . . that's a great time to do that inner, hypnotic work. Because they're saying, "I've done everything

[54] For more on this see O'Hanlon, B. (in press) O'Hanlon, W. H. (1987).

that I know how to do deliberately. I've changed my diet. I don't drink wine anymore. I don't eat chocolate anymore. I exercise and meditate regularly to reduce these. And I've gone to all the doctors that I can go to. Can you help me?'' I'd say, ''Yeah, I can help you. This is something we can do hypnosis for. This is what hypnosis is good for.'' So it's nonvoluntary, autonomic, automatic, neurological, physiological stuff hypnosis is really good for.

Alice: TMJ.

Bill: TMJ can be a combination. Like people can deliberately do TMJ exercises, wear things in their mouth . . . those are deliberate things, but if they have done all that stuff and TMJ still continues or bruxism or something, then we can do hypnosis for that.

Cindy: What do you make of it when a person has a little seizure like I did? Would you incorporate it right in?

Bill: I made of it exactly what I made of it . . . as a suggestion. Otherwise, I don't make anything of it. I let them make something of it. I slanted what you might make of it, obviously.

Cindy: You used it to say, ''Oh there was a cementing of two parts.''

Bill: It could be.

Cindy: It's happening right in front of us!

Bill: I suggest that . . . if you take that suggestion, please go for it! That's a good one. I imagined that might be what it was, and I imagined it might be something else too.

Cindy: Maybe, maybe not.

Bill: Absolutely. It either was or it wasn't. That's what I figure. . . .

Cindy: . . . To quote Bill O'Hanlon!

Bill: That's right. It was either that wonderful integration or it wasn't. I just noted it, and I thought it was important to speak to. What did you all make of it?

Katy: I wonder what Cindy makes of it, or made of it.

Bill: What did you make of it before I said something or after I said something? Both.

Cindy: It was totally involuntary. I don't know because I was really asleep . . . in a way.

Bill: Just following along.

Cindy: I was happy to buy Bill's . . .

Bill: . . . Sounded good to you . . .

Cindy: . . . I don't remember what Bill said, but what I heard him say was, "Well, sometimes that's what happens with like, two trains hitching up." I just felt like the two parts were connecting.

Bill: Sounds good to me. Metaphor, right! You got a different metaphor than I used! I used the *Certs* metaphor. I used the NLP metaphor. She created her own! See . . . now, you say, "So it sounds to me like you're on the right track . . . and that you're really . . ."

Denise: . . . Chugging along!

Bill: Chugging along . . . right! And you're really pulling all the parts of you now in the same direction. That's exactly what you do. You expand the metaphor a little in that direction. A quote from Bernard Malamud[55] that I read years ago it said, "When you're on the wrong track, every station you come to is the wrong station." When you're on the right track, not every station is the right station, but at least there's the possibility.

Jennifer: I'd like to make one more observation about the pretrance part of what we did. Cindy came in here with something that was rather focused, and you remained on that and everything you talked about had to do with getting more information about either the grandiosity or the depression, or then you renamed them. . . . It felt like I knew them both . . .

Bill: . . . A lot better . . .

Jennifer: . . . And I looked at the clock and you had only been doing it for like ten minutes, and it seemed like it was a very long time. And I thought of all the information that you had exchanged in this very short period of time and how clear things were coming. And it was helpful to watch . . . helpful to remind me to stay right on the issue of what somebody is talking about. My tendency is to go off and ask something that sounds interesting or whatever . . . you just stayed right with it.

Bill: I wouldn't have noticed that. I agree and I believe it, but I just wouldn't have noticed it.

Jennifer: You wouldn't have noticed it because you don't sit in my office and go off on tangents. (*laughter*)

Bill: But the other thing is, I think sometimes because of that . . . I wrote a case commentary for the *Family Therapy Networker*[56] about a case of Eve Lipchik's[57] . . . .and I was making all sorts of suggestions about what she could have done, and so did another person who commented on it. In the next issue of the *Family*

[55] Bernard Malamud was a renowned author. He died in 1986.

[56] See O'Hanlon, B. (1996).

[57] Eve Lipchik has published on *solution-focused* therapy with an emphasis on domestic violence. She is the codirector of ICF Consultants, Inc., in Milwaukee, Wisconsin.

Therapy Networker, Ellen Berman,[58] who's a family therapist and psychiatrist wrote in and said, "I can't believe it. Eve and the two commentators didn't ask anything about antidepressants. This guy was depressed." It was like, geez, well I'm not going to comment on everything, . . . because I get so focused on what might be helpful about it and learning more about that thing, that sometimes I don't ask about the wider things and I think sometimes that's important to remember in some situations. In some situations that focus is of benefit and in some situations it's going to be a detriment. I think both are helpful, but I think I continue to stick with that, what we joked about before is cab driver therapy . . . that is, I don't know where to go unless the person says, "Here's where I want to go. Here's what I'm concerned about." They get in my ca-b . . . and I think other therapies it's the different cab driver from the *New Yorker*, that cartoon, that basically it's . . . you get in the cab and the cab driver tells you where you want to go, "You're going to 78th and Park Ave." . . . other therapies have an idea about what's wrong with you and what needs to change about you. It's a theory of normality or pathology, and I don't have one of those. . . . I have a vague, general one . . . but not a very specific, normal, pathological one.

(Jennifer leaves the room)

Bill: Anything with that work with Cindy or what we've been talking about this morning that we need to finish off or talk about?

Alice: I did remember you started talking about somebody having problems when they drop out of context.

Bill: Yes.

Alice: I didn't totally understand that and started to sound very negative. Can you explain it better?

Bill: I was talking about my wife who's a good friend of Cindy's. They've been talking about their mutual challenges in life and Cindy was very interested in something that Steffanie had just learned. And what I was talking about is that she discovered part of the problem, and I discovered part of the problem is . . . she's been very physically ill . . . and when she gets very physically ill, that's a big challenge in itself . . . in addition what happens is she'll just drop out of relationship. She'll feel alone and she'll feel isolated . . . and often people who are chronically ill or severely ill with emotional or psychiatric or physical, I think feel isolated. That's part of the suffering of the situation. So that's what I was suggesting to Cindy who, those of you who know her here, know that she might have a tendency to feel alone with her troubles . . . or that they're all hers and that she's isolated from other people. I think she's made a good connection with Craig in terms of outside her family connection, but I think she does have a tendency to maybe take it on herself too much . . . it's, "This is me and it's

[58] See Berman, E. (1996).

all me." So I was suggesting, "One of the places that you really thrive is when you make a connection with people. You're still in the same place emotionally or psychologically, but if you're connected to other people in your context you seem to do a whole lot better than when you pull back and say, 'I'm all messed, and the only person who can handle me is Craig. The rest of the world doesn't want me. I'm a piece of shit.'" So that's what I was talking about with her . . . and again, I knew a little about her from the past and we've had some conversations and I knew she had been talking to my wife about those kind of things. I thought that was relevant for her but a little out of context for you.

Chapter 4

Evolving Conversations

This chapter illustrates an important aspect of the week: getting comments from participants and having Bill respond to those comments. This gives an opportunity to clarify or expand previous points and to add a richness and complexity for which other forums such as books and workshops are unsuited.

What's Coming Across?

Bill: So let me check in. We'll go the South American way this time if you don't mind. I want to know a couple of things. Generally what's been coming across about this work? Also, what's a little surprising that doesn't come across in the books or the workshops? If anything like that occurs to you . . . from what you've heard today or seen today or experienced today.

Karen: Let's see . . . ways that you have overcome similar obstacles before . . . and focusing on those . . . and maybe doing the same thing or something similar to overcome the problems that you have right now.

Bill: I think that's a little different from a solution-focused question which is, "When you've been depressed before, when has it been better?" This is more going to another context in competence, which I think is much more from the Ericksonian tradition than the solution-focused tradition. I think it's slightly different, so I can understand how that's kind of being highlighted in a way that it isn't in other contexts. Anything else occur?

Karen: Yeah, but right this second I'm not sure what it is.

Bill: That's fine. If you think of anything as we go around just jump in.

Denise: Well, obviously I'm focusing on how nonformal you are!

Bill: I wonder why that is!

Denise: I don't know! I'm just really struck by how it's natural, it's not this contrived like, "Okay, what was the question I should ask in this situation?" It just comes up, and sometimes those questions do come up, . . . but even then it doesn't sound like when I ask it.

Bill: You know, Michele (Weiner-Davis) and I, when we were writing our book together she was really under the sway of the Milwaukee folks and she wanted to put in these flow charts, which she had from her handouts and things that they had put out. I thought, flow charts? I mean, I can read them . . . but barely . . . and certainly that's not how I think about therapy. You know, if the client says they have an exception you pursue the exception and amplify the description. . . . It's like, yeah, I guess I do that, except when I don't. But I definitely don't think about therapy in terms of flow charts. It doesn't occur to me; that's not the way I put it together. I said, "Steve (de Shazer) can write the flow charts. We have another book to write." She said, "Yeah, I don't think of flow charts either. What am I doing?" And I thought that was nice.

Denise: Yeah, I clearly see how much I'm doing that. I'm looking at the flow chart and using that, and it's really getting in my way.

Bill: I think those are good things for teaching sometimes. They're not such good things for clinical work. I think that's an important distinction to make. I organize it a 1,2,3,4,5 when I teach, and that's a good thing to do. You've got to be wary of the 1,2,3,4,5s when you're doing clinical stuff.

Karen: You mean like the, "What's better?" or "What's changed?"

Bill: Right, or if they say "yes" to something's better, if they say "no" to something's better, where do you go from there . . . that kind of flow. There's a series of questions you'd ask this way (*moves right hand*), there's a series of questions you'd ask this way (*moves left hand*) or comments you'd make or whatever it may be. I think that's a pretty important distinction to keep in mind about what do you do when you have to communicate to other people what you do, and you're sitting there with a person in front of you.

Denise: Also, I don't know that I've ever had any training at all in trance induction. I've never really even seen it done other than maybe on tape or something . . . and didn't know what to expect. I was pretty sure you weren't going to do the old watch thing! So that was kind of a surprise . . . because you didn't do anything . . . (*laughter*) . . . you know what I mean?

Bill: Like . . . where was the stuff?! It's better to call it solution-oriented inner work because it comes out of a tradition of trance, but (it's like) "Is that trance?" and "Where's the trance induction?" I'm just speaking to her and saying, "Focus inside a bit and we're going to do the same kind of thing we do in solution-oriented stuff except I'm going to be talking and just suggesting a bunch of possibilities, and I don't know what's going to show up for you. But we're not going to be doing so much verbal interchange,'' and I'm not going to say, ''Okay, which one of those things I just said was really important to you and which brought it out?'' It's just she's going to say afterward, ''I think something happened. I'm not sure . . . it felt good . . . it was okay.'' And then it's a much more nonconscious, nonverbal process of change. I called my book about this *Solution-Oriented Hypnosis*,[59] but really it's solution-oriented inner work. It doesn't require the formal trance induction.

Denise: Yeah, that was very cool. I enjoyed watching that. I can't wait to do it.

Bill: That's the thing. If it empowers you to say, ''I don't need to know all the rigmarole about hypnosis; I'll just invite people in to do that,'' that would be great. I'd love that. I think by the end of the week it will become, ''Oh yeah, I know how to do that.'' It's not rocket science or anything.

Debbie: I don't know if there's a good analogy to make, but I read your article about narrative therapies,[60] and the trance work reminds me of White and Epston doing a letter.[61]

Bill: Really . . . that's nice.

Debbie: In a way it's like having that communication in the moment instead of after the session.

Bill: Yeah, you don't take it away so much.

Beth: But there doesn't have to be that response to it. You can just sit with it.

Bill: Yeah, I think that's nice. I think you're right. I never thought about that, but I think that's right. It is a sort of letter back to them saying, ''You know, you're this amazing person who can do this, and who's shown this, and who's told us this, and who's really done this . . . and what would you like to do with that?'' Here's a possibility, here's a possibility, here's a possibility, here's a possibility . . . and then you go away, and it's like the effect of the letter. . . . It's not just like having a letter once it has a continual transformative effect. *(looks to Debbie)* I think that's a good analogy, . . . because I rarely do write those letters, and I think they're real powerful and they're important to do. It's just not my style to do it. I'd rather do it this way . . . and there's a real valuing of the person that happens during this process. Also, again, the background that I come from . . . I was really raised from Carl Rogers as a first thing right into family therapy . . . Virginia Satir[62] and then MRI brief therapy as an interactional approach to family therapy . . . and then into neurolinguistic programming with

[59] See O'Hanlon, W. H., & Martin, M. (1992).
[60] See O'Hanlon, B. (1994).
[61] See White, M., & Epston, D. (1990).
[62] Virginia Satir was one of the original members of the MRI group. She eventually split from the group and developed *conjoint* family therapy. She published many articles and books and was a prominent teacher, trainer, and clinician. She died in 1988.

Bandler and Grinder . . . and then into Erickson's work and then to solution-oriented brief therapy. I just haven't had that psychodynamic background. So this work seems to me to bridge some of that internal stuff. All that stuff is very externally oriented. It's very directive in a lot of ways, and this stuff is so nice and unintrusive and undirective. It's still leading in some ways, but it's very internal oriented. I think some of those approaches threw out the insides. It's like a black box. All you do is manipulate the context and interactions around and change the language and the attempted solution and people solve their problems, and I think that I'm trying to both reinclude the id, psyche, and soul in this process . . . and I don't see it as incompatible with that. It's slightly different from a psychodynamic formulation of it, but hopefully those of you who have had an analytic or psychodynamic background find some commonalties there.

Beth: It feels much more active than the psychodynamic, yet it's still as respectful and as kind, and even probably more nurturing. I really like the way it opens up the possibilities, which is so key to me. I haven't read any of your books and I didn't realize that you were necessarily identified with solution-focused or solution-oriented. The only opportunity I've had to interact with you was at that one seminar, and I really liked the possibilities model that you presented there. And that fits so well with some of the narrative stuff that I had learned and some of the existential, possibilities stuff . . . and it was like, "Wow, this sort of brings it together."

Bill: And that's why I think it is misnamed, because . . . I came up solution-oriented and then Steve (de Shazer) came up with solution-focused, and we both studied Erickson's work, but after a while everybody started saying, "What you're doing is solution-focused," and I thought, "Well, not really." I like that stuff and I think it's good stuff, but that's not what I do. So I started to change the name away from it because, yes it is solution oriented, and yes it's possibility oriented, and now it's inclusive. Inclusive is that you do this work this way except when you don't . . . and that's both the internal work that I do. . . . Like with Cindy, she's saying, "It's these two," and I say, "Yeah, it's these two and they're both really valuable . . . and there's a middle place too, and there's another place too" . . . and it's inclusive and possibility oriented. It's kind of both directions . . . and also I do that so I don't get stuck in believing my own formulations.

Beth: I probably said a lot of my piece!

Bill: Maybe it was surprising this identifying with solution-oriented or solution-focused . . . or anything else?

Beth: I just hadn't . . . I guess I sort of stayed away from that, coming more from a psychodynamic sort of place . . . and what I really appreciated about that seminar was the possibility thing. It went right in there. I do plan to carry that back with me and to use that. (*looks to Denise*) And like you, I hadn't seen any trancework, . . . but it didn't seem like trancework. Again, it was just sort of speaking to her and allowing her to take with her what felt good and what felt right and leave anything else. . . . It was much like the letter. . . . You're not under any pressure to have to respond to it or think about it . . . just be with it. And that felt very comforting, very kind.

Bill: That's nice. That's the way I experience it as well. The other thing is that sometimes with this work, especially when you do more of the solution-oriented or solution-focused piece, you say, "Well this is sort of cognitive behavioral with a positive twist." But to me, it's experiential work. I really think the experiential part is much more important than the cognitive or behavioral. Those are things to include to get to the experiential, and that's what I think analytic work is getting to. . . . That's what I think existential phenomenological work is getting to. Where does the person live with the experience? That's what I want to get to. If I just do cognitive and behavioral work . . . if it gets to them where they live, I'm up for it. If it's not, to me it's like Steve Gilligan says, "Have my machine call your machine." (*laughter*) That's what they do in California! But it's just one head talking to another . . . and it's not profound for me; it's not worth doing.

Beth: And I like the way you weave the language piece into it. I think it's so important.

Bill: And that's sort of a bridge for Laurie. Laurie, you called a while ago and I didn't know how to respond. You said, "Is there anything I should be reading to prepare for this?" I thought, "Well . . . yes and no." I don't know what to say to that. "You read as much as you're moved to read," is what I would have said if I suppose I had answered it . . . and, "It depends on what you want to know. It depends on whether it's going to effect the experience for you in any sort of way." I really didn't know how to answer that. But that's my answer . . . that's great. I have no problem with you not reading anything, not knowing anything about it, or bringing just what you knew from what you saw and that appealed to you, or if you've read everything like Bob. We were joking the other day that he's read everything twice, and he's got all these obscure interviews that I've done in various places and that's a good way to come too.

Laurie: Let's see . . . nothing profound, except I think again for me, it's hearing the use of metaphor, the expansion, language . . . sort of sitting and enjoying that . . . getting a feel for that a little more . . . it's nice.

Bill: Good.

Paul: For me, I've read everything that I can lay my hands on, and I think I have a misconception from what I've read. So this was kind of a freeing experience. There was much more of a flow to it, which was a wonderful experience. It was kind of like I was the fighter for solution-focused; now I don't have to do that anymore. I can pull it all together.

Beth: Fight or not! (*laughter*)

Bill: Yeah . . . fight or not! I had an understanding of *Aikido*[63] and Steve Gilligan tells me—he's studied Aikido for a long time—that I've got it wrong. Here's my understanding. Even if I've got it wrong it's great analogy I think. (*Stands up in the middle of the room*) The deal is that they tell you you're standing on a particular position and that your opponent wants this space. The person who's coming at you wants this space. So in Aikido what you do, it's sort of like judo, you say, "Oh, you want my space? You know what? I carry my space right here. (*points to his belly*) It's in my belly. Here's my center; here's my space. You can have this spot of if you want." And the person goes down because they say, "Have my spot, please!" They just include the other person's energy, but they don't stay stuck on a position. They bring their center and their space with them wherever they move. Because if you get attached to any position, you have to defend it. And then people can attack you and sometimes they can throw you off if they're stronger or better, and/or, if you're really strong you can defend your position really well. But in Aikido they say, "Why bother? Give them your position. Don't stay on a position. Keep your center in your space." I think that's what we're talking about here. I think it's important to not have to defend it and to always keep the "or not." That doesn't mean you can't be solution focused. I think that what got communicated in terms of solution-focused got a little too closed down, and therefore, occasionally clients get ripped off or you get ripped off.

I just did a seminar in Denver at this *Therapeutic Conversations* conference. Everyone who's there is identified with solution-focused, narrative, collaborative, or Ericksonian approaches. They're all supposed to be very flexible, client centered-very active and directive in some ways but very open in other ways. But of course they've all got their blinders on and rigidities about other therapies. So I had this session, which was called "Inclusive Therapy: The Son and Daughter of Solution-Oriented Therapy."[64] What I said was, "I want to know two things from you. Here are you all, these very enlightened practitioners of this collaborative, open, flexible approach: what are your guilty pleasures?" Have you ever seen that movie review program, *Siskel and Ebert?* And every once in a while they have "guilty pleasures" movies where they would watch cheap, "B" movies that you never want to admit to your friends but you actually love! They were awful movies, but you love them anyway! So I asked, "What, as a therapist, is your guilty pleasure?" One person said, "Occasionally I make

[63] *Aikido* was developed by Morihei Ueshiba (1883–1969) or O Sensei (as he is referred to) and is a modern Japanese martial way or *budo*. Other examples of budo are judo, karate-do, and kendo (sword). The word "do," which comes from the Chinese "tao," forms part of the name and means the *way*. All these arts are disciplines that use martial training not just for defense but also as a means of character development.

[64] An audiotape recording of "Inclusive Therapy: The Son and Daughter of Solution-Oriented Therapy," presented at *Therapeutic Conversations III*, is available through InfoMedix, 12800 Garden Grove Boulevard, Suite F, Garden Grove, California, 92643. Phone, 714.530.3454.

interpretations. I used to be an analyst.'' Another person said, ''I used to be a chemical-dependency counselor, and occasionally I really confront clients and break through their denial.'' It was just like confession! (*laughter*) And they were getting freed up in the sense that they had to hide this terrible secret that they did once in a while, . . . but it worked for them, . . . when they did it it was helpful and it was workable. Then I said, ''What's the evil empire?'' They said, ''Medication,'' ''Labels,'' ''Psychoanalysis,'' and the narrative people, ''Solution-focused!'' So people were going wild raising their hands and telling what they think is the evil empire. Making interpretations, talking about the past . . . that's the evil empire . . . absolutely unacceptable and disrespectful and bad to do in therapy. What I hope happens this week is that we give you permission for the guilty pleasures when they're appropriate . . . when they really come out of your belly/mind and intuition . . . and that we dissipate the idea that there is an evil empire in psychotherapy. We're all trying to find out what helps people. I have my preferred modes to do it and I think some work better than others, but I don't think there's anything that's the evil empire. If it's done in a disrespectful way, obviously anything can be the evil empire . . . solution-focused or anything, . . . but I don't think there's generically an evil empire. Some people say ECT is the evil empire, the Peter Breggins[65] of the world and I would agree with that . . . except when it isn't . . . except when it saves that person's life and they say, ''If I hadn't had ECT I'd be dead!'' So what does Peter Breggin say about that, ''They were brainwashed?'' How does he explain it? He probably doesn't hear it. I don't know how he explains that, but I've had people tell me that. So what does he do with that data? It doesn't fit in his model.

Paul: But that kind of inclusiveness . . . is a big leap for a lot of people. I mean, it's easy to say but it's a big leap . . . if you're sort of a black and white, the whole truth or nothing but the truth kind of person.

Bill: Hopefully today you're already getting warped in that direction. By the end of the week you're going to get warped.

Beth: Warped?! (*laughter*)

Bill: By the end of this week you will be inclusive kind of folks. I'm going to leave you out in the rain and it ain't gonna fit back in the slot it used to be in! (*laughter*) You're going to have to find a whole new slot!

Alice: No surprises except what I was calling ''eclectic, wishy-washy'' is now inclusive! (*laughter*)

Bill: There you go! Now you've got a better name for it! It's more formal. . . . ''I'm inclusive!'' That dignifies it doesn't it?

Alice: That's about it.

[65] Peter Breggin, M.D., is a psychiatrist and author.

Bill: That's great, that's good enough.

Megan: I'm thinking of a lot of little things. Probably I'm surprised that it's as existential as it is . . . pleasantly surprised. Even though I've read some of your work I didn't quite realize that . . . and I liked the feeling that I had talking about the belly/mind, and that stuff. Another thing I'm really thinking of is kind of being freed from having to know the truth. I don't like really thinking that I know the truth about anything, . . . because when somebody shares something with me I realize that I was being ignorant in thinking that in the first place. I kind of like that thinking that, "Yeah, this is what I feel, and maybe I don't feel that way" and I can always change that.

Bill: Okay.

Katy: I think maybe today has helped me have more of a renewed awareness to language. But part of what I've been wanting to get out of this is I think that I'm doing a pretty good job most of the time, but I'm just not aware of it (language). I'm not as aware of the questions that I'm asking. I'm not as aware of thinking about the process. Another thing that was really helpful was the thing about working intuitively, . . . because I'm really bad at doing notes . . . and I'll sit down to do them even if I have ten minutes after a session, which is quite rare, but I just sort of don't know what to write.

Bill: (*jokingly*) "That was a pretty good session. I felt pretty good!" (*laughter*)

Katy: I really have to think about, "What did we talk about?" So that lends a different perspective for me.

Bill: A friend, the guy who does my web page[66] and did a computer program with me, created a little thing called "my notes." He's creative and he's a therapist. And what I had him do was three things . . . a list of diagnoses, so I could go into the computer and select the one; the second thing is then a checklist of things I did in the session . . . hypnosis, gave a task assignment, saw the family . . . all I have to do is check some of things which are typical things that I do. And the last thing is some stock phrases I typically use like, "Found out the client had complaint in this area," and "found there was an exception in this area," and just little phrases that I use. And I was able to build case notes really quickly, and you could do that through like a Xerox form. You wouldn't need a computer program.

Katy: That would be helpful for me. It's sort of coming through me.

Bill: Now it's a skill and a resource, not a detriment.

Katy: I need to have a different way of thinking about it and for a couple of months now I've been having an increasing aversion to paperwork, and I've

[66] Bill O'Hanlon's web page address is: http://www.brieftherapy.com

been saying, "I need to think differently about this because this is just going to grow bigger."

Bill: Good, okay.

Debbie: I'm not sure I'm going to answer your questions.

Bill: Answer different questions!

Debbie: All right! The other things I didn't talk about in my nervous introduction was that I'm really interested in storytelling, and I don't understand how it fits with working with people. So I'm observing you and your particular style of storytelling. And I'm also very interested in metaphors, so I'm also observing that. The other thing that I'm interested in that I think relates with my outdoor piece is connecting with the soul. Not many people talk about that. And I've heard you use the term a couple of times, so it feels like it's okay to use that term in here. I'll be curious to see how you discuss that or develop that piece. It feels like a piece to me. I have done a little bit of studying of spiritual psychology, and I've been a meditator. And when I'm in the outdoors it's a very soulful experience, but it's very hard to articulate and it's very hard to know how to integrate it in some tangible way into practice.

Bill: Two things come to mind as you say that. Yes, I think soul is important, and yes, I think spirituality is important for me in therapy. I think that's where it all comes from for me. I don't talk about it too much. It always ends up sounding like mundane, new age clichés. (*laughter*) I haven't found a way to talk about it yet that really speaks to it and doesn't make it very mundane and clichéd. The second thing is that one of my coauthors, Sandy Beadle, who is coauthoring a computer program with me now and she also coauthored a book, . . . *A Field Guide to Possibility-Land,*[67] she studied with some people, Steve and Rachel Kaplan,[68] who call themselves environmental psychologists. They're studying the effects of being in a natural environment versus being in an unnatural environment and how one's sense of space affects one and things like that. Really it's about what environment you're in. Occasionally I read these things in the *USA Today* or in some magazine, . . . and I saw one where Rachel had done an experiment studying people who had views of brick walls and views of fields, and grass, and trees . . . outside . . . and there was a clear difference in productivity and work morale, like how uplifting that was. And then she even did one where they put up a picture of a nature scene, if there were only brick walls available . . . and productivity rose and morale rose. And so they've been studying about how when people get alienated from nature, they're not around nature, that they get diminished in some ways. That's one thing and then how people make sense of space and how they make mental maps of space in their

[67] See O'Hanlon, B., & Beadle, S. (1994).

[68] Stephen Kaplan, Ph.D., and Rachel Kaplan, Ph.D., are environmental psychologists with an interest in the effects of nature on humans. See Kaplan, S., & Kaplan, R. (1994).

environment, things like that. I think that's one way to connect. You ask most people, it's not true for me, but if you ask, "If you had all the time off you needed and the money, or if you just had a week off and could go anyplace you wanted and do anything you wanted, . . . what would you do to kind of recharge your batteries?" Ninety percent of the people you would ask would say, "I'd go to the mountains," or "I'd go to the forest," or "I'd go to the ocean." They'll talk about the natural environment as being what nurtures their soul. Some people say, "I'd read a book," or "I'd go to a music concert," but most people will talk about being in a natural environment and nurturing their soul, and recharging, reconnecting. Jung said, "Alienation is the disease of the unsoiled." People are really alienated from their soil. He had people that were having psychotic problems especially work in gardens sometimes to reconnect with that sense of reality. One other thing . . . you were talking about the changes in your life. I have just gone through some of those changes, and what I'm talking about now is . . . is it all constructed or is there something actually going on that's being discovered as well as it gets constructed, the way you talk about it and the stories you make of it? The sense that I have is that people's lives have like these tectonic plates going on in their souls. And they're moving and the movement happens in your soul regardless of wherever you're going . . . maybe it happens because of the developmental stage you're in or the country you're born in or the family you're born in. Those influence it, . . . but there are these tectonic, underground movements that every once in a while show up in these disruptions that you go through in life.

Alice: When it shifts, it shifts.

Bill: When it shifts, it shifts, and you can either run from the shift and suppress it for a while, which some people do, or you can say, "I embrace it." And that's definitely what has happened with me. It's like my soul was moving in a particular direction, and it didn't matter what my opinion about it was. It felt like, "Guess what? This is unfolding and it's much bigger than what your stories are about it. And it's much bigger than what your conscious intentions are for your life." So that's one way of speaking about the soul. And then there's something else about spiritual purpose and spiritual life and, "Why I'm here and why I'm doing this right now." Like for me, why I'm alive and I stayed alive through my very serious depression when I had decided to kill myself . . . and that's another thing about spiritual purpose and whether I discovered that or I existentially created that, I'm not clear. It's the same effect either way, and it feels spiritual to me.

Alice: Another part of that is that if you fight that that's when you get sick. It was when I decided, "I'll stay and give it one more try," that I got cancer. It's like, how many more wake up calls do I need?

Bill: Yeah . . . time for a midcourse correction.

Paul: I made one of those about six years ago. I was making a lot of money, but I got into such a funk and depression that I quit everything and we moved. I didn't even have a job. I didn't work for eight months. I used to wake up in the middle of the night in a cold sweat, "My God I don't have a job," but it worked out.

Bill: And if you hadn't followed that?

Paul: I probably would have been . . . maybe dead.

Bill: I followed it in my career years ago. I jumped off . . . same thing. I didn't have a job. I knew what I needed to do. . . . I did it and I starved for a while. I was as poor as a church mouse and it worked out. I trust the universe in that way and I trust my soul in that way.

Lisa: I have a couple of things. Just to kind of reference what you said, Paul, I'm learning a lot about inclusiveness and one of the big parts of my job is working in a team. That's harder, sometimes, than working with the families that we work with. And part of the reason is this type of inclusiveness and differences. We obviously come up with a lot of differences. When you're working together you're different people. You view it in different ways. You have different ways of dealing with the same situation. So this is helpful to me . . . thinking about being able to include other people's ideas and thoughts about things without having to defend my own. My own are okay, and their thoughts and ideas are also okay, too. I don't have to defend them. I've found myself lots of times in the position of feeling like my insecurities tell me I need to defend my positions or my ideas. So that's very helpful. The other thoughts I had were about the trance. I'm not sure I'm going to be able to verbalize this very well, but two things occurred to me. One, you were talking about making mistakes and having that be okay, and I was thinking about that and when I get really regimented about the model, I get really frozen . . . and a lot of that is about making mistakes. You said something and it didn't feel right to Cindy, and so you went and said something else and I thought, "Oh, . . . you're human! You don't have to be perfect all the time." Just that I'm human and I can be human with my clients and what a gift that is . . . to give your clients that. And when you're doing trance you seem to be connecting with people because you're just saying whatever seems to be coming to your mind. It seems to be very automatic. I'm not sure if that's true, but that's what it appears to be for me. And it seems like you are speaking on a soul level, or a spiritual level . . . you're really connecting, somehow, with her soul. It didn't seem like you had a total understanding of where the words were coming from . . . they were just coming out. And I thought, "Wow! How scary that would be for me to do that." It's frightening as hell! Because connecting and trusting myself to that extent is huge for me right now, and that's something I couldn't even think about doing today.

Bill: That's an interesting thing. A few things come to mind. Some people get that afraid about being a parent. Like, "Will I be a good parent?" And then when your kid comes, your heart just opens up . . . and you can have doubts and is this the right thing . . . or are they going to get a fever . . . and I don't know what to do. But generally, you know how you're going to connect soul to soul with your kid. You just do. It just happens in the relationship when you open yourself up to it and it just happens organically. I remember when I was thinking about having a kid and I was like, "Oh, should I have a kid? I really want a kid, but not right now. It's not a good time." It's never a good time to have a kid . . . you can always find reasons why you should wait until next fall or this or that, . . . but you just go ahead and have a kid and it generally works out. And I was talking to this guy who was going through a bitter custody battle with his ex-wife and he had four year old and he really loved this four year old, and he just didn't have much access to her and he was just heartbroken and he said, "Bill, having kids is a lot of work. It's a pain in the butt. It's a lot of worry. It's really hard, but you know . . . and that's about this much (*shows a small amount with his fingers*) compared to this much (*opens up his arms*) love that you get and give." And I thought, "I know he's right. I have stepkids and I have a little sense of that, and I was raised in a family and I was real close to my family. I know he's right." I went and had a kid, and he was right. Absolutely there is that sense of this and this . . . and I think that I go into that similar place, soul to soul and just trusting and letting it all come out, and heart to heart . . . it really feels heart to heart to me . . . of compassion and acceptance of myself and the other person. I read an analogy one time of that with modern planes there's this thing . . . autopilot and autonavigator . . . and autopilot is [when] they set a certain course and they lock it in the computer to go from say here to Chicago. And then autonavigator has the map, and it also has a reading of where the airplane is based on radar and locational devices. And they talk back and forth to make sure the plane stays on course, but most of the time the plane is off course. And this was a book on human beings and communication and the person was saying, "Imagine if this were two human beings . . . the autonavigator and autopilot. So the autopilot goes on and that's Fred . . . and Fred says to George (the autonavigator) over here, 'Well, George . . . we're going to Chicago and I'm taking off now.' George says, 'Fine, but you're off 2 degrees to the left. You need to correct.' Fred says, 'Fine. I'll correct.' He corrects. And George says, 'You overcorrected. You're off 2 degrees to the right and you need to correct that.' Fred says again, 'Sure George.' And he's a little more testy because he's being criticized. So George says, 'Now you've overcorrected and you're 3 degrees off to the left. You need to correct.' Fred's says, 'Okay George!'" And he said all they're doing is giving information back and forth and most of the time they're off course . . . that the person's off course. And most of the time in therapy I think I'm off course and if I get real worried about, "I've got to know, and not be off course and not make mistakes," that's going to block it, . . . and if I don't pay attention to that person and I'm looking up at the ceiling . . . like Ernie Rossi . . . I'm not going to know when I'm off course. But I figure I'm off course most of the time and I also figure I have no clue what

interested in that as other people in narrative are. I don't think they covered it as well. I should have . . .

Megan: . . . Addressing the politics or . . .

Bill: . . . How they address the politics and bring it in a very personal way so it's not intrusive. It really is part and parcel to therapy, and it was in there in an initial draft and then it got kind of cut out. And I don't use that as much as they do, that political component, . . . but they think it's really essential. I didn't want it to be left out and I just thought well they'll have it . . . a whole story about Michael White, he's all about politics . . . that's why he does what he does . . . and David Epston's writing and Stephen Madigan's[71] writing about bulimia and anorexia, . . . and I figured it would be in there and it's sort of in there but it should have been in that summary article. That's the only critique I have. Otherwise, I think it's a really good overview . . . and narrative is so jargonly written. If you read some of the stuff by Michael and David, . . . Michael has this phrase that he got from this French social critic; it's called *the exoticization of the domestic and the domestication of the exotic.* That's the kind of language that they use. Basically he means making the familiar seem strange and new to you and making the strange and new seem familiar to you. Why couldn't he have just said that? I've been thinking about writing a short little book like I wrote this *Field Guide to Possibility Therapy,* . . . that will expand on that article and call it, "Narrative Therapy: The English Translation." (*laughter*) The jargon words make it so hard to get. Therapy books are generally extremely difficulty to read and very heady. Some of them are great, but most of them are so jargon filled, and narrative, unfortunately, is more jargon filled than most.

[71] Stephen Madigan is the founder of Yaletown Family Therapy in Vancouver, B.C. His teaching and writing have focused on the use of narrative therapy, in particular its application to eating disorders.

Chapter 5

Trancepersonally

Here participants learn how to do hypnosis, or what Bill calls "solution-oriented inner work." In addition to learning a model of how to do this kind of work and practicing it, participants are given a model for valuing internal experience, which can be useful in treating post-traumatic problems stemming from sexual abuse and other traumas.

Inner Work

Permission and Inclusion

One of the things that became clear to me yesterday is this inner work is new to some of you. I think I can teach it to you pretty quickly. There are two parts to this inner work or hypnotic work. One is, "How do you get people into that experientially engaged state?" It's what you might call trance or just experientially engaged—an inner focus. Then once you get there the question is, "What do you do once they're there?" When I first learned hypnosis I spent a lot of time on the first part. I actually think that's very easy to do. The second part, what to do once they're there; that was a little more perplexing to me. Let's take those two categories and then we'll do a little practice. The first thing is, "How do you get people engaged?" There are a couple of ideas about that. One is what people talked about yesterday and I think it's very, very important. When people are first starting to have this experience they're putting a lot of pressure on themselves to do it right, to do something specific, to feel something specific. The first thing I do is take pressure off however I can do that. I usually take the pressure off by giving the message, "Start where you are and be where you are. There's no other place to be to start; always start where you are." The second thing is to start to include whatever they think might be distractions or barriers to getting into the trance state or getting absorbed. You might say, "You could listen to the sounds around. You could be thinking this isn't going to work. You might be apprehensive. You might be fearful, nervous. You might be distracted.'' I call that *inclusion*. Include whatever they think might be barriers or distractions or difficulties. Another element is to give *permission*. You heard yesterday what kind of permissions I like to give, permission to do something, and permission not to have to do something. For example, ''It's okay to relax and you don't have to relax. It's okay to listen to what I'm saying and you don't have to listen to what I'm saying.'' Whatever might show up in their experience is what I want to include and give permission about. This is different from whatever might show up in their behavior. You wouldn't say, ''It's okay to hit me and you don't have to hit me.'' That's action. Or in therapy, ''It's okay to cut yourself and you don't have to cut yourself.'' No. We're talking about experience. When you get them experientially engaged, you just want to make room for whatever experiences might be there but also that they don't have to be compelled. When Cindy said yesterday, ''I knew I didn't have to go back and regress and have this yuppie childhood experience,'' that was important. It was okay for her to and she didn't have to. If she got the sense it wasn't okay to do that, she said she would have probably done it. If she got the message, ''It's not okay to do that,'' boom . . . that's where she'd go. If she got the message, ''You have to do that,'' she might go there because she was forced into it, but she'd be upset and angry . . . or she wouldn't go there out of opposition and maybe she needed to go there. It's okay to and you don't have to. You can and you might not. In addition, I mentioned yesterday that one of the things that I learned when I first did this hypnotic stuff with Erickson was to watch people and to really listen to people. The watching seems really important because if Cindy shudders at the beginning, what do we want to do at the beginning? I want make sure that I incorporate that. One way to incorporate it is just by describing it, ''Your body just shuddered.'' You want to be as descriptive and neutral you as you can get. A second way to incorporate it is by giving permission for it. If a person has his or her eyes closed and all of the sudden he or she open them, you just say, ''That's right, you just opened your eyes.'' You just describe it. ''And it's okay to open your eyes.'' And then what I usually say is, ''And you can close your eyes if that's more comfortable or you can keep them open.'' You want to widen the circle. When I used to do a lot of formal hypnosis, people would come in with this narrow definition of what hypnosis is: ''I have to be relaxed. I have to pay attention to everything you say, but I'm going to be knocked out.'' I would respond, ''You can be relaxed and you don't have to be.'' With that permission, the circle would get a little bigger. Then I could say, ''You could listen to what I say and you don't have to listen to what I say.'' And the circle gets a little bigger. And, ''You may be drifting off into your own experience and not hear what I say and not really attend to anything, or you could pay attention to the sounds around or what I'm saying or your body in the chair.'' And the circle gets a little bigger. That first element is so crucial because once you do that most people will drop right into their inner experience. If there are barriers to it and you're inviting them they will just move right into it . . . move into trance, inner experience or inner absorption or whatever you want to call it. That's the first and most important element. The first doorway, then, is permission and inclusion.

Get Rhythmic

The second doorway into this kind of experience is to get rhythmic. You may notice that when I'm doing this I'm usually speaking in this hyperactive way . . . and then . . . when I did that stuff with Cindy (*slows down*) . . . there was a lot more space . . . between . . . the words. I slow down . . . a little. (*returns to regular way of speaking*) And how I did that was that I keyed into her breathing pattern. I become like a human biofeedback machine and I speak only when she exhales. A few purposes for that. One is it slows me down from my normal hyperactive way of talking. There's a cue that we're moving into a different kind of conversation. It's more of an inner, slowed-down focus for her. The second thing is it gives her time to process in the pauses in my speech. Sometimes I even stop in the middle (*long pause*) . . . of phrases. And I might not speak every time she exhales. I might wait a couple beats. If I stop in the middle of something (*pauses*) . . . maybe she'll fill in the end in a way that's better for her than what I was going to say. Then I'll come in with what I was going to say and it may be irrelevant at that point . . . she's already gone off into her own experience. The third thing is, for those of you who are just starting out, it gives you a little time to think about what you're going to say next.

Alice: I find that the success of the induction is correlated with how relaxed and centered I am: how much I can get into trance so to speak.

Bill: Right. I typically go into trance as I'm doing it. I go into an externally focused trance that's very, very focused. And as I move into that absorbed state, they tend to move into it and we're a little more parallel. The breathing thing keeps me in sync; otherwise I can go into trance a lot quicker than most of the people that I work with. It keeps me in track with what they're doing. When their breathing slows, I slow. When it quickens, I quicken. It's like I'm following. If I lead too much I'll lose them.

Alice: It sounds more like pace and follow than pace and lead.

Bill: That's exactly right. It's like dancing after a while. It's hard to tell who's doing which because we're influencing one another. That's getting rhythmic. And you may have noticed that my head gets very rhythmic. (*moves his head very rhythmically and slowly to demonstrate*) It's like keeping time for a musician. I'm keeping time with my head. And usually when I'm talking I'm waving my arms all over, but if you noticed, during that experience (with Cindy) I was hardly moving at all . . . except for . . . my head. If the person's eyes are open that tends to be an induction in itself, because my head is very rhythmic. If their eyes are closed, they can hear a difference in the location of my voice.

Invite Dissociation

The third element then is . . . Cindy said, "I dissociate on a dime." And often to help people to get into that more belly/mind, experiential state . . . you need to split the conscious mind from the experiential life. I do that very deliberately and it's a thing I learned from Erickson. Erickson was partially paralyzed from the effects of polio.[72] And earlier in his career he had done some systematic research before he was paralyzed, before he had this infirmity because he had had polio but had recovered mostly . . . he'd done this experiment because he was a very curious guy and he experimented on lots of things. This was in like the '30s. He started to do hundreds of trance inductions with all of his students in the psychiatry and psychology programs that he supervised and taught in, and he would run subject after subject through this experiment. He would do trance with all different spatial locations for a voice. He would do trance like this (*moves head to the left*), trance like this (*moves head back*), and he found when he did trance this way (*moves head from side to side*) people would often get seasick! (*laughter*) Because they were reminded of a really bad sea voyage which a lot more people took in those days, in which there was a really rough sea, and that's how the voice location changed during a sea voyage. And after a while he learned to use the spatial locations of the voice as an induction technique. Then near the end of his life he learned to use that as his main way . . . because he mostly paralyzed . . . he had muscle deterioration from the aftereffects of polio and he would spasm sometimes, his muscle would spasm, and he'd find himself over here in the chair (*demonstrates by shifting his body to another part of the chair*), and he would use that very deliberately and he would say (*shifting to one side of the chair*), "And your conscious mind can think one thing," spasm again (*shifts to the other side of the chair*), "And your unconscious mind can think another." He would deliberately use what was naturally occurring in his body as an induction technique to dissociate. He'd say, "Okay, you have two parts now." You're really not two parts, but we can divide you into two parts especially if we start to make the distinction. If I start to talk about parent, adult, and child you'll probably start to divide yourself into three parts even though there are no Ps, As and Cs inside you. . . . We've done a lot of autopsies and never found those. (*laughter*) But people start to consider themselves parent, adult, and child . . . or id, ego, and superego. There's not such stuff inside people; it's a construction. What we're going to do is construct for people a situation where there's a critical, conscious, very deliberate mind and then noncritical, nonconscious, automatic experiential mind . . . unconscious

[72] For a biographical sketch of the life of Milton H. Erickson, M.D., see Rossi, E. L., Ryan, M. O., & Sharp, F. A. (Eds.). (1983).

mind if you want to call it that . . . that's what Erickson would call it. And we'll do that split nonverbally. (*as if to a client*—in a deliberate, strong type voice) "So maybe you're not sure you can go deeply into trance (*moves head to right and shifts voice to a softer, less deliberate type voice*) and another part of you just continues to experience what it experiences . . . at the rate at which it experiences it. Maybe you're sure you can't go into trance or you're skeptical about the process of trance, and you can just continue." Do you hear what I'm doing? (*moves head to left and uses strong voice*) The head is up over here, voice is in one location . . . certain voice tone and volume . . . (*moves head to right and shifts voice to soft tone*) another voice tone and volume over here. You're basically nonverbally, indirectly communicating to the person, "Guess what? You're at least two people now." Then after a while I'm going to be talking mostly in this voice (*motions to the right to signify the softer tone*). You invite the person to split their experience in a particular way, and that's a pretty compelling invitation into trance. The next thing to do is evoke previous trance-like experiences if this is their first experience in that inner absorbed state. It could be reminding them of a time that they meditated or prayed or some altered state in the past when they were swinging on a swing and they got dizzy, or they were lying on the grass looking up at the clouds and just getting lost in it, or reading a book and getting so absorbed in it, or watching a movie, or listening to a radio show—sometime when you'll be in that more narrow focus of attention, more innerly absorbed. I usually, of course, tell stories about that. Here's one. I was growing up in a family of eight kids, and my father read a couple of books a night. He was a big novel reader. And he did it right in the living room. Eight kids playing, yelling, screaming, fighting—absolutely he didn't respond at all to that. He would go so deeply into an inner state that in order to tell him that it was dinner you would actually have to shake him. Then he would arouse from whatever inner state he was in. He could sit in the living room and read a book and absolutely tune out the world. So that's a story that you might tell. I went to see the movie *Reds,* and I really had to go to the bathroom, but I didn't want to miss the beginning because I had read a review that said the beginning was really great. I sat right down and forgot I had to go to the bathroom. It was a really long movie if you remember that movie. They had an intermission in the middle, and at the intermission I was shocked to find out that I really had to go to the bathroom so bad I could barely walk. What happened to my consciousness? I was absorbed in something else. The other thing is when I went back and I was watching the movie, I noticed somebody come back from the candy concession after that. I never saw them leave and they were sitting right in front of me—something dropped out. You can remind the person of experiences that they might have had when they were so inner absorbed that they wouldn't notice external things or other distracting things. Going on a long car trip and spacing out is a common experience for most people. So you're going to mention common, everyday trance like states or inner absorbed states . . . or externally absorbed states . . . anything where the narrowing and focusing of attention goes on. This leads us to the next concept.

What do you do once the person's in trance? You're going to evoke experience. Here's the difference between the Ericksonian traditions and most kinds of hypnosis. Most kinds of hypnosis are trying to put new input in from the outside. Erickson was saying, "People have all the resources and answers inside. All you have to do is evoke them." So what we're trying to do at the beginning of trance is evoke an experience of trance. Once they get into trance or an inner absorbed state, we try and evoke whatever resources or skills or knowledge or experiences that might help them solve this problem. Yesterday when Cindy was in trance, I was trying to evoke the experience of whatever happened when she went to the ACoA week. Somehow a shift happened so that she was open to the possibility of going to AA and being able to balance that with her feminist sensibility. She knew that experience but didn't know how she could do it. I want to say, "I'm going to push the jukebox numbers to play that record. I don't know where it is, but you do. I'm pressing A6 because that's what you told me it is. Go and find that record and play it, and then transfer that record over to B4." I want to evoke and then transfer whatever knowledge, resources, and skills the person has. It's a very active process of directing the person to go get that and I don't know what that is, but they do. Sometimes I work with migraine headaches and I'll say, "You're an expert at getting rid of migraine headaches." They look at me strangely and I say, "No, really. I've never had a migraine headache and I wouldn't have a clue how to get rid of one. You've told me that you've taken medications and they haven't worked very well. You've gone to physicians and that hasn't worked very well. But somehow your headaches eventually go away. So your body knows exactly how to get rid of them. Probably by changing blood pressure, blood chemistry, neurological patterns, muscle patterns relaxing and tensing in different ways—breathing patterns. I don't know what else you do, but somehow your body knows how to do it because eventually you get rid of one. What I want you to do is, the next time that you have a migraine headache, I suggest that you go to the jukebox and get the pattern of how you get rid of a migraine headache and put it at the beginning of when you would have had a migraine headache." That's the simplest way that I can tell you. Somewhere they have this knowledge; you go get it and suggest that they put it where they need it. It's an evocation model rather than a reprogramming model. We're not programming from the outside, we're evoking from the inside and then suggesting different ways to use it. Evoke and then transfer it to the context that it's needed.

How do you know the person's getting with the experience? That's where trance becomes more than inner work. Sometimes what I'll do to show myself that I'm getting through to the person or to show them that I'm really getting through is I'll evoke some automatic response. That's when you're getting into the stuff that looks more like hypnosis. I don't know if it's just a bunch of words that I'm saying or if it's really getting through. How do I know? Like yesterday with Cindy, was it just a bunch of words or was it getting through to her? If she had never had that experience before, she might be skeptical. Typically what I'll do is try and evoke some automatic response that she couldn't do on her own—consciously and deliberately. A typical one is hand and arm levitation, where you invite a hand and an arm to lift up automatically. The person doesn't deliberately lift the arm. It lifts rather than them lifting it (*demonstrates the lifting motion of a hand and arm levitation*). It usually lifts in this weird way that I'm showing now. It lifts in a stepwise kind of jerky motion. It's sometimes really slow (*continues to demonstrate*). You can also suggest warmth or coolness. One hand could be warm and one cool. Or it could be tingling where the migraine headache was.

How do you do that? I typically do it in several ways. One, which was developed by Erickson, is an indirect approach in which Erickson would say, "How quickly will that arm lift up?" He'd never question that the arm would lift up. He'd just start talking about all the variations and all the possibilities of how it could lift up. He would presume that the arm was going to lift up. That's using *presupposition.*[73] How quickly will that arm lift up? Will you notice that it's lifting up? Which hand or arm will lift up first? Erickson would use all sorts of assumptions and presuppositions that would never say, "Lift your arm up." Instead he would imply, "Will your arm lift up before or after your eyes close?" That's actually a complex presupposition. You're presuming that the eyes are going to close and that the arm is going to lift up. It's a clever way of not telling the person what to do but getting them to do something anyway. Erickson learned it because he had a disability. He had polio. He decided for his health that he would try and get his upper body strong by doing some exercises over the summer before starting medical school. He took a 1,000-mile canoe trip during the summer all on his own with just $2.64, a red bandanna, shorts, and a t-shirt, and a little fishing line. During this trip he gets all sorts of things to happen. He's a proud farm kid, and even though he's been laid low by polio he's not going to ask anybody for help—he's too proud. He comes to some places on the river where it runs out and there's a land portage and he can't get the canoe across because his legs don't work. He lifts himself out of the canoe and pulls it up on the bank of the river. And usually on these portages there are pillars, so he would shimmy up the pillar. He'd put his German book that he studied in his belt, because you had to learn German to get into medical school in those days, and he'd pull himself up and sit on top of this column. Somebody would eventually come by and see this guy with the shriveled up legs, as he had atrophied leg muscles, but looking kind of strong on the top. They'd ask, "What are you doing?" He'd respond, "I'm taking a trip for my health this summer." Polio was well known and they could see what was going on and they'd look at the canoe and they'd look at him. They'd then offer to take the canoe to the next stretch of water. He'd never ask anybody. He'd indirectly get them to offer.

[73] See O'Hanlon, W. H. (1987).

When he was hungry he would row just within hailing distance of the fishing boats on the Mississippi and put his little fishing line in the water and sit there for hours and hours reading his German book. After a while the guys would hail him after they'd caught a lot of fish and extra ones they wouldn't be able to sell. They would give him fish and then end up giving him more when they heard his story about going to medical school and canoeing for his health. All through that summer he learned indirect ways of getting people to offer him things that he was too proud to ask for. He later used this as the basis for his hypnosis. He didn't like to tell people what to do. He liked to invite people in an indirect way to volunteer to do it. This was an innovation in hypnotherapy because most of the time what was used was an authoritarian approach. Certain people will go along with that and certain people will rebel against it and a wide variety of people will respond intermittently to it. This is lot more of an invitational approach.

That's one way of inviting people to lift their hand up. The second way is that more permissive way of doing it, saying, "Your hand *could* lift up automatically," or "It *can* lift up automatically." "The tingling can start in that part of your head that you used to have the migraine headaches." Some automatic experience or behavior is what we're trying to evoke. So we use generalized, permissive suggestions. Instead of "your hand will lift up," we say, "your hand can lift up."

The next technique is multiple choice options. You could say, "It could lift up slowly or quickly." "This hand could lift up or that hand could lift up," which is related to the first two—indirect suggestion and a generalized permissive suggestion. The next categories of "ways to evoke" is to tell a story. Tell a story about a time when I had hand levitation or somebody else had hand levitation or tell an even more indirect story. For instance, remember when you were a little kid and you really wanted the teacher to call on you because you knew the answer? Or the cookie jar was up high in the cupboard and you really wanted a cookie? Or for those of you who are old enough, before we had seatbelts and you'd come to a quick stop and you had your kid right next to you in the car *(puts his arm out to demonstrate stopping the kid's forward motion).* I still do it on occasion. It's an automatic response. Whatever would remind them of that experience you can remind them of metaphorically—something with automatic hand movement or automatic muscle movement.

Denise: Do people typically respond with "yes" or "no?"

Bill: No, they answer by their behavior. It either evokes something or it doesn't and you'll see it pretty quickly. That's why hand levitation is nice because you can see it. You'll start to talk about climbing in a tree and you'll start to see little movements. Then, once you see a response, you validate that response and amplify the response, invite the amplification of the response. So you say, "That's right, your finger's moving a little." You just describe it and say,

"That's right," which validates it, and then say, "And it can move a little more."

The last method is one Erickson made up. In addition to indirect suggestion, he said it was one of his few original contributions to the hypnotherapy field. He called it the *interspersal technique*.[74] This is what NLP calls *analogical marking*.[75] Basically, then idea is that you can emphasize certain phrases non verbally; either visually, auditorally, through tone, or other ways, you can emphasize certain phrases and make them specific suggestions within a larger context. So what do I mean by that? If I wanted you during trance to scratch your nose, what I could say is, "Everybody knows that when you're in trance you have to start from scratch." Now what did I do? I emphasized the words *knows* and *scratch*. If I wanted you to *lift* your *hand* I could say, "You would really like your unconscious mind to give you a *hand* in coming *up* with something that would really be helpful for you. Because you've been pretty down, and you need a *hand*. Maybe some *uplifting* experience. Something that would *move* you in the direction. So that you could *face* something that you haven't been able to *face* very easily." Did you hear the words that are emphasized? Uplifting, hand, up, move, face. Those are the words that got emphasized. Advertising people sometimes use this to maneuver us. Years ago I heard a commercial that said, "Make a *U-turn* to *Sinutab*." What's the message that's embedded there? It's you turn to Sinutab. It's the embedded suggestion. "Maybe you think you can't *go into trance*." "Maybe you don't think you can *go deeply into trance*." "Maybe you don't know how *quickly* you can *go into trance*." What are the messages? Go into trance, go deeply into trance, and go quickly into trance. When you're actually saying something else, in your whole paragraph there are marked-out portions. Bandler and Grinder in NLP called that analogical marking because it marked it out in nonverbal ways—analogically rather than digitally. Erickson called it the interspersal technique because it was interspersed through the dialogue. He actually learned it from patients who would indirectly communicate in the same way. A patient would come in and say, "I'm just under a lot of stress and I just need to *divorce* myself." Erickson would start to ask about their marriage, because they'd emphasize certain words as the indirect communication, "Follow this lead." He learned that technique from patients; then he learned to use it back.

Paul: Can you ask a person just to raise their finger? I've heard of that.

Bill: Yeah, that's much more deliberate. If you say, "I'd like you to raise your finger," they're likely to respond more deliberately. I say, "I'd like the finger to raise." It's an indirect suggestion to dissociate. It's the difference between evoking something automatically or evoking something that's a deliberate behavior or experience.

[74] See O'Hanlon, W. H. (1987).
[75] See Grinder, J., & Bandler, R. (1981).

So, again, when do you use hypnosis? When people have automatic, experiential, affective, or physiological things that you haven't been able to get to in other ways—that they haven't been able to get to by making deliberate changes.

Megan: Do you trance only with individuals? Like, what about with couples?

Bill: I've done trance with couples and sometimes both go into trance and sometimes only one does and the other one watches. I've also taught couples to go into trance together when they're in trouble rather than keep fighting head to head or conflict to conflict. I've also done it with families and groups, but typically I do hypnosis with one person. When I do family and couple work, it's usually more conscious and deliberate and we'll talk about that as the week goes on. But with this approach, it's actually easy to do hypnosis with larger groups because it's more general.

Practicing Hypnosis

Bill: Okay, I'm going to throw you in the deep end and you're going to hypnotize me. I'm an easy subject, so don't worry. And I can also coach you at the same time. We're going to do a "round robin" trance, which is each person will say one part of the induction. So the pressure's not on any one person to take the whole thing. And you're supposed to make a lot of mistakes because this is new for you. That's your job. You won't mess me up—I've got self-protective mechanisms! So you can make mistakes and I will coach you on the language that your using, you're suggestions, maybe the voice, volume, rate, and those types of things. We'll go around and you can say one phrase or you can say five minutes of things. It's okay to do what you're doing. And if you don't know what to say turn to your neighbor and get some coaching.

So, what do you need to know given this exercise? I would say go for hand levitation because that's an easy one for me. First, do some preliminary work to get me absorbed inside. Then start to invite little movements of the fingers and notice those movements and invite me to notice them. Then amplify those movements.

(Looks to Lisa) Okay, Lisa, you're going to have to start out because we're going to go the North American route this time. Do you have a basic idea of where you'd like to start, or would you like some coaching?

Lisa: I'd like a little help.

Bill: I think the main thing with the person who starts is they have to begin with where the person is.

Lisa: Like start where you are and be where you are?

Bill: That's right. Even describing, "You're sitting in the chair. Your arms are on the arms of the chair." And "It's okay to feel what you're feeling." Anything like that. We're going for generalized permission and description. And if you see my position change, like if I shift my position in the chair, then that would be a good thing to mention because it's something that's changing and you can incorporate on an ongoing basis. You can say, "That's right. You can shift your position in the chair to be more comfortable or just to shift your position." Okay, ready?

Lisa: My heart's pounding! Okay. You're sitting in your chair and your hands are on arms or whatever that is.

Bill: You have a great chance because we know we're going for hand levitation in a while and you can use a nice ambiguous phrase, "Your arms are on the arms right now." That's an interesting phrase because it implies that at some point later my arms might not be on my arms.

Lisa: Your arms are on your arms right now, and your feet are together on the floor. And they can stay together or you can cross your feet.

Bill: Just a bit of coaching. Sometimes people become very literal when they're in trance. Only speak about what you can see. My feet aren't actually on the floor. My feet are in my shoes and my shoes are on the floor. It's a small point, but sometimes you'll ask a person in trance, "Can you answer this question?" And they'll say, "Yes." That's it. They won't answer the question they'll just say, "Yes."

Debbie: So, Bill, just settle down into your breathing.

Bill: Okay, now don't tell me what to do, because I'm like Cindy. If you tell me what to do, we're going to have a tangle. You can tell me what I could do or what I can do or what I might do.

Debbie: So, Bill, you could just settle down into your breathing. You could close your eyes if you want to, or you can leave them open.

Bill: And when I close my eyes you might just say, "That's right. That's fine."

Debbie: That's fine to just close your eyes. And you can keep your mouth closed. I noticed that you're smiling, and you may smile occasionally. You may want to relax the muscles in your face.

Bill: That's nice because you say, "You may want to relax the muscles in your face." I don't have to, but as soon as you mentioned it my muscles relaxed a little. It's guiding, but you're not saying, "Do it." Now if you see my muscles tense up (*tightens facial muscles*), then you say, "Or you don't have to." You always include the other side.

Katy: You might hear sounds around you or you might not hear them.

Bill: As soon as you mention it, I'm likely to attend to it. So if you think it's a good idea for me to attend to it mention it. If you think I am attending to it, like a door slamming, then I think it's important to mention it. Otherwise, only mention what you want me to attend to. You might say, "So you could attend to the sounds inside or you don't have to. You could attend to the sounds outside." Whatever you mention first I'm going to be more likely to attend to. And then you can put in the "or not" part later.

Alice: You might find yourself letting go of some tension. It's okay to hold on to it if you need to. Your breathing is becoming more regular. You can feel your chest rise and fall. As it rises, the thoughts in your mind may wander. As it falls you'll find yourself more relaxed.

Bill: I will? Who says?

Alice: You may find yourself becoming more relaxed.

Megan: You may be sure that you're going to feel relaxed. And you may not be sure if you'll be relaxed at all. Your hands may feel the arms below them. You may remember a time back in your childhood when you were very relaxed and very much at peace with what was happening. Maybe a time at home with mom and dad.

Paul: If and when you're in a state of deep relaxation or light relation I wonder when and if you might decide to lift your arm. A little at a time or whatever.

Bill: I'm not going to start to lift my arm. That would be a conscious move. You change the phrase to, "When your arm start to lift." It has a mind of its own.

Paul: I wonder when your arm will decide to lift and at what pace that will happen. Will it be slowly or more rapid or in whatever way you choose.

Bill: Now, I guess what I would say is that's a pretty big leap for most people. Not for me, so you're on pretty solid ground with me. But for most people I do little increments on the way to it. I say, "You might notice some changes in your arms or your hands. Maybe a numbness or tingling." I'm noticing a numbness in both arms. My left hand is more numb than my right, but both are fairly numb and tingly. So, that's a step toward hand or arm levitation. You want to ease people into it a little at a time and then go for a slight movement of the thumb or finger or wrist or palm, something that you can walk them into it a little more rather than saying, "When your hand will lift up." That's a big jump for most people.

Laurie: I'm wondering, Bill, if you've found your place as a little fellow back in the family. Was it a nice day? Were there clouds outside your window?

Bill: That's too specific because I was outside already. That's a little jarring. "Were there clouds?" That's a little general.

Laurie: Okay. Were there clouds? Was it a happy time? Was it a sad time? Do you have those times now?

Beth: You may feel very relaxed. And that's okay. You might think about a time when you were a child when you were in a classroom and you knew the answer and you raised your hand. There were a number of people around and everyone was raising their hand. You may just concentrate on what you're feeling right now.

Denise: Bill, you may feel a numbness or a tingling in one or both of your hands. They may feel light. Your hand may rise very slowly. It could be your left hand or your right hand. You may want the hand to rise up toward your face. And just continue at whatever pace the hand feels comfortable with.

Bill: I think it's nice to give it a direction and a destination of the face. That's reassuring to know where it's going to go and what's happening.

Denise: The hand may go right to your cheek. Very slowly, very softly, gently.

Bill: It's actually not going very slowly. So that doesn't work.

Denise: It may rush up to your cheek. (*laughs*) Your hand may go at the pace it feels comfortable going—to your face to the cheek area. It may decide to go to another area.

Bill: That's a nice permission.

Denise: You may experience the hand getting closer to your face, maybe anticipating the arrival of your hand.

Bill: That's a nice indirect suggestion. If you say, "You may experience the hand getting closer to your face" maybe you won't so it may be dissociation or anesthesia of the hand or the face. And the hand is certainly numb, so I don't know whether I'll experience it. Sometimes they lose track of their hands and arms as they're getting closer to their face. They really don't know where they are in space.

Denise: Your hand may want to just gently touch you face.

Bill: Again, that's the dissociated form of saying, "The hand may want to." Like it has a mind of its own. What I want is one thing and what the hand wants is another. Usually we're going to have a clinical purpose for it when we're using it in therapy. And what I typically say is, "As that hand touches your face you can do that kind of integration or resolution of whatever issue you were working on. And something may come to your mind or to your body or to your emotions." You start to link one change to another change to change. Thanks, that was great! So what did you learn from that?

Debbie: The language. It's not automatic to use permissive language. You really have to catch yourself.

Bill: Right. And I think most people do better with the permissive language. Some will say, "Forget this you could, you can stuff—just tell me what to do!"

It may be too permissive for them, and then you'll need to be more directive. But I'd say that's one out of a thousand. Most people will do better if they have a lot of permission. Okay, what else?

Lisa: I think that it was really important that when you're doing that permissiveness and inclusion the first thing that you say is what they respond to.

Bill: Right. It's most likely to show up. "Are you tense?" "Yeah, now that you mention it I am tense." "I don't know how relaxed you are." "I'm not sure how relaxed I am either." All of the sudden you're associating to something or another. So what are you associating to? You're going to be guiding those associations. It's not random. You're going to be saying something very specific that's going to be more likely to invite the person to notice certain things. "I wonder if you've noticed your hands?" "No, I hadn't until you said it. Now I am." The person doesn't have to, but it's a pretty compelling invitation. For instance, some of you mentioned my childhood. I wouldn't have thought about it unless you had spoken about it.

Alice: What was the effect of being asked questions the way Laurie was?

Bill: As long as I don't feel a compulsion to answer them, or as long as they don't direct me in a place that is jarring. Again, you just have to be aware of what you're inviting people to. (*looks to Laurie*) You were inviting me to a peaceful experience and then you said, "Were you happy or were you sad?" That started a whole different train of experience for me. I happened to be happy at that time but I started thinking, "There were times when I was sad." I was off on a different road. That's what associations do. Now, I may not have gone on either of those paths, and I may have been with the clouds and what you said later was irrelevant.

Megan: Before guiding you to any place or any feeling were you just kind of into how your body was feeling?

Bill: Absolutely. I was right there. It was much more a bodily experience. Then it started to turn into a visual, emotional experience.

Continuing Conversations

Megan: Will there be different situations when you guide into one or the other?

Bill: Yes. It depends on your clinical purpose.

Denise: If you were working with someone with a conversion disorder, would it be after you'd done the hand levitation to see that there really is trance but you would begin to . . .

Bill: . . . Probably, although I weave things in from the beginning. What I would probably say is, "I really don't know how or what you need to do to be comfortable. But I can tell you that you're communicating volumes to me by your behaviors.'' I'd say that in the first sentence or two. And then we'd talk about communication and how you communicate in a lot of different ways and how a lot of communication is stuff that you don't even know that you're communicating. Then I might say, ''When I started doing hypnosis I really had to find my own voice.'' I would be weaving that in. Later I would say, ''I'm really interested in finding out what you have to say about the experience. You can stay in trance and tell me about your experience.''

Denise: You would expect them to respond verbally.

Bill: I would. And I'd say, ''And maybe your unconscious mind can tell me what you need to know, what you need to say, or what you need to do to remove the barriers to free up your communication.'' Or I might also give them a pencil and say, ''The pencil will write what needs to be written—what you really need to say.'' Then we would be working on whatever else. It doesn't exactly go, induction then treatment. It's induction-treatment, induction-treatment, induction-treatment through the whole thing, in response to whatever is going on. But we'll have much more direction than just, ''Lift your hand up to your face.'' We'll have a clinical direction. We know we want to help this person speak clearly and say what they need to say and not have a conversion disorder, so we have a clinical goal.

Denise: Would you expect if you did that one time that the person would speak clearly from then on out?

Bill: I would expect that that's possible. The idea is that once you evoke the ability, then you want to speak about it and say, ''After this experience you can use the same ability automatically to speak clearly when you need to.'' You link it to the rest of their life. I would expect that it is possible that whatever happens in the trance to happen in everyday life. It's the same thing with Cindy. We don't know what will happen with her. But do you imagine that she could find that balance in her life? Yeah.

Megan: So is it a one-time thing?

Bill: It can be. What I usually notice is one to three times with specific things like that. When I'm not getting the response within that time it's probably not going to work. It still could, but in my estimation it probably won't. I usually find some significant movement after the first, second, or third time. But certainly it can happen with just one time. I've had it happen with cluster headaches, migraine headaches, chronic pain. Also with sexual abuse issues. It doesn't necessarily solve all the problems in life, but it got them moving in the direction they wanted.

Katy: Have you done any work with folks who have had cancer?

Bill: I have—on two fronts. One is with the side effects of chemotherapy and with pain control. The other is to actually work with cancer itself. My father died of cancer, so for about five years I saw anybody for free that wanted to come in that had cancer to do either type of work—whatever they wanted. And I've done other things with cancer, too, with people that had other issues. Sometimes it's quite helpful. Sometimes people die.

Laurie: What kind of time do you spend on this in therapy? What portion of the session?

Bill: Thirty, forty minutes, twenty—minutes—somewhere in there. Some people I just do five minutes, but usually not the first time. Once they've done it sometimes that's all they want. Just a short, five to ten minute trance as part of an ongoing treatment. The rest of the time is spent just as you would in a regular therapy session.

Megan: How much have you used this with anxiety?

Bill: A lot. We do other things as well.

Megan: Can you teach them to go into that themselves?

Bill: Yeah, and sometimes you can make a tape. I actually have a tape called *Calm Beneath the Waves*[76] that I just made just a few weeks ago. It's for people that have anxiety and panic. It's also for those who get desperate in between sessions. I used to just make them for individualized clients and record them during our sessions. I'd just record what we did and then they could take them home and use them. Sometimes they will learn self-hypnosis and sometimes whatever we do in therapy is enough. They don't need anything more. So, yeah, I think it's a great thing for clients. And people will tell me, "I've relaxed before, but I've never been this relaxed." And it's not a relaxation tape. That's not what it's made for. People often relax when they're in trance. If they relax it's different than a relaxation technique. With relaxation technique, you're going to deliberately tense and relax or focus on relaxing. In trance, I could say, "You can relax deeply." And you could be as relaxed as going through an hour-long relaxation session. So what's the difference between relaxation therapy and trance? To me it's an evocation of ability. If you don't know how to relax, I can't evoke it. If you've never relaxed deeply, I can't evoke it. If you've ever relaxed, even once in your life, I can evoke it. It's the same thing with guided imagery. You were doing much more imagery, but a lot of the stuff that you all were saying didn't have anything to do with images. You weren't directing me to have images. It was experiences that you were directing me at. So it isn't always visual. It isn't always relaxation. Those are different. Ernest Hilgard[77] studied hypnosis and had people ride exercise bicycles and go into trance. He wanted to dispel the myth that trance equals relaxation. They were physiologically aroused and they were in trance. Sometimes I work with people who have

[76] Please contact *http://www.brieftherapy.com* for information on the availability of this tape.

[77] Ernest Hilgard, Ph.D., is a professor at Stanford University. He has published extensively in the areas of hypnosis and theories of learning.

been sexually abused, and they're not relaxed at all when they're doing that work. They're in trance and they're not relaxed. So it's not equal to relaxation and most people relax when they go into trance. For anxiety, of course, that's the direction we would be pointing—decreased heart rate, relaxed breathing, relaxed muscles, calm stomach, thinking more calm and clear, whatever it may be. That's where we would be going with that, but it's not necessary. It often happens spontaneously, but it's not necessary.

Alice: Is there an advantage to doing it at multiple levels in terms of the physical and the visual and evoking a memory?

Bill: I don't think so. The only advantage I can think of is that there are multiple pathways through for people and the more pathways you offer the more likely it is that they'll find a way through to whatever experience they want to go. But I don't routinely use multiple pathways, because if I'm getting through, why do I need to find another pathway? That's the only thing I'd say about that.

Megan: The different voices and the different tones didn't disrupt anything for you? No. It might for other people but probably not too much. For me, an old tranceketeer from way back, so it's okay.

Denise: Is there potential for doing damage or harm with this?

Bill: I don't think with this approach because it's so permissive. I think that people will go where they need to go. Now that doesn't mean that a person won't go to a scary or difficult place. When I've heard this about people who are lay hypnotists I think they're better directive hypnotists than I am. They say, "Go deeply" and people will. They're really good at that stuff. The only worry I have about this is with dentists or doctors doing hypnosis who aren't trained in psychotherapy. When I first went to hypnosis workshops, they used to say, "Beware of the abreaction." They'd say that you can put people in trance and get a really severe abreaction. It happens occasionally. So I learned all these techniques to contain the abreaction. And I did hypnosis for years and wondered, "Where's the abreaction?" Finally, after years, I figured out that what they meant by abreaction was that people start to cry or get scared or go into a painful experience. Geez, people do that all the time in my office and they're not in trance! (*laughter*) That's just therapy to me. But it didn't freak me out. I was waiting for this terrible, psychotic, really weird abreaction and I had all theses minor type things that to me were just part of regular therapy. I realized that why this scares the doctors and dentists is because it's emotions and traumatic memories. (*laughter*) But that's the stuff of life! We're therapists, so we're comfortable with that. If you're not comfortable with that then you probably haven't been doing therapy that long. And general physicians are not that comfortable being with people when they're emotionally upset. So I was saying, "Oh, that's the abreaction? Why do I need to contain that?" There's no need to contain that. If it doesn't freak you out they won't get freaked out and they'll move through it. Last time Cindy had a very traumatic experience when she was in trance and she was saying, "Am I going to go back there again?" I was like, "I don't know." It was okay with her and it was okay with me. She was willing to do it again. It didn't bother her. She's had other traumatic experiences that had nothing to do with trance. She's gone into that place before. It's a familiar place to her. Was she freaked out about it? No. But did she prefer to go there? No. Was she willing? Yeah. It wasn't that bad. Did she trust that I wasn't going to freak out and say, "Snap out of it?" Yeah.

Megan: How do you end the trance?

Bill: Before I talk about that, are there any other comments or reactions?

Katy: Can you do this with children?

Bill: Yeah. Some kids you can only do a little with them because they won't sit still. Other kids really get into it and like it. There are other techniques you can use with children. I don't do much hypnosis and inner work with children, but I learned a technique years ago that I've never used but I think is very clever. (*looks toward Katy*) "Do you know how to use your dreaming arm? Well, it's this arm (*lifts Katy's right arm*). That arm won't go down any faster than you'll be able to see your favorite cartoon or movie or scene from that movie again and again as many times as you want. It will go down a little at a time as you're seeing your favorite scene." So, you engage them in what they're interested in, and the arm hangs up there for a while and starts to drift down.

Katy: It's still up there! (*laughter*)

Bill: You better see that favorite cartoon or movie scene soon! So you adapt the technique. You can do, "Simon says sit in the chair. Simon says uncross your legs. Simon says close your eyes. Simon says you could think of this." There's a bunch of books on using hypnosis with children, and the prevailing idea is that children are much better trance subjects. There imaginations are unfettered. Of course, it depends on the child and his or her situation, but generally, kids are better trance subjects. I think with most kids you want to use a more active technique, rather than just a verbal one—something that engages them physically.

Okay, so how do you complete a trance experience? Usually, what I say is something about putting yourself all back together in a way that works for you and reorienting all the way to the present time and the present place at your own rate and your own pace—something that is a generalized suggestion.

Denise: Do you say that directly as opposed to, "You can?"

Bill: Yes, because you're really engaging much more of the conscious part of them. And I change my voice tone. I change my volume, my rhythm, all those cues are saying, "Time to change." Sometime before that or even before the inner work, I do a "cleanup." I say, "Anything that I say or that I said that hasn't been helpful to you, you can tune it out, ignore it, leave it behind, or just skip it. Anything that I've said that hasn't been helpful to you that you still want to use you might change into something that's more helpful to you. And you only need to use what's been helpful to you about this experience.'' That's an indirect suggestion that they will use it, and also that they can tune out whatever stuff I've been offbase about. After this general type cleanup, I'll then have them come all the way back.

Now, what happens if they don't come out of trance? First of all, it's only happened twice in the eighteen years that I've been doing hypnosis that a person hasn't come out of trance in a fairly timely manner. I think if you switch your voice and your tone and your breathing, you're really inviting them out and back to everyday reality. Sometimes they're so absorbed in their inner experience they really don't hear you. I learned this in a particular way when I was doing inner work with a woman. She started with her hands on the arms of the chair and she had both hands lift up while we were doing this work. And then her hands went down to her thighs. So at the end I said, ''It's time to come out.'' I'm waiting and waiting and waiting and it's not happening. I had someone else on the hour, so I didn't have more time. I said, ''It's time to come out. Please come out, I've got somebody else waiting.'' Still she didn't respond. So I remembered something that I had learned from Erickson called the handshake induction. He did it like this. (*looks to Paul and shakes his hand*) ''I'm glad to meet you Paul, my name is Bill.'' Then he'd do the trancework, and at the end he would say, ''O'Hanlon.'' (*laughter*) And for everything in between the person would have amnesia. He would just reorient to the moment right before they went into trance. So I thought, ''Maybe if I reorient her to the moment right before she went into trance she'll come right out.'' I said, ''I'm going to lift up your hands.'' And I lifted them up and put them on the arms of the chair, and as soon as I touched her she came out. So you can engage the client differently and that can bring them out. For instance, if they're a little groggy you can say, ''Let's set the time for next week.'' Or you can joke with them and say, ''Earth to client, this is ground control.''

Megan: Do you usually talk about what they were experiencing?

Bill: I usually say, ''Is there anything in particular that stands out about that experience?'' I'm very vague, rather than, ''What did you feel or think or see?'' I also see if there's anything they want to ask. Whatever they want to ask I'm willing to tell them what I did, what I saw, what I observed, what I thought of.

Now with some people you want to use the word trance or hypnosis and with others you don't. I'm moving away from it, but I still have that in my background. I learned hypnosis and I've been doing that, but it's not exactly rocket science and it doesn't look like trance. Where's the big trance induction? It's more like, ''You can go inside and experience what you want to experience.'' And it's automatic experience. That's why it's like trance, because it's trance-like behavior. You don't need to use the concept ''hypnosis,'' which freaks out most of the people you say it to, and you have to demystify it and debrief them on what hypnosis is and then move into the work that you do. So why bother? Just do inner work. When I first learned this I had a certain repertoire of therapeutic skills, and this added a whole new piece that allowed me to work with more problems than I could work with before. Somebody came in a few years after I learned trance and said, "Can you do hypnosis for warts?"[78] Now if somebody came to you for therapy for warts, maybe you'd try and do stress control or something like that, but what would you do about warts? Go to your dermatologist. She's done that. They'd burned off or frozen off the warts every month for twenty-two months, and it was the middle of winter and she went out of the dermatologist's office and put her hands on the steering wheel and they were freezing—she was in such pain. She ached so much that she knew she had to do something else. So she went back into the dermatologist's office and said, "Is there anything that you can do other than what you've been doing? It hasn't been working and they keep coming back." He said, "I hate to say it, but I read an article in a dermatology journal that said that hypnosis could be helpful. But I don't know anyone who does it; I think it's quackery." She said, "I know somebody who does it." She was a therapist who had been to one of my workshops and knew I did hypnosis. She came to see me and in three sessions her warts were gone. I still see her at therapy conferences and she shows me! (*holds up his hands*) (*laughter*) Twelve years later, no warts. I never *did warts* when I was a therapist. I wouldn't have known what to do. But with hypnosis I had a way to do it. I figured that there was a way her body grew the warts and there was a way that her body got rid of them. From what I knew and she knew, it probably had to do with withdrawing the nutrients from the blood vessels.

Megan: Did you or she come up with that?

Bill: We talked about it together. And I learned from Erickson who worked with a person with warts.[79] He had the person step in the coldest water and the hottest water. Stand in each for five minutes—the hottest water she could stand and the coldest water she could stand. So I had the woman I worked with do that. And she'd actually read the same book I'd read about Erickson, so she knew when I was using an Erickson technique and she told me that. I said, "That's fine. That doesn't matter." For me, the point was to get her body to know how to change blood flow—to remind her that she knew how to change blood flow. Blood could flow into the feet or out of the feet depending on whether it was hot or cold. That would remind her that she could rapidly change blood flow and that she could withdraw the blood from the warts. She did, indeed, do that. After the first time they became worse. After the second time they were better. After the third time they went away, and they've never come back.

Alice: Can you say more about what you mean about eliciting resources?

[78] For a synopsis of this case see O'Hanlon, B. (in press).

[79] See Rosen, S. (1982).

Bill: Yes. I think the first thing to say is, like solution-oriented therapy, you go to a time or a place in the person's life when they had a similar experience and something better happened. Or something similar to what you want to have happen happened. Within their life experience is the first place to look—within their life experience about the problem or something very similar to the problem. The second place to look is more universal life experiences that people have. To stay on the warts case, I thought that she had blushed at some time in her life. The next place I went is that when she ate food the blood would flow to the middle of her body to help digest it. What do those things have in common? I start to think of there being a *class of problems and a class of solutions.*[80] Warts are the specific problem. The class of problems is that blood is flowing to some growth on her body that she doesn't like. The class of solutions is to change blood flow and withdraw blood flow from that part of her body. How do I evoke that? I do it through evocation of actual experiences in her life related to blood flow and to her warts. Then I go a little farther toward specific experiences in changes in blood flow. I then go for task assignments like having her stand in hot and cold water—to evoke the experience within her. Next I talk about images. I used to live in Arizona in a place called Casa Grande and they used to grow cotton there—out in the middle of the desert. They used an irrigation method to do this. They would have an irrigation ditch and rows of cotton, so they would use irrigation troughs between the rows. They would use these U-shaped tubes in the irrigation ditch, which ran by all the fields and into the troughs. Because water seeks its own level, they would let it go from the irrigation ditch into the trough between the cotton rows. They could cut down on pesticide use and costs if they put the water into the troughs and as soon as the cotton started to come up, stop the flow, because as the cotton grew so did the weeds. By withdrawing the water, the hot desert sun would bake the weeds. The cotton would start to wither too, but not nearly as quickly as the weeds. Then they would restore the water and the cotton would grow some more and the weeds would eventually start to grow again—and they would repeat the process of withdrawing the water and nutrients. After the weeds had died down they would start the water again and because of this process they didn't have to use as many pesticides. In a similar way your body can withdraw blood flow and nutrients. So I'm using a general image and even though she's never been to Arizona, she can relate to that general analogy or metaphor. The last thing I do is general permissive suggestion: "Your body can get rid of the warts, can withdraw the blood flow; can make them go away." They're just general permissive suggestions. I just say it "can." I don't use the other side—"and it doesn't have to." I only suggest that these things can happen.

So what would you do with a case of anxiety using that same model? In trance, we might say, "There may be times that you can't even remember when

[80] See Figure 5.1, *Class of Problems/Class of Solutions Model.* For further reading see O'Hanlon, W. H. (1987).

Class of Problems/Class of Solutions Model

Specific Presenting Problem ··········> Specific Intervention ··········> **TRANSFER TO PROBLEM CONTEXT**

Analogy
Anecdote
Trance phenomenon
Task
Interpersonal move

DERIVE (Specific Presenting Problem → Class of Problems)

EVOKE (Class of Solutions → Specific Intervention)

Class of Problems ··········> Class of Solutions
(pattern of experience)
(resource/skill)

Figure 5.1

your heart rate calmed down when you were anxious. You don't even know how you did it or what changed. Your heart rate clamed down, your muscles changed, your breathing changed—go back to that time and get it and bring it back to where you need it in the present and the future.'' That's the first kind of suggestion. The second kind is, ''Remember when you run and your heart rate speeds up and when you stop your heart rate slows down?'' It doesn't have anything to do with anxiety, but it's a similar kind of thing. Go to what your body knows about how that happened, and make it slow down. The third is image. So calm beneath the waves—that's the image. ''On the surface there's a lot of agitation in the ocean, but if you go beneath the surface and go diving and go to a certain depth you'll find absolute calmness. Just like that, there's someplace in you that can be really, really calm even while there's agitation on the surface.'' The next one is generalized permissive suggestion: ''Your body can calm down—it can be relaxed. You can calm down even more. You can find yourself starting to think anxious thoughts and your body can still be calm.''

Megan: Could it be something as simple as a train slowing?

Bill: Yeah, it could be. That's great. Where I get it is from the client. They start to talk and would use a metaphor and an image would come to my mind. So how about if you play an anxious person and begin to talk as you're talking about your problems?

Megan: ''When I'm in a room full of lots of people I feel it coming on and I can't get out.''

Bill: Great. I would say, ''Sometimes you have a sense that you're in a room and that you've painted yourself in a corner. And have you seen one of those cartoons where the cartoon character paints a door and doorknob behind them and turns the doorknob and gets out of the room? Something in you can find a way to paint a door and doorknob and get out of that place where you feel trapped.'' For me, I can't know about these images and associations until the person starts talking. I don't think about it consciously; the ideas just occur to me.

Karen: Is that something that you developed?

Bill: Yeah. The best analogy that I can use is something that I think most of us have but that I have made more explicit because I have to teach. I have file folders in my mind that I call ''classes of solutions.'' As soon as someone starts to talk I pull out my preferred file folders. I make sense of the problem in a particular way based on my ideas about how people have problems, and, usually, when I do hypnosis, mine have to do with very literal body things. For instance, how would a body do anxiety? Not, what does this mean, what is their childhood about. I don't typically go to that place. Some of you would and that makes sense for you. To me, if I were a body, how would I make myself anxious? I would speed up my heart rate, tense up my muscles, get this gurgling acid stuff going on in my stomach, breath more shallowly, think racing thoughts—I think of that stuff and then wonder, if I were a body and wanted to not do anxiety, what would I do? I'd slow my heart rate, relax my muscles, breath more deeply, regularly, and slowly, think more clearly and slowly—from that, images and ideas and analogies would come to mind that I or the other person has had from experiences. I would then want to evoke those things. I'm thinking, here's my file folder for nonanxiety. I have a bunch of images, ideas, and analogies about how a heart slows down—on how breathing changes. And I have everyday situations in which I can remind the person in which that happens.

For pain control I have like eleven file folders because I've done a lot of work with that. There's anesthesia, analgesia, time distortion, remembering a pain-free time, anticipating in the future a pain-free time, changing the sensation from pain to a tingling or a warmth or a coolness, changing the location of the pain, reducing the intensity of the pain, separating remembered pain from experienced pain and anticipated pain—separating it into three parts—interpretation of the pain versus the sensation of the pain, and there are one or two others. So I have these file folders that are filed in my solutions file cabinet, and I automatically go to them. If I had never done work with pain control I wouldn't have any there. You have some file folders in the areas you have expertise in. In these file folders are usually stories, images, and general suggestions—and I think it's definitely learned over time. I told no stories when I first did therapy. I had no analogies, no images. They didn't occur to me. It was clearly learned behavior—I learned ways of thinking.

Karen: Do you think you have to know a lot about the problem?

Bill: I think the more I know the better, but generally, no, I don't. I was treating a neighbor of mine who was a plastic surgeon. She was a workaholic and very busy and I heard from her husband and my son, who played with their kid, that she had been down for the count for days because of severe back pain. She had been treated with cortisone injections, but it hasn't worked. She can't do her surgery. So I say to her husband, "Tell her this is what I do for a living. I will come over and I will do hypnosis with her." A week goes past and I hear she's gotten better; then I hear she's down for the count again. So Sunday I go over there and she's resting and she tells her husband to bring her out to the living room. He does and she teaches me, medically, what her problem is. She describes a sheath where the nerves are supposed to go, but the nerves are swollen that's why they've used cortisone. But you can't get right to that place, so you have to use general cortisone and that's not good for you. A reduction of the inflammation of the nerves needs to happen so they can fit into the sheath—that's why there's pain. I had no clue about that. In that case that was a very helpful image. So, I explained to her what trance was—a narrowing focus of attention and automatic behavior—and asked her if she had experienced something like that before. She said, "Oh yeah. When I have to do microsurgery we do it through a microscope. And it's so small, my hands have to be absolutely still because if I move a little I might damage something. And there's a way that I do it that I'm absolutely still. Hours can go by and I'm so calm and still and focused." I said, "Are there any other times?" She said, "When I go cross-country skiing I can think and make my hands and feet warm." So she told me what her trance abilities were. I used those and the image of the sheath and the nerves. So the more I know, the better. If I don't know I'll make it up and hopefully it will translate into her own experience.

Alice: Did it work?

Bill: It did. She bought me a sweater for Christmas! (*laughter*) You know, more than that, she was a virtuoso hypnotic subject who started using it for lots of things after that. In fact, the next week she had dental pain and couldn't get in right away and she used it for that—in between patients. She said, "I just went into trance and zapped it!" (*laughter*) Okay, what else do you need to know before you feel comfortable doing this with your clients or patients?

Debbie: I think practice. And also a little, tiny note beside me.

Bill: Yeah, a cheat sheet—that's a good idea. The other thing is finding those clients and patients that you trust the most and say, "I learned this new thing. I don't know exactly what I'm doing yet, but I know a bit and I need to practice. I practiced in the training I went to, and I need to practice with people with real issues. Would you be willing to do it?" It's a good way to introduce it. There was a person I worked with who learned it in a very short time and I asked her how she did it and she said, "I just listen to you all and then I go in with clients and say, 'I don't know what I'm doing, would you be willing to try this?'" Some would say, "Hypnosis, sure." Others would say, "Hypnosis, no way." She tried it with a bunch of people and learned it in a couple of weeks. It took me like six years to get confident enough to try it. She learned it right away. I think there are different ways of going about it. What else?

Laurie: I think you said earlier that you don't do it with everybody.

Bill: I don't. It's partly based on the presenting problem, and it's partly based on my sense. When I first learned hypnosis at these workshops, they would say, "You have to get the patient to trust you." I think that's wrong. I think that you actually have to trust the person. This is probably more important when you're starting out. Now I feel safe enough about doing hypnosis with anyone that I felt it was clinically indicated and they were willing. The clinical implications aren't always clear. I think you'll see times this week when it won't even emerge as a topic and some situations where it will. Typically, when I do couple or family therapy there's no mention of it. When I do individual sometimes there is and sometimes there isn't. It depends on the nature of the presenting problem. I tend to divide problems into voluntary and involuntary. Now lots of people will say, "I can't help it," or "I'm stuck with my problem"—what I mean is, if I asked you to do your symptom, could you do it deliberately or could you not do it deliberately? If you said, "I smoke and I want to stop," we'd do other things if I was to help you with that. If you said, "I have warts," I'd say, "Show me how you do your warts or don't do your warts." You couldn't do that—it's crazy. Migraine headache, anxiety—same thing. "Maybe I can think of some things that make me anxious, but I can't really get rid of the anxiety. I've tried deliberate efforts." Those things are amenable for hypnosis. The other stuff isn't. Yelling at your kids—that's not a hypnotic problem. Now maybe you could calm down more so you wouldn't yell at your kids. You could resolve some issue so you wouldn't get triggered. Maybe that would be a thing to use hypnosis for—that's more in that nonvoluntary realm. Something goes off for you experientially and then you yell at your kids. But for the behavior part, I wouldn't do hypnosis. There are people who do hypnosis for smoking and weight control. I rarely do that. I don't think it works very well overall. I also don't think that's what hypnosis is for. It's for experiential, physiological, perceptual, automatic aspects of experience—not for deliberate, conscious thinking.

Debbie: What about something like nail biting?

Bill: I typically wouldn't do hypnosis for that. I think there are more conscious deliberate things you can do. You could have the person bite nine nails and let one grow. That would be something very deliberate that they could do that could change the pattern and show that they have the possibility of not biting their nails. It doesn't mean that hypnosis might not work for that. It might work, but it wouldn't be the first thing that I tried. Nail biting is a deliberate behavior. Now, oftentimes the person experiences it automatically. They don't know when they're doing it, but they could bring it up to consciousness. So they may not be aware of it at first, but you can bring it to their conscious attention and it's something that they were aware of that they could change. They may not want to change it, or choose to change it, but they could change it. You could say, "Show me nail biting" or "Show me not nail biting" and they could do both.

Karen: How important is motivation?

Bill: I think it's important for people to want to make changes in their lives, but they don't have to be entirely unambivalent about it for hypnosis. I think in therapy it's pretty important to find out what people are motivated for rather than what they're not motivated for—like the involuntary clients that come in or kids that come in and don't have a clue why they're there. I probably wouldn't do hypnosis with those kids. If the kid said, "I really have a bad temper and I really get frustrated," and you had done enough with the voluntary work and they really keep their behavior in check but get really frustrated, you might do hypnosis. If the kid is motivated for that, great. If the kid comes in with bad grades and they're not very motivated to change those grades, I wouldn't hypnotize them to do better. It would be just like trying to get them to do homework. If they're not willing it's like beating your head against the wall. I'd work with the parents, the teachers—make sure there are consequences so the kid gets more motivated. Then if the kid comes in and says he wants help focusing because he gets distracted easily, I could work with him hypnotically. Being able to sit down and do homework—that's not a hypnotic thing. So I think it is important to have motivation and figure out what the person wants, but they don't have to be one hundred percent clear that they can and will do that. All they have to say is, "I think I'd like this." I think Cindy said that yesterday. It was like, "I don't have a sense that I can do this." After we talked she had a sense she could do it. So it wasn't like, "I'm committed to doing this and I'll do whatever I need to do." She was more like, "If this can be done I'm willing, but I don't know whether it can be done." I don't know if you would say that it was a problem with motivation, but it was her ambivalence about the whole thing. I don't think you have to express a belief or desire in trance to go into trance. But I typically wouldn't put a person in trance if they didn't express at least a willingness. I can put someone into trance who hasn't given me permission and hasn't asked for trance. Some of you will go into trance when I do trance. I can guarantee it—even though you didn't ask for it. You can probably stop it if you want to, but you will go into trance.

Katy: Yesterday I was having a hard time because I was looking at your head and had to look away every now and then to stay alert.

Bill: Exactly.

Karen: So you don't have to be concentrating to go into a trance?

Bill: Absolutely not. You may have to concentrate not to do it. You don't have to concentrate or fixate on anything—it can happen without that. Erickson used to hypnotize one person while he was talking to another person. Very weird. It scared me when I read it because I was thinking of going to a hypnotist at the time, and I was thinking, "They're going to put me in trance, tell me come back every week and pay them $45 an hour, which was the going rate at that time, and forget the suggestion." So I thought, "I'll bring a tape recorder along." But then I figured, "They'll just tell me that every time I listened to the tape I wouldn't be able to hear that part." Then I thought, "I'll bring a friend along." Then I read the *Uncommon Therapy*[81] book about Erickson, where a woman brought her roommate in who was really messed up and would never seek therapy: Erickson suggested that the woman act as if she was getting the therapy and her roommate was to come along to protect her. He hypnotized the roommate and did some really serious work with her because she was suicidal and wasn't willing to come in and deal with it. So I thought, "Oh great, now I can't bring a friend because they can just hypnotize that person too!" I ended up skipping the whole thing. Now I think it's silly. I think one has protective mechanisms inside, and I think that woman probably went along with it because she needed some serious help and it was a face-saving way to go into it. That's my explanation anyway. I wouldn't try that experiment.

Lisa: You said that you sometimes use it with couples?

Bill: Occasionally I have.

Lisa: What would be a context in which you might use it?

Bill: Well, I don't use it often with couples, but there's one example that comes immediately to mind. I had a guy come and see me for phobias—three phobias. We cleared those up with hypnosis, and his wife was a therapist, as was he, and she said, "Do you mind if I sit in?" We said, "Fine." I really didn't focus on her, but she always went into trance when he did. So the phobias were cleared up after a few sessions and I said to them, "You know, these phobias have been a big part of your life and you've adapted to them. Do you think this is going to mess up your marriage in any way?" They both said, "We don't think so, but if it does we're willing to handle it." A year later they came back and their marriage was all screwed up. They were having lots of severe arguments that they couldn't seem to get out of. We tried various things and it wasn't working very well. But he was such a great trance subject and she had gone into trance with him before, so one day I said to him, "Why don't you go into trance when you're in this place where you're just defensive and going back at her? You're really good at it. Just get in touch with your soft underbelly and come from that loving place." He said, "That would work for me." She said, "I could do that too." So I said, "Why don't you both just look at each other in the eyes and go into trance." And, actually, it didn't work for her. She would come out of trance and go at him again. But it would work for him. He would go into a different place and respond differently and they would somehow find their way out. So the trance was a way of shifting their attention and awareness and

[81] See Haley, J. (1973).

experience at that moment. That's one application. I suppose one could think of doing trancework with one person in front of the other to help him or her understand where this defensive behavior comes from, and give him or her some empathy and compassion for it. But, again, it would probably be to evoke something. Say your partner says something and immediately you go into an age-regressed, "I'm going to be abandoned" state. If you wanted to do hypnosis with that, you could interrupt that process and get them into a "I'm loved and I'm not going to be abandoned," or an "I'm okay on my own" state.

Valuing Internal Experience

Bill: You know, I have written a lot over the years, but I only really disagree with a couple of the things that I've said. I tried to get around a philosophical problem in the first book[82] that I did with Jim Wilk[83] by banishing internal experience to be considered in psychotherapy. It was a dumb idea, but we had to do it because it was too complex to take up in the book. It was a stupid thing. We were saying, "Stay with the observable." This was a radical behaviorist stance. It was an epistemological and phenomenological stance saying, "They have their own phenomenology and you'll never entirely understand. So stick with what they describe and what you know. You'll get what goes inside fully, so don't even bother to try and consider that you will ever get it." I disagree with that now. There was one other thing that I disagree with. I've definitely focused and honed the expression of what I do, but generally I don't disagree with what I've said in the past.

Lately I've been putting out more audiotapes because people seem to like them. I have a tape called *Moving On*[84] that I did on resolving sexual abuse that therapists will buy and give to their clients. And I've received such touching letters. Someone will write and say, "I was afraid of hypnosis and I was in therapy for sexual abuse and I wasn't doing well. I listened to your tape and it's the safest, most wonderful experience, and it's really helped me move on. I've never met you, but thank you." To get a letter like that once in your life is amazing to me.

[82] See O'Hanlon, B., & Wilk, J. (1987).
[83] Jim Wilk is a psychotherapist and workshop leader who resides in England.
[84] *For more information on this tape please contact http://www.brieftherapy.com.*

Chapter 6

"Jill and Eric"

One of the partners from whom the seminar was renting office space for the week brought a couple she was seeing for a consultation. Again, this consultation was done with participants in the room, showing the open and collaborative nature of this work.

Therapy with a Couple[85]

Bill: I specifically asked not to know anything about you. I know that may be frustrating for you, but we don't have to go over the whole thing again. I'm the forest for the trees kind of guy. I want to come in and be a consultant for you. So I'd like to find out, in twenty-five words or less, a summary of where you've been, what's brought you to this place, where you think you are now, and where are the troublesome and stuck places, and where you want to go—so I can get an overview. Sometimes I describe this as like going for chemical dependency treatment—they do an intervention and you may still have issues to deal with the rest of your life, but this gets you moving off of whatever you're stuck on. So where are you now, what do you think you get stuck on—as a couple or individually, whatever you're here for—and I don't even know if you've been in counseling before.

Jill: Oh, you really don't know anything!

Bill: I really don't. And I want to come with fresh eyes. Sometimes I get referrals when I'm back home and sometimes they send the case notes ahead or the medical records ahead, and I read these things and I think, "Gosh, this doesn't sound good. I don't think I can do anything about that." (*laughter from Jill*)

[85] Cindy, the therapist for the couple, enters the room as an observer.

But if I don't read them before I meet the people and then I meet them I think, "Wow! What great people. There are lots of chances here." Then I read the medical record and it's like, "Oh yeah, I heard all that stuff, but these are the people in front of me." So, I don't want to get swayed by that stuff. I want to get my own impressions. After that long preamble, what the heck brings you here? Where are you now? What's happened up until now? And where do you want to go? You can answer any of those questions or all of those questions.

Eric: The primary purpose here is for us, jointly, to try and keep our marriage. Although I'm young, it has been difficult because of a lot of issues that I've brought to the marriage. I'm previously married and divorced. I have a son from a prior relationship.

Bill: How old?

Eric: He is going to be three next month. His mother and I did not marry. It has been a very strongly litigated situation that has brought a lot of stress to me and I've brought to the relationship here that has made it very difficult.

Bill: Litigated for child support, for custody or for. . . .

Eric: Litigated for visitation. I didn't see him for one year. We were in the court system. On Tuesday we're supposed to be getting a court order where we can finally begin overnights. I refer to it as the "prevent defense"—prevent me from seeing Christopher and maybe she can get what she wants, which was packaged financially and all that stuff. That has brought a lot of tension. Plus me being me creates tension. We've gone up and down and up and down and we're trying to get to more of an even keel.

Bill: That's brought extra, added stresses you wouldn't have had if you had just gotten together and everything was fresh and new and there wasn't any of this stuff going on?

Jill: (*laughing*) We assume that.

Bill: Yeah, you assume that, but you don't know. Regardless of that, this stuff is here, that stuff is out there and it's affecting you. But there are things that happen in your relationship that sometimes don't work based on whatever is going on with either of you and what's going on out there. Okay, I got that sense. And what kind of progress have you made on it so far? What brought you initially for counseling, if you came for that? If not, what brings you now?

Jill: Originally I moved out.

Bill: That's a pretty strong statement.

Jill: I'm trying to remember if it was before I came in here or after I came in here. I think it was after I started. For me, I was struggling with how do I support my husband and help him through the rough times and still get what I need out of the relationship and have the kind of life I want and still deal with all these outside influences? It was real tough to balance those out. I think we've made an incredible amount of progress. I would give Cindy full credit for that. I think she very definitely made a success story there. Especially in the last month to two months we have made an incredible amount of progress of being able to find ways to talk to each other that don't create fights and nastiness. I think that's been a big thing for both of us. The last two weeks have been downright enjoyable!

Eric: I think the difference is we know when not to deal with it.

Bill: When to leave it alone.

Eric: Walk away from it, let things settle down. (*looks at Jill*) I think in our last session here you saw how open and receptive I could be—when you brought it up in the safeness here.

Bill: Even tough stuff in the right circumstances in the right way you can deal with a lot better as long as you, at those tense moments, have not tried to engage in the tough or even not-so-tough stuff.

Eric: And in the fact that time had passed and I was in a different place. I could be much more receptive and say, "Yeah, I screwed up. I'm responsible for that."

Jill: Plus defensiveness on both our parts. I think I have learned, as hard as it is for me sometimes, when I really want to jump on something and say, "Let's deal with it," or even worse is I would feel that I wasn't being heard and I would force an issue at a time when all I was going to get from him was defensiveness if I did that. I think that my being able to step back a little bit, and even swallow some things, which for a stubborn Irish woman like myself is not an easy thing, and being able to bring it here has made it easier to take. I think we're at the point where we're hopefully beginning to take some of what we do here and bring it home.

Bill: Okay.

Eric: One other thing. She's five months pregnant.

Jill: Five months this week.

Bill: Five months pregnant.

Eric: We're trying to get stuff settled from the past and so forth and get a fresh beginning here with the baby due the first part December.

Bill: I once went to a seminar. One of these self-help seminars—a human potential thing. And, they said at the beginning of the seminar, "Our purpose here is to get you to get rid of all the problems you've been dealing with and give you a whole set of new and bigger problems." And people laughed, and I thought, "I like that because I'm so tired of the same old problems I've been dealing with for years. I want new problems.'' So, how will you know, if you can make a guess about this, when you're pretty sure, ''Hey, we've made enough progress. The work that Cindy has done with us has really contributed. It has translated out there and we're doing okay. We're on our own and we can come back for checkups or tune-ups.'' How will you know when you've made enough progress? What I'm doing is trying to set the compass: where you've been, where are you now, and where do you want to go. And that will probably come back to what still needs to be fine tuned. It sounds like you're going in a good direction. What still needs to be fine tuned or handled now?

Jill: From my point of view, at this point, we've made a whole lot of progress. It's not a regular routine at home. Right now our routine at home is more or less to wait until we go and see Cindy—as issues come up. With most of the big issues, we've really gotten to a point where we can discuss them reasonably and logically. I think for me there's only one sticking area that's not really even a sticking area because think I understand what's going on there; it's just tough for me emotionally sometimes to deal with it. At this point I would say that we're at the stage where it's a matter of practicing what we do—practicing what we do in here and making that transition to taking it home.

Bill: You've had some of those discussions and you'd have more of those discussions, and they don't go too badly. They're not perfect, but they don't go too badly. And ultimately you decide, ''Let's stop on this one, we're not getting anywhere, and come back to it later. Or you say, ''Hey, we've resolved this one,'' or ''We're doing pretty well on this one.'' So if you have more of those experiences—and how many more is kind of hard to tell—and how much longer is hard to tell. But when you're not saving all the really sticky stuff that might get you in trouble for Cindy's office, then you'll have a sense, ''I think we're okay now, doing pretty well, and we're pretty confident that we can go off on our own.''

Eric: I agree with Jill in a large part, that we are getting there. It's almost like we can phase down the frequency with which we come in.

Bill: Sort of build up that muscle between times.

Jill: Funny you should say that!

Eric: It's almost like we don't have crises every week, but after a couple weeks we've got a few things accumulated. I think last session we really broke through. Jill was expecting some really strong defense on my part, and I just agreed. And maybe because we're getting to the point where I'm feeling less of a need to defend myself and perhaps she feels less of a need that there can be more of the open, nonaggressive conversations happening at home which means we bring less to the office.

Bill: Can you teach me so I can understand a little better? (*looks to Eric*) Pretend I'm Jill for a second. If I were going to bring an issue to you and have it be most likely to get you to be defensive—for us to have a flare-up—how would I do that? And, conversely, if I were to bring an issue to you and have it most likely that you would really hear me and that you would respond in a nondefensive way; teach me both.

Eric: That's easy because we've done that recently. (*laughter*) My business is based in my home—the office upstairs—and coming in while I'm on the computer is the absolute worst time.

Bill: The timing of it is good and the place is really good—to choose that, that would be a good invitation to a flare-up.

Eric: Yep.

Bill: What else?

Eric: A good time is probably in the morning. That generally, probably doesn't work if it's something of substance. If it's minor stuff like functions, duties, things that need to be taken care of—generally in the morning I'm still rushing. I'm either trying to get work done to go get my son or get the house vacuumed or something like that. After supper I'm spent—come seven or eight o'clock. Probably right after she comes home from work, assuming that I haven't got stuff spread throughout the house and I'm still working and before, perhaps, supper or on weekends.

Bill: Those would be the best times to approach you rather than the worst times?

Eric: Yes. (*looks to Jill*) Is that accurate?

Jill: Yeah, I would say so.

Bill: And how—once I approached you before dinner time, if that were the right time—how would I approach you? What voice tones, what voice volumes, what words, would be most likely to get a defensive response from you and least likely?

Eric: Probably saying, "I was thinking about this today. Let me know if you've got a few minutes you can talk about it." Just like you did this morning when I was on the computer and you came in and said something.

Jill: Yeah, but I was asking at a bad time this morning! (*laughter*)

Bill: Because you said, "Later."

Jill: I asked first.

Bill: You asked first and instead of saying, "We need to deal with this now," what was the opposite of it?

Eric: (*To Jill*) What were you asking?

Jill: If I just went ahead and asked. If I just went ahead and barged right in to what I was doing. . .

Bill: To ask about a time when you could ask was okay. To ask when you're feeling pressure or it's not the right time or you're feeling caught in it right then wouldn't have been good.

Jill: If I had just said, "I need to do this today," or "I need to know if you're going to do this today," instead of saying—what I said, I believe, was, "I have a couple things I'd like to ask you before I leave." And then I waited to see. If I hadn't got any response, I just would have left, because I would have known that he was disgruntled.

Bill: Right. (It was like) "What's a good time for you?"—more multiple choice options or a little freedom as to when to respond.

Jill: It was a really a good thing for us because what happens is I need to get an answer. . . .

Bill: By a certain time.

Jill: For me it's a little different in terms of time frames. My morning is my time to ask questions and get things resolved so I can get on with my day. When I come home at night I'm just as likely to want to veg out, because I'm going to an office everyday. I'd just like to relax and do dinner and maybe do some work that I do at home and not get into it.

Eric: We've got some incompatibility there because of me and the odd hours that I'm doing.

Bill: Time—weird hours, yeah.

Eric: And, also, we've identified that working out of the house is a problem, because I have a tendency to spread everything out. I'll have plans all over the house and they never to seem to get quite put away on a daily basis. I'm sorry, a weekly basis!

Bill: On a yearly or monthly basis!

Jill: (*laughing*) Let's just say that I live in Eric's office!

Bill: Well, I work from home and I understand.

Eric: Part of the package is I need to get an office out of the house.

Bill: And that's partly dependent on resolving this financial stuff and other things.

Eric: Yeah.

Bill: Okay, so that would take a little pressure off—and you'd go to the office and things would be spread around there.

Eric: Or possibly converting the second floor of the barn.

Jill: And I also think that part of it is that Eric lived in this house seven or eight years before I ever came into the picture.

Bill: So you're the interloper in these plans.

Jill: It was bad enough I was coming into his house and taking space, but now I was coming into his office. Before that it was okay to have his office all over the house. For me to start making it, ''Well this is the living room, this is where the family should live!''

Eric: And at first we consolidated the office from the whole house to two bedrooms, and then she took one of the bedrooms for her office.

Jill: And when Christopher was supposed to start overnights we converted my office into his bedroom. So now we're sharing an office, which is really a unique experience. Actually it's been okay.

Eric: You've gone back to your real office.

Jill: Well, we're not doing it eight hours a day. I was working at home too, and we were both working out of the home at that point.

Bill: Okay, the same thing back—for Jill. How would I approach you the worst? What times? We've already sort of found out about that, but, what times and how would I approach you—what voice tones, what voice volumes, what facial expressions, what words—would get the worst response and also the best?

Jill: My morning is my best time to talk about things, although I would also say weekends. For me. When I'm vegging out in front of the TV and not really paying attention to it really—those kinds of times are times when I can forget what I'm doing and talk about something. The worst times to get me are when I'm trying to get out to go someplace, because I'm not listening. I'm just focusing and you're interrupting me and I don't want to be bothered.

Bill: I'm on my way out and this is kind of a distraction and it's like tugging at your coat sleeves.

Jill: I guess that's something we actually have in common—or when I'm working—when I'm on the computer, when I'm writing, when I'm on the phone. I don't want somebody talking to me when I'm on the phone because I want to focus on the person I'm talking to. So those are some of the worst times you can approach me. The worst way that you can say things to me is just ''you''—you do this, you do this, you do this—I'm gonna get pissed right off the bat. I'm just gonna be mad because to me that doesn't do anything productive, and I have allowed it to put me on the defensive and I stop listening. I don't care what's being said. It's just not real productive.

Bill: An he's shifted that recently?

Jill: Yeah. When we started out it was a little more general as far as I didn't like the way I was being spoken to and had a real problem with it. I think we've narrowed it down to when I approached him at bad time what seemed to be happening is it became all "you" statements, which made me want to fight more. That would escalate into a real horror show.

Bill: Both of you were able to identify that the "you" start is a bad invitation and it's more likely you get that when somebody's approached at a different time.

Jill: I guess as far as a positive way to approach me I would have to say that I also like being asked, "Do you have a few minutes so we could talk about this?" or "I would like to talk about a specific thing." It also gets back to something we've been working on in here which is "I" statements. "I" statements are really hard. There's no doubt about it. It's much easier to see what's wrong with somebody else and what they do.

Bill: Yeah, we have a problem and I know where it is! (*laughter*) I know where it exists! I'm pretty clear about that!

Jill: And we have made a lot of progress. We haven't done it consistently at home yet, but I think we have both seen it to this point. I think that was a lot of what I heard in our last session is that we're on the same track as far as how we want to communicate, and now it's a matter of working it into our daily behavior—so it becomes second nature and I don't think about it anymore it's just the way I do it, and it allows us to respect each other.

Bill: I have a couple ideas, two or three ideas—just to find out, because we're doing an overview of trying to see the forest through the trees. It's just what I've learned from my own relationship and other people's relationships. I just want to check, based on what you've said, a few things. One is that sometimes with couples when you get into that defensive mode it's nice to be able to move into a different mode, and I sometimes tell a story to couples. I was involved with my now ex-wife when she was just going through a divorce and she had a four year old. He was just going through a tough time and just kept clinging to her—when she would have me over or other people would be over. It got really bad, and he would just cling to her leg and she was trying to cook dinner for people or whatever, and I would watch and I'm a family therapist and I've learned that you don't get in the middle of this stuff—don't triangulate—that's our rule as family therapists. You never get in the middle of a two-person relationship or you're into it like cats and dogs. So I learned to just bite my tongue, but I thought she's not handling this in a very good way, but I didn't want to criticize her; it's her child. He just kept escalating and escalating and becoming more of a problem—clingy and needy. Finally, I saw her after a couple of weeks, and I was just about to break my rule and she just leans down and says, "I know what you need. You need love." And I thought, "Great, reinforce it!" And she reached down and hugged him. Immediately, within a week, he stopped. He entirely stopped his behavior. I was like, "I don't get it. She reinforces his behavior and it stops?" And I thought, "No, you can think about it another way." He was really scared and really needy and she reassured him and then he was off on his own. He was fine. So occasionally when I see couples and when they get into those defensive modes I think, "If you could just remember he's like that little four year old who's clinging to his mother's leg or she's like that little four year old who's clinging to her mother's leg, instead of this, 'Why is she doing this to me or why is he doing this to me?'" And you can age regress them in your mind and say, "You know, when he gets defensive like that he's just that little four year old." You just soften your heart and say, "He's scared, defensive, worried, hurt." And the same way, "She's this scared or hurt or angry little girl and she's really freaked out," instead of, "I've got to get her to shape up." It's just like compassion. Not even going over and hugging the person—which may be one thing to do—but just this sense of opening your heart for that moment and realizing, "This isn't about me so much." I mean, it's certainly about me, but it's also about this other person, and they're really hurting and they're really scared. And at other moments, like you somehow listened in the office when you said, "You're right." And that was hard for you—you were just in that place of telling the truth and compassion and that was so much more of an effective approach, and she softened.

Eric: That is probably my single biggest weakness—is that is really hard for me. (*laughter throughout room*) (*looks at Jill*) And you're much better at that than I am, and you probably would rather have me hug you at that point. (*laughing*) That is the absolute worst thing for me at that point!

Bill: (*laughing*) I don't want contact at that moment—forget it, no way!

Eric: I know that's one of the things that I have to work on. I did a little bit last time. I've known it, but it's just one of those buttons for me. I fully accept it.

Bill: My wife is actually the same way now. When she gets angry—it's like distance—physical distance and emotional distance. That freaked me out, of course. I'm wiped out at that point. I'm either angry or I'm hurt or scared or whatever it may be, and she's done something that maybe you could do. She can't reach out and give me a hug; that's way, way too much for her. That would be the opposite of what she feels like doing. But I've asked, because somehow I want some reassurance—are we still related—do you like me in the universe? (*laughter*) She's actually done this (*Bill touches Eric on the hand with his index finger*)

Jill: (*laughing*) Oh God, I can see it now!

Bill: It has a profound effect. It's like she's willing to touch me at this moment so it isn't like I'm the lowest Paleolithic pond scum in the universe. I think she actually may like me after this is done.

Eric: It takes me a while to let it down and go back to being normal.

Bill: Right, right. (*pointing at Jill*) She's actually been quicker, so I'm giving her a challenge. She's been able to do it right in the middle of it sometimes.

Eric: A hug and a kiss might be difficult, but I could do that!

Jill: And I will tell you, he's not incapable of it all the time. I have to give him credit. There are times when he does not get defensive and he does give me a hug and listen to what I say. He may not agree but I think part of what we've gotten to is it's okay that we don't agree. We don't have to prove each other out.

Bill: Right. You've got to a place where that's okay, but when he's really hooked in and he's on it. . . .

Jill: . . . At that point I'm better at backing off.

Bill: Right, or just even saying somehow we've still got a relationship beyond this disagreement or upset at the moment. I guess that's what it is for me. It's like, somehow it's not over and she doesn't think I'm the worst slime in the universe.

Eric: I don't think that I give any indications that it's over.

Bill: Oh no, that's clearly my fear and my stuff. But it goes a long way to have that little—because I know it's like repulsion, magnetic forces you have to got through to get over there! (*laughter*) It's really difficult for you.

Jill: Especially when I'm emotional about it, because when I'm asking for it, obviously and that's about the last thing he could do. If I could be calm and logical. . . .

Bill: . . . Yeah, say, "Perhaps it would be good for you to give me a hug sometime when you're available to." (*laughter*)

Eric: That would be a great tension breaker too! (*laughter*)

Bill: That humor helps doesn't it!

Jill: Actually, I think what's happened a lot in the last couple of months, at least for myself, is I've gotten to a point where, well, I went a long time not being sure whether I was going to stay here or not. Eric can tell you; I came in here, actually about half way through our therapy, and said, "You know, I come in here every time deciding that we have to start talking about how we're going to separate." And I end up waiting and waiting and waiting, and that was when a lot of things broke for me. I think I was holding back a lot of things. I don't know what I was waiting for! (*laughter*) It just fell out of the sky I guess. The difference between that time and right now is that I, right now, am not even considering leaving. I was considering leaving for most of the second half of our therapy. I was like, this is still an option for me because I just don't see what I need to see here, and I was really struggling with that for a long time. And I would say that in the last couple of weeks that it has been something that's changed. I still have a few issues that I think we need to work on. There's actually one thing that I can think of that we need to work on as far as being able to talk about it and how we deal with it and how we respect our differences, because Eric and I are very, very different from each other and sometimes that's very hard for me to accept. I've been working very hard on that. The only thing that really helps me with that is I want the same thing back. When I think about it selfishly it works. When I say, "I know I want him to respect my differences," then I've got to give the same thing back. That's been the big difference for me in the last couple of weeks. A major change for me has been that I feel like we can get through almost anything. I walked into a situation—new marriages are tough anyway—he's already had a couple and I've never been married before. At forty years old I decide to get married all of the sudden and have kids, and then you add this very difficult court situation where there's all sorts of personal nasties going on, and this poor child, who I adore to tears, is getting torn apart. And, of course, I didn't do what you did, I put myself right in between Christopher and Eric on several occasions because I got very attached. We started having him at a very young age. And I got very angry with both of them—with his mother and his father. It was just, "I can't believe you two are being this stupid!" And there are times when that made things worse, obviously. But I think that we've worked out a lot of that.

Bill: So you think that having the relationship forge in this very difficult time, when it goes on, will make it stronger—because it's like, shit, we've been through all the crap that anybody could face. It's been harder than most human beings have to deal with in a lifetime. We did that in our first six months or a year or whatever it was.

Jill: The fact that we made it two years—I get brownie points for that one!

Bill: Absolutely!

Eric: On our first date I told her everything and I put it on the table and said, "If this is too much, I'm not the right person for you." (*laughter*)

Bill: If she knew what it was *really* she would have. . . .

Jill: . . . I went home and said, "Yeah, right. I'm going to talk to this guy again." Actually, that was one of the things that attracted me to him was that he was honest about it. Honesty is like number one. We've all got suitcases piled up in our closets, but being honest about it was the key for me because I'd been lied to a lot prior to that time.

Bill: He wasn't prettying it up for you!

Jill: He didn't leave much to the imagination!

Eric: But then again, her best friend worked with my former wife.

Jill: I worked with your former wife!

Eric: Oh yeah, that's right too! (*laughter*)

Bill: They had a sense of perspective on that. Enough said, maybe, about that. The third thing I was thinking of, just as an idea that I thought I would check out, sometimes what I've seen and done in my own relationship and with couples is just patterns. It's like you get into patterns and they turn into ruts—and somehow to break you out of patterns—I've just got a couple of ideas. Sometimes when you get those tough moments of communication, you're trying to communicate in the same way that you've always communicated, and you've changed that with the messages and the timing and all that kind of stuff—but even changing the mode of communication. I had a couple that I was seeing that started to get into this escalating pattern which turned into violence—actually her violence toward him. She would want to deal with something right then, sort of one of those things you were talking about, but much more adamant and violent than you're talking about. And they had children, and she would want to deal with it right then, and he would say, "Not in front of the kids." He just had this thing, "Let's not do it in front of the kids. Let's go into another room or do it another time when the kids aren't here," because they would get loud even if they went into another room. So he'd try and cool her down—bad move to try and cool her down. She'd escalate some more. They'd end up screaming in front of the kids, which he hates, and he's trying to be really calm. He doesn't respond like he's taking it seriously, and she finally gets so mad she starts hitting him—slapping him. Then he wrestles her—terrible situation. They just didn't know how to get out of it. It would only happen every once in a while, but it was bad stuff and it was getting both of them to think that they didn't want to be in the relationship. So one of the things she said was, "At that moment I just need to know that I'm heard, and he just tries to stop me. And that just makes me crazy, and I'll do anything to get a response from him." He says, "I don't want her to get angry and yell and scream and then have the kids hear it. And I stop listening as soon as she gets loud, so she gets more frustrated." I said how about this—I said to her, "You go in the other room, get a tape recorder and you record what you have to say to him." Then you go out and say, "It's on the tape recorder and you've got to go in and respond within five minutes." He goes in and listens to it. He can listen to it at whatever volume he needs to listen to it. (*laughter*) If she screamed into the tape recorder he could turn it down, but he has to leave a response within five minutes or ten minutes or whatever it may be. And then she can go in and listen to it, and if it's satisfactory that's great. If it's not she has to say, "You have to go in listen again; that wasn't okay." This was just to break up the pattern. It sounds like with Cindy you've made a lot of progress. You're going in the right direction and it sounds like you're going to finish this thing off, but I guess I want a relapse prevention plan in case you ever got into one of these places, because it started to tear the fabric of your relationship (*looks to Jill*) when you were thinking, "This isn't worth it. I don't think I can handle this. I'm not gonna stay." We want to make sure the fabric never gets rent again. You may leave the fabric alone and not pull on it, and save it for Cindy's office or save it for a better time or whatever, but if you're ever in the middle of that I think it would be important to have some sort or relapse prevention plan so that nothing more gets rent in terms of the fabric of your love for one another and your connection to one another. So does anything like that appeal to you or that you can think of that might work? Something that changes the pattern? And I'm even talking about silly things, like I had a couple one time, when I was supervising somebody, and they said, "I couldn't get this couple to stop fighting." Finally, I just told them to do anything absurd to change it. And what we came up with together was that anytime they started a fight they'd have to go into the bathroom, and he'd have to take off all of his clothes and lie in the bathtub and she'd have to sit on the toilet next to him and they could continue to fight. (*laughter*) And they would just burst out laughing; they couldn't fight anymore. It was a perfect way of interrupting whatever the patterns were. So whatever it may be—you have to put your shoes on the wrong feet, anything that breaks up the pattern. Can you think of anything like that that might work? It sounds like you both have a good sense of humor, so something that involves humor. . . . Get squirt guns and squirt each other or whatever.

Jill: I like that idea! (*laughter*)

Bill: You like that, huh! Just go non-verbal! No more talking!

Jill: Christopher and I both have our spray bottles. He would jump right in and help me!

Bill: He would! Oh, that would be teams!

Jill: Although that kind of blows the rule about no spraying in the house.

Bill: That's right, you'd have to go outside.

Eric: (*laughing*) In the winter!

Bill: Yeah, in the winter—that makes it an ordeal even. You have to stand back to back. Christopher counts ten paces, then you turn around and fire at will. Christopher has to figure out who won.

Eric: Let's get some real squirt guns.

Jill: That's could work. That could seriously work. I think at this point I've probably experienced more frustration, because for him it's, "Not now." Although I think in the last couple of weeks I've turned that around a couple of times, because I found myself doing the same thing. I decided, "Stop, right now. I'm done talking about it." I do a lot of writing so that's generally what I do—I leave. I leave the situation, I go. Put it down on paper somehow.

Bill: Then it's at least out where you're not going around and around.

Jill: I've been known to come in here with a notebook. That works generally. I have a harder time when I walk away from something like that—dealing with emotion. I'm more likely, I think, to sit on it and chew on it and it will stay with me a few days. When I get mad it stays with me because, it doesn't get processed a lot. It kind of stays there and it will affect you for the next few days.

Eric: And I need the time to process because I'm not quick on my feet.

Bill: Right, she's much quicker and you need a little time to let it percolate through and figure out what's going on—so some balance between those two.

Jill: I like the idea of squirt guns. Can I have a supersoaker?

Eric: No, I'm going to get you a little one! I'm going to get a big supersoaker. (*laughter*)

Bill: The other thing I was going to say is by the winter you won't need this. You'll have mastered these wonderful communication. . . .

Eric: (*laughing*) . . . Are you dreaming? (*laughter*)

Bill: And so maybe you'll only need this for the summer and the fall.

Jill: I've said it already; we have made a lot of progress, and I don't want to speak for both of us, but I know the last few weeks in terms of just feeling somewhere back to what we felt at the beginning of our relationship—only better. That wonderful thing that you hear that happens in relationships when you get to the point where you have this wonderful—you're just kind of being really nice to each other. Then you get married and, of course, you get married and that stops. (*laughter*) But then you get to the core—it just really deepens—you get to the next level. That's something that I'm feeling happening and I think that's changed a lot about how I feel—having seen us get through this, especially having so many doubts that we would get through it.

Eric: I've got a lot more respect for you with the efforts that you've made that are very clear and apparent to me—in making changes so it works. And I think that's part of a deepening love too. It's true; we're getting there.

Jill: I think we both respect that we have circumstances that are, I don't want to call them unusual because I think that it happens a lot more than people have any idea, but I think that there's a lot more tension. Most of our friends—I don't think that Kate and Larry or Patty and Vince have any of the outside influences that we have in this relationship going into it—they don't have the outsiders who affect their daily lives like we do. It's been a very difficult situation and as Cindy has said to us a couple of times and we've actually managed to turn that to our advantage in that if we gave up, Christopher's mother would win. And that's something that neither one of us wants. It has been pretty nasty—towards myself as well—I mean somebody who's tried to stay out of it as best I could. It was very hard for me, because I walked into it more than ready to give her the benefit of the doubt and be nice to her.

Bill: Now it's down to a more one-sided story.

Jill: I am definitely on the other side of the fence now. I've never seen anything like this. I've never been involved in anything like this in my life. I've never been inside of a courtroom until this year.

Bill: It's a terrible, legal soap opera.

Eric: Nine hearings so far.

Bill: Or nonhearings it sounds like.

Jill: And that was a whole other thing that Eric and I are still working on, but that was something that also made it very difficult. The idea is when Christopher is with us he's ours, until I do something that he doesn't like. Then he's his kid.

Eric: I pulled rank. I fully admit that I have.

Jill: And if we wanted to be a family and we wanted to treat it like a family without those inside influences that can't be. Especially with other kids coming in.

Bill: That shifted for you recently?

Jill: Yeah, it's getting there.

Eric: I recognized I was doing it, but we were in so much of a defense posture. I mean, one of those hearings went for a week—forty hours of trial—just to get visitation in place. It's almost like we're living on three separate chessboards.

Bill: 3D chess.

Eric: I have to recognize that and alter some of what would be natural, easy decisions and that was a source of a lot of tension between us. And I pulled that rank. . . .

Jill: I felt like, here I am, I'm treating this child as my own, I love him to death, and as far as I'm concerned he is my kid. And I walked into this knowing that he was there and I made a decision very early on and he's my first child. This is my first baby, but not my first kid. So I've gone into it with that attitude and I think I got frustrated when he had to make decisions based on court instead of what I considered good family values. I felt like I wasn't being heard and that I wasn't being treated as an equal in the parenting situation.

Eric: And you weren't.

Jill: His family always tells me that to be a stepmom and to be the way I am about it is, they think, really neat. I can't imagine doing it any other way, but from what I understand it's not a common thing.

Bill: It's unusual—definitely. Can you explain to me, both of you—I'm going to ask you a couple of individual questions and a couple question—What would you say is the quality or qualities of Jill that have allowed her or helped her to both deal with the situation and overcome it and that kind of loving stepmother that is unusual? What would you name those qualities if you could give them names?

Eric: Being the loving stepmother—it's just the way she chooses to live her life. I've got a lot of friends who are in second marriages and so forth and if Christopher didn't spend his time with his other mother, it would be just he was her birth child. I don't know a word to describe that.

Bill: Would you say that's commitment?

Eric: It's so many quality words or values—loving, giving, caring.

Bill: Loving, giving, caring, committed—and how about making it through the challenges of your marriage—to what quality would you attribute that?

Eric: Craziness.

Bill: Craziness. Absolutely.

Eric: One word can't describe it all, because it's a combination of so many.

Bill: What would you say about your relationship that has survived the challenges, these external and internal challenges? What's the quality in it? I've heard humor as part of it. It would be one of the things that I would label—the ability to step back and laugh—to see the humor in it.

Eric: Just all the perseverance, being able to see beyond the immediate problem, willing to be patient to get to that level. I guess patience is the biggest one. And commitment to be able to see beyond the disasters of the moment.

Bill: So it's long-term vision—patience and persistence. And humor I already identified. And would you say that too, Jill? Any that you would add in terms of couple or Eric's qualities?

Jill: His honesty.

Bill: Honesty—you mentioned that before.

Jill: Yeah. His honesty is very important to me, and it's something that he carries through in all of the aspects of his life. His sense of humor is definitely important. Sympathy—there's a certain amount of sympathy if I get him at the right time. And his love for me. I have never doubted that Eric loved me. Not ever, ever doubted that. Anything that we've ever gone through or been through, it's funny, that's never been an issue. It's not that he didn't love me, it's just maybe that we're different. I would say that that's a big thing too. Patience has been a big part of it on both of our parts. It's being able to see beyond the end of our noses and being able to say, "Okay, here's the little picture and here's the big picture. The big picture's still there!"

Bill: That's an interesting thing—both of you, one of the things that you've been learning is when the pressure is on of the moment, for the court, in your relationship, whatever it may be, that being able to take along with you and have some patience and say, "There will be a time when we'll go in and see Cindy," or "We'll deal with this at a better time." (*looks to Jill*) Or, you saying, "I'd like to take up these issues with you" and having a little bit of patience and saying, "Before I leave for work." And that gives him a half an hour or an hour—a window of opportunity to choose that time—that kind of patience seems really important.

Jill: Give and take is a very hard thing to learn. I lived alone for seven years before I met Eric. I had everything the way I wanted it in my house.

Eric: Same thing for me.

Bill: Except the child and the husband part.

Jill: The child and the husband part, right! (*laughter*) Just having to ask for things that I never had to ask for before. I went, "What do you mean? I'm forty years old, I don't have to ask for this! I'm just going to get it." It doesn't always work that way, and for me, the change with Eric is he's been a little more willing to give. I generally know not to bug him when he's on the computer or on the phone, but if it's something I need an answer for I'm a little more comfortable saying, "I need to ask you this," and letting him take the lead from there. And he will do it sometimes, like this morning, he did it. In the past I would have got an immediate huffy response and I would have gone off mad for the rest of the day.

Bill: As far as I can tell, the forest for the trees sounds, because I didn't hear about you beforehand, like you're really on the right track—and that you're actually moving, you're moving well. It's not slow progress. It's amazing and good progress. I think that's one of the values of me. You're all so close to it, it is really hard to see the forest for the trees. I'm telling you the big picture looks good. The big picture of the basic qualities of each other and the relationship look good. The direction you're moving in looks good. I agree with you that you'll know when it's time to be on your own more and just check in every once in a while—when it's happening more and more at home that things like this morning happened (*looks to Jill*)—when you check in and it's not the huffy response. Somehow you've found your way to move with your differences and your styles. What's coming more to the foreground is the love and the patience, and the compassion for one another, and the humor, rather than those outside influences. I sometimes remind people, you know when you're first in love and your seized by it? People look at you and go, "What's going on with you?" And you're like, "I'm in love." They can tell. You're driving down the street and even if it's bad traffic or somebody cuts you off, it's like, "Ah, I'm in love. What's the difference?" The outside stuff doesn't really dampen that. Sometimes I describe it like there's this light that's glowing. People are saying, "You're glowing." And then the court stuff gets dumped on it, a hurtful thing that happens gets dumped on it, everyday habits dampen that, and it's like a pile of manure gets thrown on the light, and then there's not so much glow coming out of there anymore. And you still know that love is underneath there, but you're not feeling it so strongly and those outside influences come in more strongly. And what I hear and see from the things that you've been doing is you've been washing away the manure from the light and the glow seems to be there a lot more. It never went away, but it got covered over a little. And when you've got that glow going there, there's a whole lot of credit in the bank to cash a few checks. But if your account is tapped out and there's not much of that glow there, any little thing bounces a check with your partner. It sounds like the glow is coming back a lot more and you're into that deeper, second level of glow, if you will, and second level of realization. You're dealing with things now and getting it out of the way, and it sounds like you're getting more and more built up in the bank. So it isn't like anything that happens is a crisis for the relationship.

Jill: I know what I've been feeling the last couple of weeks is just that warmth is back—that glow or whatever you want to call it. There's been a lot more of that warmth between us. It's been more enjoyable being with each other than it has been in a long time. (*laughs*) And when I think about how we started out with Cindy!

Eric: I think I walked out in one of the first meetings.

Bill: A compassionate, patient guy like you walked out of a meeting! (*laughter*) You really have grown.

Jill: The funny thing is that ended up being one of the things that kept me going in it, because he did come back into the therapy.

Bill: Ah, hard to do but he did.

Jill: He stuck it out. And I'm sure that there were a few other times in here that I pushed his buttons and he wanted to get up and leave again, but he didn't. I could still see that the commitment was there. It was, how did we see what was there? You've been saying, "The forest for the trees." I have to tell you that we told Cindy when she asked us about the session I said, "Yeah, Cindy, that's okay, but what if we're cured by the time he gets here?" (*laughter*)

Bill: (*In a funny voice*) You're too healthy for me and I'm not going to do a demonstration! (*laughter*) I need to show them how to fix problems! Come on, act a little crazier up here! I hope that what I've said is really a fine tuning of what you've done and a recognition of it. I think that's pretty important. You're going along and you are pretty close to it and it's like, "Where are we in this process?" (*looks to Jill*) You said, "In the second half" of your therapy. I thought was a really interesting phrase, because you have a sense of where it's going and how long it's going to be and where you are in it—it's the first time I've heard it.

Jill: It's funny, I had a very set time frame when I started. About a couple of months into it I would have told you that we were going to be in here for life, and it's just been lately that we've been seeing some success. It took a while just to get to the point where we were really talking about what we needed to talk about.

Bill: It sounds like you're absolutely to that place that you're talking about. I don't think that anyone can predict that, but I think thats when you start to see more of those signs and feel more of those signs in your everyday life—things like what happened this morning—it was essentially glitch free, and that's noticeable. When that's not even noticeable anymore, and you're like, "Of course we do that," that's when it's time to say, "We'll come in and have a checkup every once in a while."

Group Observations, Reflections, and Feedback

Bill: I'd like to invite comments and questions from the other folks because we're like forest for the trees here; we're in the middle of it. I'm having a conversation with you, and maybe they can hear something or see something that we couldn't, or maybe they'll just have questions about your experience or my ideas or what I was doing here.

Laurie: When you first came in here it was a little off-putting, right?

Jill: Absolutely.

Laurie: How long did it take you to settle in and become connected with Bill?

Bill: To feel a little more comfortable and not so self-conscious. . . .

Laurie: Yeah.

Eric: (*looks at Bill*) I just focused on you and ignored everyone else. I've spoken a lot and I feel that I live my life openly enough that I was real comfortable talking about it.

Jill: I thought more about keeping some things general and not getting into some specific areas which would be hard for me to do in front of a large group of people. But once we got started I didn't think about it.

Debbie: What was helpful?

Jill: It was good to talk about all of the good things for a change—we've been through a lot of hell and back. And it was really nice to have a lot of good things to say. Cindy had said, "You can have issues that are good issues" and to sit down and pay a little attention to those.

Eric: Like I said, I'm slow on my feet. While I'm driving home I'll be reprocessing everything and perhaps see where you were going with things and understand the process that was occurring a little bit more too.

Beth: I think one of the things that I noticed was, Bill, when you asked them to describe each other's qualities that was carrying them through the relationship and building, as you described them they felt very big and encompassing the relationship. (*to Eric*) I think you said it was hard to describe just one thing, that she has a lot of qualities and that deepened your love for her. That felt very warm for me—like the light you were talking about coming back up.

Eric: It's a bit uncharacteristic of me and I think that might have caught her off guard too. A little bit out of character, but I feel comfortable about it.

Paul: One thing I'll remember is we really do learn to appreciate the small things. That's what really makes things work.

Jill: It's funny how that seems to be the thing we always take for granted, until they get brought to the forefront.

Eric: It seems like the stuff that was nitpicky in the past doesn't matter anymore.

Jill: Or it's changed because it's either one or the other. It's either not important or it's been something that we took a little time with because the little things are important. Like, what you did this morning made a big difference.

Laurie: When you were working with Bill, did you both feel you were heard or was there a time when it felt like, "I wonder why he doesn't pay a little more attention to me." Was there ever a time like that?

Jill: Nope.

Eric: Not for me.

Megan: I'm wondering how it felt to know that Bill had some similar situations or stories that he could share with you.

Eric: I picked up on that right off. The comfort level being created early on there—it was disclosed real early that you were divorced and that was something in common—and the child there—I think sharing some commonality creates some comfort.

Bill: That's an interesting question, and I think part of it may be because we have a context as therapists. Many of the people here received training that's said, "Never talk about yourself. Never disclose any personal information about yourself." It's part of my tradition—I was trained as a humanistic—to really equalize the relationship a lot more by saying, "Yeah, me too." It's a lot more open, but especially on the East Coast, where there's an analytic tradition, you don't ever reveal; it's, "Why do you ask?" But the other thing is, is it off-putting? Some people say he talks about himself a lot. So both of those things.

Is it not so great to talk about yourself? Or, is it narcissistic talking about yourself a lot? And you say, "Well, it felt like a commonality."

Eric: That just makes it more personal and gives more friendliness to it.

Jill: Plus there's a lot of trust. It's a lot easier to trust someone who extends that kind of trust to you. I've been through a lot of therapy for a lot of different things. I had a very rough couple of years. I started learning that you shop for a therapist. You just don't go into any therapist. You go in and you test them out and if you don't like them you don't have stay there. For me, one of the big things was to sit down and say, "I want someone who's going to tell me what they think." I don't want you to sit there and nod your head. I've been listened to. I've gotten it all out. I want somebody who's going to tell me what they think. That's why I'm here. I'm looking for a solution to this. I want suggestions. I'm intelligent enough to decide whether I want to do it or not, but give me some ideas. Otherwise, why am I coming here?

Bill: We were trained to say, "What do you think you should do?"

Jill: I used to get this one a lot, "Oh." (*laughter*)

Bill: Yeah, I'll have to master that one. I've never actually said that. I've always had more to say than that. (*laughter*) Cindy, do you have any questions, comments?

Cindy: I'd like to know, How was it different being with Bill than it is with me? And if it's better with me, you can tell me about that later! (*laughter*)

Jill: Aren't you a former student of his? I think you should know how well that you've done with us.

Cindy: I consider myself an ongoing student of his.

Bill: I consider her a colleague of mine, but we have different perceptions of that.

Jill: For me it was a little different because I don't know you as well as I know Cindy. Cindy's been through a lot with me the last year. There's a lot of personality that's gone on between us, and I feel closeness to Cindy. However, I was comfortable with you.

Cindy: What about in terms of what he was doing? Is it similar to what I do?

Bill: Style or method.

Jill: There were a lot of things I heard that were almost exactly out of your mouth. (*laughter*)

Cindy: Can you talk about any difference between working in a solution-oriented style, which is what we've been doing, and working in some of the other styles that you've had therapy in?

Jill: Oh, absolutely.

Cindy: These people come from lots of different backgrounds, not necessarily solution-oriented.

Jill: I've had several different types of treatment. I think solution-oriented therapy, even if you're dealing with someone who's got a severe problem and is having trouble functioning in the real world, they've got to be able to see that light at the end of the tunnel. They've got to be able to think that they can be normal or whatever word you want to use for that. For me, always working with someone who has my goals at heart and listens to what my goals are and helps me to get there is very important. I cannot stand sitting in an office and having someone sitting there nodding their head. I can appreciate the value of understanding your history and what's happened in your life and in your family and knowing how it affects you, but once you understand that it's time to move on. That was one of my biggest problems with former therapists that I had. (It was like) "Let's analyze this thing that happened to you." I'm like, "I'm done with this. This I where I live now. I live in the here and now. I can't do anything about the past. To me it's extremely important to always keep in mind what the patient wants and where that patient wants to be—make sure that you're hearing them.

Eric: I've also have had some other therapy. I'm real straightforward and businesslike, and I thought that was a waste of my time. I wasn't getting anything out of it.

Jill: We knew how we liked things and didn't like things and I think we both come from a lot of experience of learning what didn't work and finding what does work.

Continuing Conversations

Bill: Okay, there was no hypnosis. There's wasn't even any mention of it. Why not? Obviously, each had issues that we could have done hypnosis for, but that wasn't what was pressing. What did you note about the interview in terms of the technicalities of this approach—what you've been learning so far and hearing so far.

Alice: What impressed me was the questions you didn't ask—all those little side tracks that I would have gone down. And how you kept to, "What's working for you," "How do you keep that going," "What are the qualities that keep that going?"

Bill: Did you hear any of those solution-oriented questions? The ones you learned?

Denise: You asked, "What are the qualities that support the relationship?"

Debbie: Also, "How can you prevent a relapse?"

Megan: Then you said, "If I was your wife. . . ."

Bill: What was the purpose of that? What was I doing there?

Alice: How do you do the symptom and how do you do the solution.

Bill: That's right, and to get a very specific description of it. It's one step removed for one of them when I say, "I'm your partner now." They're still describing what Jill and Eric do, but it's not quite so loaded being one step removed. I could have gotten much more specific descriptions, but that was okay. That level was okay.

And, again, one of the difficulties I have when people first learn this is they say it's so "positive." We want to talk about problems too. You ask, "Tell me about when it doesn't work" and "Tell me about when it does work." We go back and forth between problems and solutions. I think sometimes people have a misunderstanding that we can only talk about positives, what works, or solutions. With some clients that's what they want to talk about. I get a little worried about the shadow stuff or the problem stuff and so I bounce back and forth—as long as you don't focus on what's so negative and problematic in their relationship and as long as you don't exclusively focus on what works.

Paul: You did talk about patterns getting set and how to deal with that.

Bill: And that was something that I brought up. If you see someone like *Scott Miller,*[86] he follows the client very closely and doesn't add anything more. He wouldn't say, "Hug the four year old." It's very minimalist in that approach. I'm not. I've got ideas and I introduce them.

Denise: That was interesting how in getting them to look at what would work for them you described your situation and what works in your own relationship without saying to them, "This is what you should do."

Bill: Yes, it's one step removed. It's like that indirect hypnotic approach that I was talking about, "Your hand could lift up before or after your eyes close." Some people's hands lift up slowly, and some people's hands lift up quickly. You're not saying, "Your hand lift up quickly." Instead, your saying, "You can take it or leave it." It's more of a possibility way of saying it. But, of course, as you say it, it's going to be very influential in their thinking. It's going to steer their thinking and emotions in a certain direction. So it's going to be more likely that they'll consider that and they'll consider the myriad of possibilities, negative and positive. To Jill and Eric, I said, "You can tape record things. You can write them out. You could do squirt guns." What showed up? You know how you get that response? They laugh. They joke about who's going to have the biggest "supersoaker." They take it and run with it. So you're providing possibilities, and they take it and make it into an actuality. And they'll either do it outside of this office or they won't. Time will tell.

[86] Scott Miller, Ph.D., is a developer of solution-focused approaches to psychotherapy and author of numerous books and articles. He resides in Chicago, Illinois.

Paul: And they really don't have to do it.

Bill: It's okay with me if they don't do it—ever. Just the idea may be tickling enough for them, and maybe they need to do it. Maybe it will appeal to Cindy and she'll take it up with him, "Did you get the squirt guns yet?" Maybe she won't. It's what appeals to you and what appeals to them and what gets focused on.

Megan: I really liked the idea of the light. And you used your hands to help them picture it. I thought it was really interesting how they took that and she used "warmth" and used new words.

Bill: She changed it a little bit. I used the checkbook metaphor, which they didn't really take up. They took the warmth metaphor—she took the warmth metaphor.

Okay. So what surprised you about that conversation? Anything that you have read in the books or heard in the conferences—things that you expected—that you don't do—that you have done—that you thought, "Oh, I didn't know other people did that." Or what's something that you might carry back into your practice from that conversation?

Beth: For me, the self-disclosure. I've seen it done before and I've done it some in my practice, but it's so anti what I've been taught. It's hard for me to take the leap into that and to feel comfortable doing that. But it was very comfortable to watch it happen. It certainly added to the treatment. I can see it as a very positive thing, but it's hard for me personally to take the leap into that most of the time.

Bill: My joke is, "I don't think they put you in jail for self-disclosure. I think you get a fine or a ticket!" It really is such a tradition, "Do not reveal any personal information. It will contaminate the therapy. It will be bad for the patient." I understand that, and, actually, with some people it would be a bad idea.

Beth: You really do have to know how to use it and when to use it.

Bill: Right. And it depends on whether it's a teaching story or whether you're working out your issues on their time. It is an addition—a joining and an equalizing move. When he said, "You've been there"—there was a commonality, and I think that's what I hear most from my clients.

The other thing is, I have a friend in Buffalo and his wife was in psychoanalysis for many years and she loved it. She thought it was great. And we had many conversations about it, and it was good for me to hear positive experiences and great growth. She was in it for years and years with several different people, but she was with one of the people for five years—in analysis. The person was a very well known analyst and really good, she said. The woman said that he said almost nothing in the therapy—very, very little. He just created a great environment and occasionally would give an interpretation. Three times in the five years she was in analysis with him he told a story. It was the most he ever talked in the analysis. And the stories were told at particular turning points in the therapy, as she remembers now. It wasn't so clear in the midst of it that they were turning points. All she remembers from the therapy are those three stories. She remembers the emotions of the therapy. He never really said a word that was self-revealing. He was there as a presence—a very strong and containing presence and occasionally gave interpretations. But, he said very, very little except for those three stories. That was very powerful for me. It was like, "Three stories? That's what she remembers?" My clients often say things like, "You know that story you told me? I still think of that and still use that." That's a pretty powerful keg for emotions and learning and solutions and ideas.

If I had a question in my mind, and I went back and forth on it a little and it really stuck in my mind, I would put it out on the table. I would say, "I'm wondering whether this is a useful question or whether just by examining this I would be presuming something or creating something that maybe isn't a problem." I think that's a collaborative way. If you've got it as a hypothesis or concern, or if your colleagues may have it, or if your supervisor may have it, then you could say, "I don't have this concern, but I think my supervisor or my colleagues would have this concern that maybe I'm giving short shrift to this. Like, maybe you needed this problem or maybe it's pulled you together in some ways. How are you going to keep this thing on track when this thing is no longer there? What do you think about that?" That's the way I would open it up. It's not like you can never think a psychodynamic thought or a problem-oriented thought. If that occurs to you, that's fine. Just give it to your clients as a partnership rather than, "I've got this hidden agenda. The symptom serves a function and they don't know about it, and I've got to somehow maneuver it around so they don't get back into the symptom."

The point of having your eyes and your ears here is that there are crucial issues here that I wouldn't bring up. You can say, "My sensibility says that at least it could be a concern to open up." It's not a bad thing to open up—it depends on how you do it. This discussion we have after the session is very powerful. There are ten or eleven or twelve different minds, different ears—hearing different aspects of it, highlighting different aspects. We can't possibly do that when it's just me and the couple. As long as you don't impose it on people.

Chapter 7

Pathways with Possibilities

This chapter begins with the process of getting comments again from participants and continues with a discussion of some methods of acknowledgment combined with opening possibilities for change. Some role playing helps make these skills concrete.

What's Coming Across?

Bill: What's been coming clear for you? What's stood out for you? What's still muddy for you? If you were going to describe for a friend or a colleague who wasn't here now and say, "Here's what's been going on this week and here's what I've gotten and what this work is about," what would you say?

Lisa: I think the strongest thing is the sense of collaboration. That has a new meaning for me. And I think the self-disclosure—I have done it before, but I work in teams and my partner's like, "I can't believe that you did that." I get a lot of negative feedback on any type of self-disclosure at all. So, I think just the whole level of collaboration I really like. Right before I came here I closed with a family—which is always very hard for me. They were like, "You can stop by." I was like, "This is really hard, but that's not something that we can do. We're not allowed to do that." He was like, "I don't understand that. We had this relationship and now we can't have a relationship." I didn't know how to react to that and I'm still not sure. I don't know why, but that really sat with me. Its like, "Why is it exactly that I can't do that?" You know, no boundaries—the big "B" word. I'm just free associating here. But I just don't see it as a big deal. I see it as important. I see it as I have a relationship with this person and they took a risk to have this relationship with me and why can't that relationship continue? It may have to be different because I'm not saying that I have to be friends with them or go out to dinner with them, but why is that not okay? I guess I'm saying that I don't have an answer, but I'm struggling with that whole thing. It's very helpful—the collaborative work. I think people take huge risks with us, and if I'm asking them to do that why is that I can't do that too? It's like the therapist being on a pedestal and not being human. What made me think of that was when you talked about sharing your inner thought process like, "I had this thought" and saying that your supervisor might say this. We do so much of keeping that stuff inside of us like it will contaminate the process. I've been trained that you're really not supposed to be human.

Bill: Check your humanity at the door.

Lisa: Right, but then that's your tool. So I'm always confused because my tool is myself and I'm not supposed to bring it in here. But I think I am feeling more comfortable about it.

Bill: And it's very interesting to me to take it to that level where you're saying, "I feel like saying this and revealing something about myself and my partner over here is going to give me a lot of crap for it later." It's like, "Why did you say that? You're not supposed to reveal any of yourself." It's just like pulling the covers on the whole process. Okay, that's a great experience.

Debbie: It was interesting this morning when you did the trance stuff. I feel like I'm not interested in trancework, but the language seemed important.

Bill: Right. Even if you never do formal trance work, the language is important.

Debbie: I think the session was also helpful—to see the techniques being used. Both sessions. The one yesterday and the one today were very different.

Bill: They were different.

Debbie: I feel like some things are coming together. The one thing that is happening for me now is I'm doing home-based work now, and it's been a real shift for me to go from a clinic to that. I'm trying to be very focused, and so I'm trying to think about how to apply this to circumstances where there are constant interruptions. It's improvisation for me in this situation.

Bill: And can you understand what I said yesterday? I can't separate the hypnotic and the nonhypnotic. I tried for a while, but I couldn't—because it's the language that's important. Even if you never do hypnosis, it's really important to understand the language. I'll use it in nonhypnotic sessions in a slightly different way, but it's very inclusive and possibility oriented.

Katy: There was something that Denise said yesterday about being formulaic. I do ask, "What's better" or something similar to that often, and it was helpful for me to think about asking, "What would be a useful question?" So that was helpful. Also, just watching you work with clients on a human level is helpful. And I think that's helpful for clients, because it is very intense going into relationships in home-based work. And to just be done with it and say, "I can't talk to you'' isn't very good role modeling. There are boundary issues, but I think it's damaging to clients. I've started to tell more stories even though it's not very well supported in the general population in the field. There aren't a lot of people promoting it. I've learned more about knowing that I do good work and trusting that. I'm just trying to continue to be more aware of that.

Bill: Great.

Alice: In spite of training, people end up being human and telling stories. I probably won't know until next week or next month how all of this turns out. But if I were to go back, like in my peer supervision group, I'd say, ''You know what they say about brief therapy and how you use client resources? Well, this is about how to do that.'' That's the way I would describe it.

Megan: For me, the place that I came from—these thoughts and ideas are very much okay. It feels very comfortable for me. It's a really nice feeling to know, ''That's okay and that's okay.'' All these different things that I've seen and heard and that I really like reinforce that for me. The inner work for me is like, ''Wow!'' It's very new to me, as I mentioned yesterday. And I think even more today I had these lights that went off and it was like, ''Oh my God! Maybe there is a different way that I hadn't even thought about—a different level to work on some of this stuff.'' I'm thinking of a couple of different clients in particular. I can't wait, when I get the nerve, to try this because I can see this actually being very helpful for them.

Bill: *When* I get the nerve! (*laughter*)

Megan: Yeah. If we talk about it for another day or two, I might feel more comfortable. But for things like panic, that people can't really rationalize—they don't understand it—I can work on a different level which is really amazing to me.

Bill: When I came across Erickson's work I was really interested in the family and interactional parts of it. Then I got more interested in what Jay Haley wrote about, the strategic parts of it with individuals. Like how Erickson did pattern intervention with people. Then I became interested in the inner work, and to me, they're all of one piece. I just can't separate them. It's the same philosophy, just a different methodology and application. There's very similar language and very similar sensibility and just the focus is a bit different. I like that. What I like about de Shazer and Berg's model is it's very pure in one way, but it leaves a lot out. de Shazer knows how to do hypnosis. He knows it real well. He learned it a long time ago and has used it in the past. Now he just declares it unnecessary. I don't think that's so.

Megan: I've never seen that the solutions stuff and the experiential and spiritual stuff can actually go together. I like that.

Bill: Right. They are together.

Paul: When I came I wanted to take a leap forward, to become committed to solution or inclusive therapy and I think that's happened. I don't have this need to justify what I do to other people. I think it was affirming because I think I do a lot of this already and it's nice to know that I'm on the right track. It's pretty hard to make a serious mistake that's really going to hurt somebody, because you can always check in with them and they can give you feedback. So for me it's been an integrating process. And I like the collaborative piece. I guess it's possible to do something horrendous, but if you're half-way moralistic and believe what you do and have respect for people it's pretty hard to do.

Bill: Yeah. As long as you keep checking with them and putting it on the table you're not going to go too far. Sometimes you'll have a rude awakening and they'll say, "What you're doing isn't helpful." And I think that's good.

Laurie: Much like Alice, I am not really great in terms of what is the impact today or yesterday. This is building beautifully with what I did at Cambridge Family. It's great—reinforcing. Before I work with a couple I go over questions. I have thought about where we are in the treatment and I write down two or three or five questions that I want to bring up—at least just to have them there as my security blanket. It's so I know that I can keep opening up so that they are going to have the possibility of a different experience. So I'm in the middle of the trip and you're taking it in, but sometimes when you get home you can reflect and begin to pull out the significant, meaningful things. That's that piece. As far as the inner work, I just love the idea, but I'm scared to death. I don't know what it is. I'm excited about the possibility—whether I could use it, I don't know.

Bill: Well, we'll find out by the end of the week—or we won't! (*laughter*)

Laurie: So it's great, and I'm in the middle of a journey!

Bill: You're building something and you're in the middle of a journey! (*laughter*)

Karen: The trancework, or hypnotherapy, I really didn't expect to see it this week at all. I feel like I've been enlightened and it's not so hocus pocus. I'm very impressed with it. I don't know that I feel comfortable doing it right now.

Bill: Not yet.

Karen: Right—not yet. But I think it's very helpful.

Bill: Mostly I do workshops about non-inner work and about solution-oriented work and other types of things. Because the assumptions are rather challenging from traditional therapy, sometimes people will stand up, and they'll be in a struggle with it or they'll be angry, but when I do a two-day hypnosis workshop[87] no one attacks, there are no stops or resistance to it. It's like, "Yes, this is

[87] See O'Hanlon, W. H., & Martin, M. (1992).

clearly valuable and powerful. And, I don't know whether I can, but I want to be able to use this.'' It's a little surprising. So I'm thinking, ''Why don't I just do all hypnosis workshops so I can skip the arguments!'' (*laughter*) It's an easy workshop to do, and people do learn it in two days and can use it right away. It's such a powerful way of working for me.

Alice: I've been to two-day workshops on hypnosis and they get so hung up on trance induction that I get turned off and don't use it.

Bill: I think that's right.

Beth: You have a way of demystifying it.

Bill: And I also answer what I think is the $64,000 question. That is, ''Now that you have them in trance, what do you do?'' That is a much more interesting question.

Beth: I like that your work is very open. What I've appreciated about the last couple of days is that you've offered a lot of possibilities for me. You've put a smorgasbord of ideas out there for me—different techniques, ideas, and possibilities. It's nice to choose one this day and choose the next one another day, or not choose it all. It has a sense of a parallel process to what you might do in therapy.

Bill: Absolutely. And I hope the parallel effect has the sense of affirmation and validation and possibility.

Denise: I have this mental image of how I've been representing solution-based work in my own therapy and in teaching it—it's like straight lines and right angles. I haven't been able to figure out what I've been doing wrong. I know that there's something missing. In here, watching you, it just feels like there aren't any right angles or straight lines to it. I think part of it is that I haven't been inclusive enough of anything. I've been like, ''This is solution therapy. This is how it's done. It's not done another way; it's this way.'' It's more clear to me. Now, as I think about it, I think I've held people back in my teaching. That's been incredibly useful to me. I was also thinking about self-disclosure. I work in a setting where they don't even like to see it being done on a tape. It just makes people so uncomfortable. And I've never been good at not self-disclosing in any aspect of my life! (*laughter*) So I do self-disclose. It's within boundaries, and I don't just share anything that I would think is inappropriate for the moment.

What Do You Call It?

Bill: I've come up with a term that is inclusive of solution-oriented and solution focused. I call it solution-oriented, because it's oriented toward solutions, but it's not focused on them. We'll talk about other things. I thought that solution-oriented was a nice inclusive term, but then people do one or the other and they call de Shazer's stuff solution-oriented and it upsets him, and they call my stuff solution-focused, and it upsets me because that's not exactly what I do. So just call it solution-based. You could also say competence-based or resource-based. Those are all nice, inclusive terms. I think that's a kinder and gentler way to talk about it. I don't like to be pinned down so that's why I came up with "possibility therapy," which I think emphasizes the acknowledgment piece much more than solution-based work had. I thought it was in there in solution-based work, but it really was emphasized how important the acknowledgment and validation is as well as opening possibilities. There are multiple ways of opening possibilities besides focusing on solutions and finding resources. Inclusive therapy goes a little beyond that because I think we've made certain things guilty pleasures that you only do behind closed doors and don't admit to your solution-based colleagues that you do them. We've also made other things the evil empire, like medication, labels, psychoanalysis or whatever it may be. We just don't deal with that. We don't bring it in. In addition, the inclusiveness of, "You can and you don't have to" and, "You can and not at the same time."[88]

Acknowledgment and Possibility

Bill: I'd like to talk more about the use of language. Please go to the handout called Acknowledgment and Possibility.[89] As I was thinking about it, I have a friend who's a neurolinguistic programmer, Connirae Andreas,[90] and she called it "slight of mouth." I call it "Carl Rogers[91] with a twist," because what I realized was that people would say, "Briefer therapies, solution-focused kind of therapies haven't articulated so well how they acknowledge people." Someone asked me in a workshop many years ago, "You know, all this directive stuff, change-oriented stuff, whatever happened to Carl Rogers?" And I said, "Oh, Carl Rogers is the first five minutes. If you don't do that stuff, people aren't going to follow you wherever you're going to go." That was sort of a throwaway line at the time, but as the years went on, I realized that that was what was missing from the descriptions of the solution-based stuff. We weren't talking about how much you have to acknowledge people. But I also didn't want to give a false impression, because some people have the idea you have to acknowledge for a session or two and really listen to people's history or their feelings before you introduce the possibility of change. I say it goes on both

[88] For an overview of Bill's evolution as a clinician, workshop presenter, and writer, see O'Hanlon, S., & Bertolino, B. (Eds.). (in press).

[89] Return to Figure 2.1, *Acknowledgment and Possibility*.

[90] Connirae Andreas is a teacher, author, and innovator of neurolinguistic programming (NLP). She lives in Boulder, Colorado.

[91] Carl Rogers, Ph.D., developed a humanistic approach that later became known as "person-centered" psychotherapy. He died in 1987.

ways. It's both/and. It's not either/or. It's not do the acknowledgment and validation and listening to people and then suggest the possibility for change. People would say, "How do you do that and how do you know when people are ready to make changes, when they're ready to move on?" I do continued forays into possibility-land through language while I'm acknowledging that you can do both at the same time. This was an attempt to articulate some of it (*referring back to Figure 2.1*).

There are a number of other ways in which I and other people and you do this, but I just thought I'd make some of them explicit. The first part is "Carl Rogers with a twist." When clients report things that sound discouraging, statements of impossibilities or difficulties, instead of just reflecting those back and saying, "Okay, so you're really discouraged," you put it in the past tense. That's one way to do it. You put holes in the generalities that they're making like, "I'm always depressed." So, you say, "You're really depressed most of the time." You start to introduce possibility talk into acknowledgment, and when your clients start to take up that possibility talk, then you know they're ready to move on. And it could be the first minute that you respond that way and it could be the seventh session that they start to take that up. I think your clients lead you as long as you continue to open possibilities and acknowledge. If you don't acknowledge, typically they're going to feel alienated, not heard, or angry or they're going to show you how sick they are of your Pollyanna positive. So this is a way to continue to acknowledge, validate, and really stay with them very carefully and introduce a little bit of a twist—a twist into possibilities.

These methods are used much like Carl Rogers' reflective talk. When the clients tell you something that seems pretty closed down or blaming, difficult, or discouraging such as, "I've been to a hundred of you therapists and none of you are helping," something that's challenging for the therapist, that seems like resistance, that's when you'd use the Carl Rogers with a twist. So the first and most obvious one as I said is to just reflect in the past tense. It's not a major shift in the person's life, but it starts to do what the White House calls "spin control." You start to spin this talk into the past. Yes, you've had a problem, whether you have a problem at this second and in the future. Yes, you've been discouraged, whether you're discouraged at this moment and in the future. So, when I was talking to the couple, you probably didn't know it, but I used that kind of reflective language again and again. She'd say, "We're really having a tough time." I'd say, "You've had a tough time." She'd say, "Whenever I approach him like that." Then I'd say, "So a lot of times when you approach him like that, it hasn't worked." All of a sudden you're putting it someplace where it's in the past and its not so globalized like, "Always when I approach him." I don't know if you noticed, but later in the session, she said, "Well, you know, not every time when I approach him like that." When she first brought it up, it was every time you approach him in the morning when he's on the computer you get a bad response. Later, she amended that. What do you think that was about? Spontaneous? Perhaps. It may have been about the kind of language shifts that I continued to do through the session. So besides those blatant kind of interventions that are obvious to people, there are multiple little language interventions that are going on throughout the session of acknowledgment and possibility. The first one is reflect by reflecting in a past tense what they just told you and they brought into the present tense as a problem or a discouraging statement or a blaming statement.

The second one is to take a global or general statement and reflect it as a partial statement. You can't go too partial or it will seem like invalidation or minimization. If the person says, "Nobody likes me," and you say, "Occasionally people don't like you," it's too big of a leap. So, you say, "So most of the time people really don't like you; almost all of the time people don't like you." The third one is to take a statement that claims truth or reality and reflect it as a perception, idea, or sense statement. "So your sense of it is that people don't like you." "You've gotten the sense that every time you approach him in the morning when he's working on the computer, you'll get a bad response." "Your perception is he's angry at you at that moment; his perception is he's not angry at you." It's just a reflection that's saying, "That's not the truth or reality, but that's certainly the way it seems to you now." So you validate, "That's a valid perception, a valid thought, you're not a bad person for having it and I can understand how you might have it, it just may not be the truth." but, you're not going through that long explanation; you're just doing it with a little spin.

(*Refers back to Figure 2.1*) On the bottom are three techniques that not only reflect people's past experiences but try to move them a little more into a future with possibilities. You're gonna spin things a little more into the future, rather that just reflect in the present something that has a little more possibility open. You're going to invite them into a future with possibilities. So I call this the "moving walkway," like in airports when you get on one of those moving walkways and it takes you to where you want to go. You don't even have to do anything to get there. You just have to be on the moving walkway. Clients don't have to do anything here. All they have to do is listen to this language and they are invited into possibility-land. So the first one is that typically they're going to talk about the past and problems. That's what I do with clients, couples, and families first—just have them talk about what's wrong. As soon as they talk about what's wrong, I almost immediately lead them into, "So this is what you'd like instead?" With the couple yesterday, "You'd really like to find more consistent ways to approach one another so the communication went better and you worked things out?" They're talking about how he blows up, she gets defensive, he gets defensive, and that's fine, I acknowledge that, and at the same time I say, "This is what you'd like." They say, "Yeah, that's right, this is what we'd like." "Then more consistently do that at home. Work things out like we do in the office." So they don't really notice it, but all of the sudden, their consciousness and attention start to be on the future and what they want, rather than on the past and what they don't want. So we're moving them into possibility-land in that way.

The second method is to move them into the future by using words like "yet" and "so far." That's what I did with Karen yesterday. She said, "I'm not sure I can do this." I said, "So, you're not sure you can do it yet." It's just adding a little more possibility to that statement. Okay? "So far you've been really confused about this or uncertain that you can do it so far." So far. That doesn't say anything about the future and it sort of implies that in the future you will be there.

The last category I have listed here is being even a little more presuppositional and positive that that future will come about. For example, "When you're confident about doing hypnosis, you'll first try it with your friends and then try it with some clients." *When,* we're not saying *if,* we're saying *when* that happens. It's that language of seeding expectancy—when this happens, this will happen.

The client might say, "When I got depressed one time I called a friend," and I might say in response, "So when you get depressed you call a friend." That's a shift in the tense too. Now you're bringing something from the past up to the present. Or you could put it into the future: "So, if you ever get depressed in the future, you can call a friend; you'll call a friend." Now that moves it into the future. So you can use the present tense and shift into the present tense when you want something more into the present or more into the future. Again, this doesn't magically transform people's lives, but the cumulative effect of this is an automatic—if we were to go back and listen to the audiotape of the interview, you can hear this process going on again and again and again throughout the session. Much of it doesn't take and some of it does.

I think it would be best at this point for somebody to role play a client and I'll do this kind of conversation; then I'll role play a client and you can all practice in a round robin way. I think that's the only way to get it; to notice it again and again and then start to get it automatic in your behavior. I want a client that's really troublesome and resistant.

Alice: Well, I thought I'd take off in a creative way, not doing a particular client.

Bill: Okay, good.

Alice: "I've heard about this stuff and I just don't . . . my history is such that all that stuff, gosh, I don't see any way this can move any of that."

Bill: "As of right now, it seems pretty discouraging to you. You're not sure that whatever anybody can do but especially this brief, solution stuff could even speak to what's going on with you."

Alice: "Yeah. How am I even going to be able to trust you enough?"

Bill: "You're not sure you can trust me or maybe anybody. But certainly with me it's in doubt for you right now."

Alice: "Just take doubt. I live in doubt. I doubt all the time. I doubt everything."

Bill: "So doubt's a pretty constant companion for you and a lot of times it really gets in the way of that trust, maybe self-trust as well as trusting other people like me."

Alice: "Oh, yeah. I doubt whether I can do any of this stuff. I'm looking at a new job, and, gee, I don't think I can do it. I've never had any self-confidence. You can't just inject self-confidence."

Bill: "So you've had some challenges in self-confidence and sometimes when you've gone to do something new like get a new job, it's been really hard for you to trust yourself or to feel the confidence that you can even do it."

Alice: "Sometimes? All the time. Every time. Every time I try something new."

Bill: "So pretty much every time when you've tried something new, you've had to deal with this lack of self-confidence. This really has pulled the rug out from under you anytime you've tried to take a step forward."

Alice: "Yeah. It's amazing that I've done anything."

Bill: Okay, that's great. So did you hear it? It's just unremitting again and again and again. But at least this person doesn't get pissed off, like, "You don't get it, you just don't get it," and gradually through the course of a conversation, there can be one thing that clicks for this person or opens up a possibility. Again, it may take the whole session. My attempt is not to try to fix and change and say, "Oh, you have distorted thinking and that's really wrong," just to join and put in some possibility.

Again, if you just stay with the person, keep reflecting, opening up possibilities, my sense is that eventually, they'll move to that, "I don't know when it will be," or "I don't know where it will be." That'll be the next step. And then you follow that wherever it goes. So, what did you hear? Did you hear any of those? They go by very quickly.

Debbie: It was hard for me to pick up. I heard you reflecting her stuff back and I heard a little bit of possibilities in the language, but I'm still having a hard time getting it exactly.

Katy: It was almost all in the past tense.

Bill: A lot of it in past tense, yeah. You said, "Almost all in the past tense," very good, not generalizing. So some of it was that globalization—she said "nothing." I said "almost nothing." "It has pulled the rug out from under you." There was a lot of globalization, and I was doing more partial and then the idea of "right now." "Right now it doesn't seem to you." That's more narrow in time, rather than global in time. "I've never been able to trust anyone. I never will be able to trust anyone." That's more global and I say, "Right now, it seems like to you that you really can't trust anybody." I was doing mostly reflection of the first three because when the client first starts you want to just generally meet them where they are and they're going to be talking about where they're coming from rather than where they're going. That's the natural tendency for people. So usually I start with the first three. Not always, sometimes I mix them. "So, so far it's been really hard for you to trust people." That's a mixture—"so far"—of the two. So far implies a future in which you could.

So, another client? Discouraging, hostile, resistant, borderline.

Debbie: I have a client—just a little background—this is a woman who has four children, one on the way. They've been in and out of foster care. She has been battered in two relationships. And her children have been taken from her by Department of Social Services. There's a whole bunch of treaters involved.

"Well, Bill, what if they take my children?"

Bill: "So one of the things you've been afraid of is that they're gonna take your children for good or they're gonna take your children. Yep, sounds pretty scary."

Debbie: "There's nobody I can trust. I can't trust you. I can't trust any of these other people because they could turn around and stab me in the back."

Bill: "Because your kids might be taken away, it seems like you can't really trust anybody now, not me or anybody else because anybody could turn around and testify against you or you don't know what information they might be gathering about you that could go against you. So it's really hard to trust people right now. It's tough."

Debbie: "Nobody helps me with the kids. I'm here all by myself. The father doesn't help. Nobody's telling him he has to shape up."

Bill: "So a lot of times you think it's pretty unfair that all the pressure's on you, you're not getting much help, and you're feeling pretty alone in all this. The other people are saying, "You better get it together or you're gonna lose your kids," but they're not saying here's how to get it together or here's help to get it together. So that's been pretty frustrating for you."

Debbie: "Now you guys made me put a restraining order on my boyfriend, from my kids, so he can't even be here to help me."

Bill: "Right. So what help you could've gotten before from your boyfriend has been blocked by the legal stuff, and you're feeling like all the cards have been stacked against you at this point."

Debbie: "Yep."

Bill: "So it's pretty frustrating to work with all these people, and its pretty hard to find your sense of hope in all that."

Debbie: "And I'm about to have a baby. Whose gonna be there for me? I don't have a crib, I don't have money for food. I don't have anything."

Bill: "So that's pretty overwhelming facing another baby and less resources and support than you had before. One of the things is, 'I maybe want to trust you or work with you but who can I turn to because I'm not sure who to trust or I'm pretty sure nobody's trustworthy right now.'"

Debbie: "Yeah, nobody's trustworthy. My mother used to stand and watch me get my head smashed into the floor. Who can I trust?"

Bill: "So even your background has been a pretty long history of nontrustworthy people, and maybe in recent years you were making some changes in that, but right now it seems like, 'Yep. That was probably right. People aren't trustworthy.' From early on until now. Right now, you can't see any possibility that people could be trustworthy in the future, me or anybody else."

Okay, that's good. Get it? Its not like, "I'm gonna talk you out of this." Its being really *there* and continued possibilities. It's like, "Yep. I understand, *and* there are possibilities." Do any of them come alive for you right now? Not yet, not yet, so far it's been not yet, but I haven't alienated her so far, as far as I can tell. I haven't pissed her off, she doesn't say, "You don't understand!" At least we're not going down that road. We're not going down the road to possibilities yet either, but they're there. Did you hear some of them as they went by?

Debbie: I heard language of, "You don't trust anyone yet."

Denise: It's so subtle that it's remarkable.

Bill: Can some of you say some of the phrases that you heard?

Lisa: "At this point.

Bill: At this point—right now. That makes it more limited in time than forever in the past and forever in the future. What else?

Karen: "You've *been* feeling."

Bill: "You've been feeling like you can't trust people. The way it's been for you." What else? There was a possibility statement in each one of these reflections. Absolutely. There's acknowledgment and possibility in each. Again, just like with Carl Rogers, you don't have to repeat the exact words they say. I was adding some more.

Megan: I even thought I heard when you were saying something about that you *could* not trust anybody. You seemed to be emphasizing that word. And you were validating that she couldn't trust.

Bill: Yeah, there may have been a little of that interspersal technique, like when you're talking about hypnosis, saying, "So, you're not even sure you *could* trust." That may be an automatic pattern for me, because I learned it with hypnotic patterns and it may be part and parcel of what I do in nonhypnotic therapy. Switching again one of the ways to connect. "So, you're not even sure you can *feel safe right now!*'' Wow, feel safe. And the person starts to feel a little more safe. Was that an indirect suggestion? I don't know.

Megan: It seems to me that these methods recruit your clients into a partnership with you.

Bill: I was in Vancouver and I was teaching a workshop and these three people came up and said, ''We work in a residential treatment center for teens who've been sexually abused, and they will not talk about their sexual abuse.'' I said, ''What's your big thing about having them talk about it?'' and they said, ''that's the way you get over it.'' I said, ''Well, that's the way *you* get over it, but (*laughter*) okay, if you really want them to do it, here's what I would do.'' They said, ''They're totally in denial and say they've handled it already; they'll say they don't need to talk about it.'' So I said I recommend—they have groups—you go into the group and you say, ''Gee, we've got a whole new crew of kids coming in after you all leave. You've said you've handled this issue and resolved it, could you give us some ideas and advice about how you've handled it so well so we can do a little better with the next group?'' They do this and the kids say, ''Well, you got to talk about it. You can't keep it inside. Just keep talking about it and talking about it until you get it all out.'' It's like when they're helping other people they're much more healthy than when they're not talking. That's what occurred to me in this. Asking the person to be a consultant lifts the person up a little to be that. They *are* an expert in some ways. It also highlights for them what they need to do at their best moments. That's another technique—making the client a consultant and expert on the problem and process of solution, both after they've solved the problem and as they are solving it or facing it.

Denise: Do you determine at some point that this is not the customer, the client?

Bill: The first thing is that in my experience almost everyone who shows up in your office is a customer. I disagree with the idea that there are complaintants and visitors and window shoppers and customers.[92] There are certainly people that are more motivated for change, but I think in my time as a therapist I think I've had one person in twenty-two years that wasn't a customer. It was a sixty-seven-year-old chunky, strong man with a butch haircut.

Denise: Sounds like an ex-Marine.

Bill: Yeah, ex-Navy, which is part of the story. And he says, ''Hello. Glad to meet you,'' with a very hearty handshake. He doesn't look like your classic therapy client. ''My insurance man told me you could hypnotize me to make me stop smoking.'' I said, ''He lied. I've never hypnotized anyone to make them stop smoking. First of all, I rarely hypnotize people for smoking. Second of all, I can't *make* you stop smoking, regardless of whether I hypnotize you or not.

[92] For discussion on visitors and customers see de Shazer, S. (1988).

But you're here, tell me about it.'' He tells me this story. Basically, he was in the Navy in World War II, he drank like a fish—absolutely, clearly an alcoholic. Smoked like a smokestack, chain smoking, roll your own in those days, and he ate quite well. He was discharged from the Navy in '46 or '47. They told him he wasn't going to live ten years the way he drank, smoked, and ate. I didn't even know they knew about it in those days, but they did. Well, this is the 1980s when we're having this conversation and I say, well, they were wrong. He said, ''But five years ago my doctor said I had breathing problems, cholesterol problems, so I changed to a healthy diet, stopped drinking when I was sixty. The only pleasure left to me is smoking. I go for a physical each year, and the doctor said I don't have to stop smoking but that someday I might.'' No breathing problems from it. His insurance guy says he's at risk for cancer and emphysema. I asked him if he wanted to stop smoking and he said no. I said I bet if you go for your physical and your doctor says, ''You have to stop smoking; it's bad for you and hurting your health,'' you would stop smoking. He said yes. I said, ''If you have trouble with that, you should give me a call because I could probably help you, but if the doctor doesn't say that, live out your time and smoke to your heart's content!'' He said, ''Thank you, young man,'' and off he goes. That was it—the only noncustomer I ever had.

Debbie: But you introduced the possibility of stopping smoking.

Bill: Absolutely. I think he could. In a millisecond. The guy stopped drinking altogether, changed his diet because the doctor said he had to.

I've had people come in like, ''Well, my parents want me to change,'' but they're motivated for something. They come in looking like they're not motivated, and truly they're not as motivated as mom is, like in this case we just did. But I'd still work with him if he were willing to come in and see me, even on an intermittent basis.

Denise: I did tell her when she called the second time that I wanted her there as well. It was clear something else was going on.

Laurie: If mom came in, how would you deal with her? How might you deal with her?

Bill: It's the same kind of thing as we did with the couple yesterday and as we've just been talking about. ''So you really think he's been sitting around the house too long and he needs to go get a job. He's saying you bug him too much and that that has the effect of getting him to dig in his heels and he's not gonna do it.'' So then we'd talk about that, and changing the pattern and each person's understanding of the situation and what each person wanted and how each person perceives the situation, and we'd change the viewing and change the doing and validate each person while we're doing it.

Lisa: That's what I find really hard sometimes. Like with that case I was just talking about—the kids have all these ideas about things they want to change, and they don't want to talk about the past abuse and trauma and say, "Why is she bringing all this up."

Bill: And mom's saying, "These kids are this and they haven't dealt with this."

Lisa: Yeah, and so I feel like I'm trying to play this balancing act of validating her, because every time I try to move into some kind of possibilities with them, it fells very—I think I'm getting the message loud and clear—invalidating to her and she keeps going back to, "Well, they never do anything."

Bill: "So, mom, you're saying these kids don't do anything around the house and they don't obey and they're saying they want to change and you're saying, 'Oh, that's just a great act.' "

Lisa: Pulling the wool over my eyes.

Bill: They're pulling the wool over your eyes, and you're saying they're just not facing the truth and they're saying, "Oh, mom, you're just exaggerating things and you're not telling it the way it is."

Lisa: So if I talk about the dynamic that's going on instead. . . .

Bill: Yeah. Once I validate and I open up possibilities, then I start to move into changes in the patterns. "Okay, what's one thing that they could do in the next week that would absolutely shock you and be in the direction you want it to be in? Well if they cleaned up their room, or if they started talking about the sexual abuse and wrote a little thing about it. That would really convince you that they were being sincere in their efforts or that they were cooperating?" Start to add one thing to blow mother's stereotype of that. Like this guy, mother says he's lazy, no good, whatever. You figure out what that is and what's in that box and you get him to act anywhere outside that box, at least once, probably ten times. "These kids don't obey, they're . . . " Whatever that is, find out what that looks like and sounds like and get them to act anywhere outside that box.

Denise: Suppose her reply was, "He'd quit hanging out with that gang."

Bill: All right, so that's one thing. What else? Because that's probably not going to happen.

Denise: He won't talk. He won't say anything to us.

Bill: All right, so if he talked to you a little more during the week, that would really show you something's going on, something's changing?

Denise: Okay, that's helpful.

Bill: If she says one is not negotiable, forget it—but if something else that equals he's making changes or he's motivated—that's what I want to know. And there are ten things on the list and, same thing, I want to know what that looks like. Anything that would convince her. Five things. Two things. Anything. You can get it from exceptions sometimes, but sometimes they're not open for exceptions. Or you just say, "If you had other kids and your kids were taken back to hell from where they came and some children were dropped off who were actually reasonable and cooperative, what would those children do during the week?" (*laughter*) "If Satan came to claim his own?"

Megan: Would you kid and say something like that?

Bill: I would, absolutely. No question about it. I would try a more reasonable approach and after awhile I would be joking. "If Satan came to claim his own and took your kids away. . . ." I think the kids would laugh, too. I think the kids would like it because you lighten it up just a bit and say, "Okay, if two clones were substituted for these two children who we know are the demon seed, what would they be doing?" I've asked people, and they absolutely cannot answer with the person who's sitting in front of them. You know, "What would your husband do if he were being loving to you?" "He can't. He's just selfish." "Okay, *Phil Donahue Show.* Your husband is out of the picture and you're now married to Phil. He's this sensitive New Age feminist guy. What would he be doing, because I know your schmuck of a husband will never do this, but what would Phil be doing?" And then I get a description of the behavior and coach the husband to do one little piece of that. He's not gonna do all of it, he's gonna do one little piece. "He could do this—he could hold your hand; that's genetically possible for him. We know the other things are not possible given who he is." I do use that humor stuff when I get to that point. Again and again and again I've tried the reasonable one, I start to go with really blatant humor that highlights things like mother does think these kids are the spawn of Satan. It's funny in some ways; it's not funny in other ways. But, that's the way people get through really terrible things sometimes, they joke about them in that sort of dark humor way. And I would.

Laurie: Okay, we have the Phil Donahue thing.

Bill: We get a description of Phil Donahue's loving behaviors.

Laurie: Right. Loving behaviors. Then do you negotiate, "Now do you think he could even do that?"

Bill: No, I just turn right to him and I just say, "She's got a stereotype of you. She's clear you're genetically, personality wise, history wise, developmentally incapable of this. Wouldn't it be great to make her wrong? (*laughter*) Because she is so righteous about this, isn't she? So all you have to do is hold her hand, listen to her for fifteen minutes, 'cause she's sure you're genetically incapable of doing that. She's sure that that isn't you and that it's not a possibility for you. I think your muscles work like that, but maybe I'm wrong. If you just do one of those things, we'll blow her stereotype and we'll both have a good laugh at how wrong she was about you."

Megan: Do you think that sometimes you get them to say what they would do differently and put it in an action statement and the other person doesn't even necessarily know that that's what they need to do? They're doing something else or they've never heard that from the other person?

Bill: That's exactly right.

Karen: What if he feels like you're taking her side?

Bill: I would say, "Yes, because I think you understand that if you don't make these changes, you are going to be flailed for the next twenty-five years of your marriage, because it doesn't sound like you two are getting divorced. All you get to do is be punished by her for the next twenty-five years. So, yes, I'm on her side and I'm on your side. That is, I'd better take her side because otherwise she's just gonna keep wailing on you, and I better take your side because I think we can get her to where she actually sees that you're a reasonable guy who loves her and is trying to do his best." Then he feels really joined and so does she.

Well, let's do some practice here. I will be the client and you all use these acknowledgment and possibility statements. The first thing to remember is that you're not trying to *convince* the person out of it. You're not just trying to fix their distorted thinking. This is the way they perceive the world and think of the world, feel about the world, their points of view about the world, their lives and their situations. So you're just trying to join the person and then add a little possibility for something to shift, whatever it may be. I've got to get myself into a particular client.

All right, well, "I'm living with my parents now. It sucks. And I've been to see you counselors before and you've never done me any good. My mother's as good as any of you. She has better advice than most of you. But I don't take the advice. I sit around all day, I'm depressed, I'm bitter. Life didn't work out for me. I just feel like getting a gun and killing people. My mother said I had to come in here because I lay around all day and I'm depressed. I'm living with my parents. She said I couldn't live with them anymore unless I got some help. So I'm here."

Denise: "So, up to now, things have been pretty crappy for you."

Bill: "Well actually for years they were pretty good but, you know, life didn't work out for me. I wanted to be a rock star and it just didn't work out. Now look at me. I'm here in Nebraska. I was in California at the time, it just didn't work out. Here in Nebraska, its not gonna work out. Don't try to tell me it is, because it's not. I'm over the hill, I'm burned out. It didn't work out. My dream didn't happen. There's nothing to live for."

Megan: "Wow! So up to now, things really haven't worked out, but you have had some difficult times in the past, up to now."

Bill: "Difficult times? Yeah, right!"

Megan: "Pretty bad. Pretty rough."

Bill: "Real rough. Real rough and they're gonna be rough for other people now. It's been rough enough for me, but it'll be rough for other people. That's all I can say."

Debbie: "So I hear you saying that it's been really rough in the past and I also heard you say there have been some times when things have gone well. Can you tell me a little about that?"

Bill: "I had a girlfriend at one point. I was in a rock band. It looked like I would make it. But, you know, the music business is really weird and the deck was stacked against me and I didn't make it. Now I don't have the girlfriend, I'm living at my parents' house. Look at me! I'm thirty-eight years old, I'm living at my parents' house; I'm broken down; I'm depressed; Haven't got any money, no job, no prospects for a job. Look at me."

Paul: "So at this point you're feeling hopeless."

Bill: "Yeah, I am hopeless. Not feeling hopeless. I am hopeless. If anybody could see the truth about it, they'd see that I really was hopeless. There's no chance for me. My life is blown."

Megan: "You're feeling like there aren't a lot of chances."

Bill: "No more chances. I had my shot. I didn't make it."

Megan: "No more?"

Bill: "No more. I had my shot at it. I didn't make it. I don't know what else to do. I didn't have a backup plan."

Denise: "So sometimes there are some other options, but you don't really see any options at this point."

Bill: "No. I wasn't a good student. I'm bright enough, but I don't have any skills."

Megan: "If you'd go back now and talk about that backup plan that you didn't make, how would that backup plan look?"

Bill: "I would've studied harder in school. I would've gotten some sort of major or something in college. I would've gone and got some major that you can earn some money. I don't want to work as a clerk at 7-11. I'm smarter than that."

Alice: "So you feel like you've come up against a brick wall and haven't seen your way around it yet."

Bill: "Yeah. I am up against a brick wall."

Laurie: "Have you ever experienced a brick wall in the past that you could draw from in getting through the brick wall? Have you ever found a way over it?"

Bill: "Well, I used to think I could, but, no, I really haven't. I used to think I could though, if I just persisted enough and tried hard enough, but it really didn't happen."

Paul: "So right now, you don't think you can change this situation."

Bill: "Right."

Alice: "And all old the ways of working don't seem to work at this point and you haven't found a new way yet."

Bill: "No. I can't even imagine what the new way would be. I don't have any energy for anything. I don't. All I've got is bitterness and anger eating me up inside."

Paul: "I'm curious, do you still play your instrument?"

Bill: "No. I haven't played it in years, a couple years. Why bother?"

Alice: "You still haven't found the energy yet to find a way out of this."

Bill: "I don't think I'm going to. The only thing I have energy for is hatred and bitterness. I'm mean to my parents. They're being nice to me—they're letting me live in their house—but I'm mean to them. I yell at them all the time. I tell them they're stupid. They should kick me out."

Laurie: "So right now you feel like you're being sort of the meanest kid they ever had."

Bill: "The only kid they ever had. They don't deserve it, but I can't help it. I'm bitter. Life has screwed me over."

Denise: "What would have to change for your parents to have some inkling that you may not be quite the demon seed that you think you are?"

Bill: "I don't think I'm a demon seed, I just think I'm a bitter person whose life is screwed over. I'd have to talk to them a little nicer. They're feeding me, housing me. I shouldn't repay them with bitterness and screaming at them."

Denise: "What would you say that would be nicer, what will you say that's nicer?"

Bill: " 'Good morning.' If I say 'good morning,' it would be laced with sarcasm."

Denise: "What's the opposite of that—the nicer one?"

Bill: "Just 'good morning.' But I don't feel the energy for that. I am bitter. I can't pretend."

Alice: "You just haven't found a way through that yet."

Bill: "I don't think I will. Life is done with me."

Lisa: "So at this point, bitterness and anger stand in your way of having the kinds of relationships you'd like to have with your family."

Bill: "I don't even know if I'd like to have them, I just think its not right to not treat them politely because they haven't done anything wrong to me. They never abused me. It just didn't work out for me."

Megan: "So, so far, you've shown a lot of your anger and bitterness in a sarcastic way toward your parents."

Bill: "Yeah. They're pretty frustrated with it, but they love me and they put up with it and they probably will continue to, but it's sick. I'm just striking out at them; they didn't do anything wrong."

Paul: "So when do you think you might possibly maybe once in a great while say 'good morning' in a more nice way?"

Bill: "When I first went there, I did. I was grateful they took me in because I couldn't pay my rent in California and they really gave me a ticket to get back here and I was grateful and I was nice. But, you know, I still had a little hope at that point. Maybe I'd come back here and something would go better."

Megan: "So hope was the difference."

Bill: "Yeah. I don't have any hope now. I had a little then, but it was false hope."

Denise: "Your perception is that you really have a level of gratitude toward your parents that you've experienced."

Bill: "Yeah, I'm a human being. They raised me and took me in now. They're nice people; kind of boring, but nice."

Debbie: "You described that you had a little hope. Can you describe what that false hope was?"

Bill: "I thought maybe I'd come back to Nebraska and get it together, get a new band, and give it another try or maybe get a regular job or get another girlfriend or whatever. I don't know, but nothing's happened since I moved here. It's been three years. Here I am living in my parents' house. I'm a loser."

Megan: "So, so far, this dream hasn't crystallized and you haven't seen any movement, but how could you make that first step?"

Bill: "I don't know because I'm such a bitter loser. Who wants to go out with someone whose thirty-eight years old, bitter against the world, hates everybody. That's not a very attractive picture, is it?"

Denise: "I read an article about George Harrison who was the Beatle. Had women, had everything, money, fame. All the other Beatles went their way and he just fell into drug abuse; nobody talked about his music. Over the years, he's managed to pull his life back together. People respect him again. People are trying to get all the Beatles together. He's getting interviews, his financial situation is getting better, he's clean and off drugs."

Bill: "Well, if I had all George Harrison's money, I could do it, too."

Denise: "He doesn't have all that money. He lost all that, too."

Bill: "Yeah, but he has the George Harrison name and he could get a record contract. I couldn't."
The guy's smart. You're not gonna get him with that! I think its a good point, though, to have somebody whose fallen and made a comeback. Okay, so this guy was hard, actually. My favorite line from this guy was he said, "You're not telling me anything my mother doesn't tell me." I told him to bring his mother in and he did. She was really, really good! She was not your standard "give advice." She had paradoxical interventions for him, she used humor, she broke up the pattern between them, she would stand on her head if he was weird to her. She was very creative, really likable. I told her, "You've done everything I would have done."

Lisa: So did anything pull him out?

Bill: No, absolutely not. Very bitter.

Denise: Does he still come?

Bill: No. He came to see me a few times. When his mother came in for that session, it was the last session because he saw that his mother absolutely was as good a therapist as I was.

Paul: Was he a customer?

Bill: Yeah, he was a customer. He really wanted to change, he just couldn't find a way out of it, and I couldn't find a way out of it. He wasn't an entirely motivated customer because he thought it was all over. His story about his life was that he had burned out, it was all over, and there was no possibility for him. I never changed him. Saw him three times.

Debbie: So in that kind of situation, if you look at family dynamics, let's say, were there things there that you felt that needed to shift and were there ways that you would suggest a shift occurring?

Bill: That's partly why I got her in there, and I didn't see that, no. I thought I didn't get the father in, so maybe I would've seen something different. Actually, I got the sense that it was fairly much his issue at that point. It's not a family dynamic issue. The way he described his earlier life, there wasn't that negative dynamic. He was on the path and he just fell off. He got involved in bad drugs, was in a band, and could have been Kurt Cobain, but he didn't have his moment of glory.

Debbie: What if you had a session with the mother and the son and you said, "What would happen if your parents told you couldn't live in this household anymore?"

Bill: We spoke about that. She said, "I have said that and it will happen. It will happen. We have set a time limit, because I can see that just letting him live there to get it together is not happening. In six months if he doesn't get it together, he will be gone. He knows that. It scares the hell out of him. He doesn't want to kill himself."

Denise: That was what I was wondering—the suicidality.

Bill: I would say he could have been homicidal, and it was a little worrisome. He mostly talked about that. And she talked about it. She said, "I'm afraid he's gonna be one of these guys that goes up to the tower and starts shooting people. We will not let him have any guns. We will make sure he doesn't have enough money to get guns. He's just gonna have to go out and get it together." She was proud of all that.

Debbie: So then actually the intervention was in progress.

Bill: She was gonna do the intervention, but I didn't have anything else to add. Truly, I did not. I searched for, "What about your forgotten dreams" and "Yeah, this didn't happen, but there are other dreams"—all that stuff. He wasn't available for that. He didn't believe that that was possible.

Megan: So for someone like him, what do you think about medications? Does that enter your mind as something that he should try if he wasn't already on them?

Bill: Yeah. He had been on them. He first saw a psychiatrist; then he saw a psychologist who referred him to me as a hostile gesture, I later understood. (*laughter*)

Denise: Payback!

Bill: Yeah, it was like, "You think you're really good, you think you're really cool, but I have this guy!"

Megan: Did the psychiatrist put him on anything?

Bill: They had him on antidepressants, and I think he'd been on other things in the past. I'm not sure. It's been eight years.

Megan: So it was nothing you remember making a big change?

Bill: No, no. He said it was legitimized drug abuse. He was very bitter about the whole thing; it didn't really make a difference for him. He actually wasn't severely depressed. He was very hostile, much more hostile and bitter than depressed.

Lisa: It wasn't really clear to me that he wanted to change that about himself.

Bill: If I could change him, but it wasn't that he could do it, but he wanted the change.

Karen: Did you ever focus on his not taking responsibility?

Bill: Yeah. And so did his mother. She said, "As long as you expect someone else to take away the bitterness for you, it will not happen. You need to get off your butt. You need to do something about it, and in six months you will have that opportunity or you won't do it and it'll be on your shoulders and that's it. You keep expecting some miracle to happen. Now you're expecting the therapist to make you not bitter." She was very clear about it and I thought, "That's right." He said, "Yeah, I know, but so what; I can't help it, that's the way I am."

Chapter 8

"Lynn"

This illustrates another individual consultation, this one without inner work, followed by observations and discussions with the seminar participants.

Individual Therapy without Hypnosis

Bill: Okay. First thing is you should probably introduce yourself. First name.

Lynn: My name is Lynn.

Bill: I'm Bill, and I asked not to know anything about you before this. You may think, "That's frustrating, I have to go over the whole thing," but I'm coming in from the outside and hopefully I can see the forest for the trees, and I'm really gonna be trying to figure out where you've been, where you are, where you're gonna go, and what we might be able to do. There's a certain urgency or focus for both of us here in that is a one-time thing. I have a certain sense like I've only got this time to really be a consultant for you, to make a difference, so I get a little more focused and a little more excited about the possibilities for just whatever little fine-tuning or big shift that you want to make within this time. I am absolutely committed to making either the big shift or fine tuning, whatever you want. I don't even know what's brought you today or if you've seen somebody before for something, so if you can bring me up to date on that and focus us a little on where we are today and where you want to go.

Lynn: That's a big chunk. It's taken me about a year to do that with Jennifer.

Bill: Okay.

Lynn: I might as well start at day one. I was born into a family as a replacement child, as best as I can understand. My brother died young and as I was born into the family, my parents seemed to be looking back, grieving. As I was brought up, there was not a lot of attention shown or love given to me.

Bill: There may have been love there, but they weren't available to express it at that point.

Lynn: Right. They were not even able to support each other through what had happened to them. And I can't think of a harder thing than losing your own child, now that I have kids. My father died of cancer when I was about six and a half. So, within a very short time, another foundation, against my ability to control it, was taken away. My mother, as a result of having lost a child and her husband, became an alcoholic. That was her way of numbing her pain. Again, that's how I see it as an adult now. As a child, I think the perspective, was complete abandonment. As a child you don't know if your father left because you could have done something better. You don't have a clear perspective because you can't process the information. I lived with a lot of fear at home without a lot of basis for caring or demonstrative caring given to me. I pretty much took care of myself. I had an older sister. She's eight years older. I looked to her to be more of the mother figure and she was the one that kind of assumed that role. My mother's alcoholism went on for a long time and to the extreme; bed ridden, hiding it, keeping the secret, don't tell anyone, afraid the neighbors would find out, all of those pretty clichéd images of an alcoholic. After several years, three or four years, I came home one day after school and my mother became physically abusive and started to come after me. I ran. There was a woman named Mrs. Williams that I would go to when my sister was not around. My sister was then at college, so I had no place to go, no point of reference. I was really on my own without the security of knowing she was available. So I ran to Mrs. Williams, three and a half miles, nonstop, except once to throw up and obviously I was a mess when I got to her house. She took one look at me and asked me if I wanted to go to the police. I said I did and we went and got an officer and went back to my house. My mother came to the door, she was livid, wild, and angry because part of that was I had broken the secret. I had brought in an external public eye to the situation. The officer asked me if I wanted to stay there. I said no and we turned around and left and I stayed at Mrs. Williams' house that night. In the meantime, they brought in one of my mother's sisters, my sister came back from college, and all those references that know how to deal with my mother came to help. That became a punctuation to that episode. My mother did stop drinking, but she still carried the traits, was not demonstrative with caring, was pretty unavailable, but did all the right things—she was there at home, and she didn't drink. I'm looking back on it and realizing she had quite a bit of depression. That prompted a lot of her reaction, and she didn't have the help that's available now. So, about three years ago, when my mother died, I found a lot of the stuff coming back in very unconscious ways. My mother died and my first child, a boy, was turning six and a half. So I started to feel like I was relooking at myself at six and a half and all that had happened to me and, quite unconsciously, a lot of knee-jerk reactions, a lot of odd things frightened me.

The main one that frightens me is I started very infrequently shoplifting. It was one of what I think of now as many self-destructive things I did to myself, whether it was eating a lot of junk that wasn't good or not exercising or shoplifting—all ways to destroy my stability. So I'm looking at that, is that my addiction or my comfort in that stress zone of when I was a kid? I don't know. I'm still looking at that. So the one thing that I would like to focus on, I think, because it is most destructive to my stability, is shoplifting. I don't need to shoplift. I haven't been recently, but it doesn't mean I wouldn't come into that feeling again. What triggered shoplifting this last time for me was my relationship with my husband. I'd found I married my mother. I don't have a recognizable show of caring. I find myself in that same emotionally desolate situation in the home front that I was in as a kid. As a kid, I couldn't control it; now I can. My knee-jerk reaction was to get the fulfillment through other ways, helping myself feel good, whether it was shoplifting, eating, whatever small compulsion or big compulsion I could find. It was so subtle, it didn't seem like a big deal. It didn't seem like an overwhelming addiction on any level, but I don't want to lose my family. I don't want to destroy that stability. Family is very important to me because, not experiencing that as a child, it's very important for me to do that now. I guess I need to pass it off to you to get some prompting.

Bill: Yes. That's good. I've got some prompting to give, or some questions or some comments so far. I guess a couple of things come to mind. The first thing is that I do hear a story and there's a good part to that because I get a sense of perspective on it. I've heard a lot of stories. I guess there's a particular thing that stands out and a particular thing that I have to tell you that I've heard in other stories that I think stands out in addition. The first thing is that I always think about what doesn't fit with this picture when you tell a story. That day that you ran to Mrs. Williams and vomited on the way, that wouldn't have been predicted given your background. Like, the lack of support, lack of love and the difficult circumstances. People accommodate to these situations, like the violence seems normal, the alcoholism seems normal, the craziness seems normal. They just accommodate to it, and that day you didn't accommodate. You didn't just stay there or just run off and hide for a little while and come back. You didn't go to Mrs. Williams, and say no, let's not call the police, somehow I need to keep the secret. You didn't do that. That wasn't to be expected. What do you think, how would you explain that you were able to do that that day and actually, it seems to me, to cause your mother to stop drinking? As a child you had a big impact with that one intervention, if you will. That's what we know about domestic violence generally. I read a research study that said all the clever therapeutic things that we ever might do in the world don't really make that much of a difference in domestic violence. What makes a difference is going public, whether its calling the police, telling the neighbor, telling the relatives, having it spill out onto the street. Whatever it may be. Going public makes the biggest difference in stopping domestic violence. You went public in some way with the secret. How do you explain that happening and how do you explain that it was about you, that wherewithal that you had to do that? That wouldn't have been predicted from your background. So that's the first thing I need to know, if you could talk about that a little bit.

Lynn: As best I can remember, I was extremely frightened but had hit that point of complete, "I can't take this anymore." I hit my barometer, whatever that was. I don't know why that day I was able to make the change. I think it was because she became actually physically violent instead of just emotionally violent and that was something that I could see. It wasn't so subtle and undermining as the emotional manipulation that I had had before. I do see a direct relationship between that going public and the going public in terms of getting caught shop-lifting to bring attention to my current situation with [my husband] James. I see that as there's something there, but I'm not real clear.

Bill: Okay. That's fine. And what do you think the quality is that you had and that you have such that you can't just go along with the situation with James, the situation with your mother? Some people do go along with it—yes they can't stand it, yes its terrible and its horrible and they go along with it and they're victim to it and they never get to that breaking point where they say, "I can't stand it anymore, I'm gonna speak up or I'm gonna shoplift and get this out and deal with it," or they never come to therapy or whatever it may be. What would you call that? How would you name what this is about with you such that you did that and that other people who live the same scenarios or a similar one wouldn't have done that?

Lynn: Somewhere along the line, and I'm not sure if it was from the home-front or from school and the nameless faces of people that supported me in public spaces like school, somewhere I believe I had a sense of what was right and what was wrong and what was fair and what was unfair and I hit a point of this is extremely crazy, this is extremely unfair.

Bill: Mmm. Okay. So you did have sort of a reality check—right and wrong, crazy and sane, fair and unfair. A lot of people in those situations do not. They lose all sense of perspective of what's normal. There's a book, *An Elephant in the Living Room*,[93] and there's this elephant in the living room and nobody talks about it, nobody mentions it, nobody notices it. They all know its there but they become so used to it, nobody ever speaks about it. You noticed the elephant in the living room, you spoke about it, somehow, under dire circumstances, but you did. That's an interesting thing. I guess another thing comes to mind that doesn't fit with this picture; then I want to add the other thing I was going to say.

Some people with such backgrounds either choose not to become parents, or when they're parents they don't do very well at it or don't have these kinds of

[93] See Hastings, J. M., & Typpo, M. H. (1984).

sensibilities of caring for their children in the same way. I got the glimmer, and maybe I'm taking too big a leap here, that you do care for your children. Family is very important to you, so you do care for your children and you're not with your children the way your mother was with you. What do you think? Again that was not to be predicted, with your background of emotional deprivation. Your sister was there and maybe that was part of it and we'll talk about that, but how do you explain that you've become a better mother than you had as a role model as parents?

Lynn: Since day one, my sixth sense of the energetic level has been developed almost like a blind person. I was always having to be aware of the energy within a space when I walked into it. So I'm very clear on the invisible energetics between relationships, between people in rooms and in locations. Being a good mom, I overcompensate for what I considered a not-good childhood. I don't have role models, I have ideals. And those ideals made the extreme of family and how the kids should be treated.

Bill: Sometimes those ideals are a bit hard to live up to, but generally they're better than the lack of standards, lack of role models and they've pulled you in a better direction.

Lynn: Yes. Yes. So I care for my children, they're very well cared for, on emotional levels and physical levels. I treat them as people, I don't diminish them and they don't become nonexistent as I felt as a kid. I didn't have a word of acknowledgment or hope in the home. That was fairly prevalent at that societal time, too, I think, but not to that extent.

Bill: That's an interesting thing and again that doesn't entirely fit with the picture of how you grew up. It wouldn't be predicted. It wouldn't be expected. And that may be related to the third thing which is that I knew this guy Patrick Carnes,[94] he's written books about sexual addiction. He and I were at a conference together, and he told a story that still really speaks to me strongly. He grew up and had every kind of dysfunction in his childhood that you could possible have, sexual addiction in his family, physical abuse, sexual abuse from a priest he went to see as a Catholic kid, emotional abuse and all sorts of craziness at home. His family had certain expectations and certain things to be predicted such as they didn't go to college. In part, the way he dealt with the craziness at home is he escaped at school, did really well and read a lot, escaped into books. He would go to the library and take out books. The librarian at school took an interest in him and they developed a relationship. She started setting books out and she'd say, "Patrick, I saved this one for you. I knew it was the kind of book you'd like. It just came in. Here, you take it out." He loved these books. As luck would have it or as maybe her plan was, when he went from elementary

[94] Patrick Carnes, Ph.D., has published and lectured extensively in the area of sexual addictions. He lives in Arizona.

school into high school, she transferred to the high school. She was his librarian mostly through grade school and high school.

Lynn: Sounds like a guardian angel.

Bill: Yeah, absolutely. And that was the way he felt. He said, "She was my fair witness," from the book *Stranger in a Strange Land* by Robert Heinlein,[95] the person who can just see you as you are, and she loved him, clearly. He felt that. He didn't really feel it at home. He said years later he had finally gotten sober, dealt with his sexual addiction, 12-step program. He was doing better and he got a Ph.D. A Ph.D. in his family wasn't to be done! He wrote his first book. He was giving a lecture where he lived in Minneapolis to a group of volunteers who were helping the elderly people with meals on wheels and things like that and he was telling them how important they might be in a person's life. They may not be, but they might be. He told the story about the librarian and how she really was responsible for him getting a Ph.D. and writing a book. So, there's a guy in the audience who was like, "Dr. Carnes, Dr. Carnes" in the middle of the lecture. "I just want you to know that I heard that story from the other side. I know the other side of that story. Everyday, my wife came home from the library and told me about this wonderful kid who loved books and loved to read and how it made her whole job worthwhile. More than that, she's sitting right next to me. This is my wife, the librarian." Patrick Carnes said, "If you have one person that can see you as you are, who loves you or cares for you as you are, that seems to be enough. That's all somebody needs, seemingly." That was enough to give him the alternative model to say about his family maybe they're the crazy ones, and I'm not so crazy. Maybe *this* is screwed up, not *me*. He thought he was screwed up most of the time. He still does a lot. But there was some seed of a possibility there and he followed that alternative path. All he needed was a little opening, like Indiana Jones getting out right before the thing goes down. He got that opening and there he goes out that opening and he took that path. He had other struggles, too. It wasn't all easy, but I think of that when I think of your sister, Mrs. Williams, people at school. I don't know. Who else?

Lynn: There were a lot of nameless faces. I did the same thing. I was a straight A student because that was the only place I was given the kind of feedback for actions. There were nameless faces all along. There was not a consistent person, but there was that seed and that's what I have come to understand that saved me or seemed to have saved me. I do the same with what I learned. I use that. I'm a fairly public artist in the area who works with all facets of life from prison inmates to children to adults to do that. If I can reach one kid, one person to give that seed or build self-esteem, that is my sole mission. That is what I do. So I see a lot in that story. It could've been me. (*tearful*)

Bill: Maybe somebody else'll be telling that story about you later.

[95] See Heinlein, R. A. (1961).

So, given all that, these two things that don't fit with the picture, maybe three things, and the fact that somehow you had people who cared for you and loved you and took you in, I'm curious as to how. If you were going to be a consultant for someone like that and you'd say, "Here are the materials you've got to make a new picture of your life, a new sculpture for your life, a new art piece for your life. You've got these materials, how would you make a picture that dealt successfully with the barrenness in the relationship that you're experiencing, your marital relationship, and with some of the compulsions and addictions like shoplifting, especially shoplifting? What picture would you make of that, given those materials? I'm just saying, "Here are the materials and what's the picture that could be made given those materials?"

Lynn: The good picture? What I would like to see happen?

Bill: Yeah, right. Or how could these materials be used to stand in opposition to compulsion or self-sabotage or self-harm or whatever?

Lynn: I think maybe I'm a little stuck right there. I don't know. I keep thinking that what I would like to have come from my mate and my family homefront is the unconditional love, trust, understanding, and support.

Bill: Sure, that would be great.

Lynn: I don't know how to elicit that. I don't know if I'm supposed to try and solicit that. I don't know if I'm just supposed to be me and allow family to wash away like a wave or build and stay with me. I don't know what my next step is.

Bill: That's what I need you to teach me. I have ideas about it but I need you to teach me something like how does art evoke? I think art evokes; it's not just sitting there. It evokes a response from people. How does art evoke a response from you?

Lynn: My understanding lately is that the art I do is collaborative. It's a partnership. Its working together in communities to build one piece and to show that each twig makes a difference. Each person adds a part to a piece and because of that intention and energetic level of so many intentions to one piece that all come together to this one art piece it holds much more energy prompted from its viewer than I can by myself.

Bill: Okay, so a couple of things come to mind in terms of that for me.

I was doing a workshop in San Francisco and I was riding back to the airport with a woman from the workshop. She said, "I do diversity training." We were talking about diversity and she said, "I liked the fact that you didn't talk about having to integrate everything, because I don't like integration. Integration is the old metaphor for the United States, the melting pot. We're all supposed to be the same." We were joking and I said, "When it was the melting pot it all looked like white middle class males." She laughed and said, "The metaphor we're using in diversity training is tossed salad.'' Obviously, if we move in to the art thing, basically what she's saying is you want to honor multiple voices and visions and sensibilities. Different people would want different salads and if you made a different salad in collaboration with other people they'd say ''Oh, let's put a little of this in, I like croutons, I don't like croutons'' and so forth. You could mix it all together and it would really be a unique creation, a collaborative creation but it isn't better than any salad other people would make, it's just different because it's a collaboration of the people who do it. And when you're saying art is really a contribution of each one's unique sensibility, vision, energetic sense of things and each one of those gets honored.

Lynn: I'm putting that to the family, or that's how I'm hearing it right now, that all of those diversity of thoughts, interjections, and participation make that salad that is home and I can pick and choose what I need to make my salad be okay and it's not right or wrong—that other people within the family unit can do the same and at least that's kind of what I'm hearing, and maybe being less judgmental toward the mix is a starting point to allowing that salad just to be.

Bill: I didn't know what you would make of that.

Lynn: I kept going back to the family.

Bill: That's where I was pointed initially. I guess that's the sense that I have and I'll tell you two things about it.

I had a woman that I saw in counseling a while ago, and she was labeled schizophrenic. There was something that was off about that. I didn't really see her that way, although she had a lot of the symptomatology and she could have easily been diagnosed that by a traditional person. She was a poet, a really neat person and I like her a lot and every once in a while she'd have hallucinations. They seemed to be an anomaly in her life rather than a regularity in her life. We started talking about it and I asked her to teach me about what that was all about. When does it happen? How does it happen? Basically, what we came to after a lot of discussion is that she was a college student, an artist, and she would overspend for one reason or another. She had a monthly allotment of money and she would spend it by the 10th of the month, basically. Then she would have to go to her mother and kind of subtly suggest to her that she was out of money. Her mother knew and would resist talking about it but finally they'd get into it and her mother would give her money reluctantly because the stepfather would get angry for giving money, rescuing and catering to this kid and not letting her stand on her own two feet. Then, mother would give a lecture to her. Every month, it was the same scenario. As soon as she would go home from mother's house she would start hallucinating. Some months she'd be hospitalized, some not.

So I said, ''Okay, it seems pretty clear that there's a pattern here. Let's see how we can break the pattern.'' She said that her mother literally drove her crazy. "Okay, well until you get the money thing handled you're probably going to repeat this pattern with your mother. Let's see if we can make shifts in it that are in your power. Here's the only thing I can think of, why don't you pretend that you're a movie director and you're gonna try to get your mother to be a mother perfectly, as obnoxiously lovable as she is. As soon as you ask her for money, as soon as she responds, you're gonna say, "Okay, mom, here's the lecture part. Really get into it. Tell me I'm irresponsible." Be in it as the movie director. She said, "Well, that might work. I get so frustrated with her." I said, "Why get frustrated? You both do the same thing every time. Why not embrace it, come at it with open arms, and choose it. If it's gonna happen, you might as well choose it, that's what I figure."

So, somehow, that came to mind in terms of your family, especially your husband. It's like "Wow, wouldn't it be so amazingly different experientially and energetically for you if you came to him and said, "Boy, that is the closed down unemotional, unconnected piece that he brings to this art?" It's so wonderful. It really is a unique contribution, rather than, "Ugh!" and the, "How come you can't?" stuff.

The second thing I can say about this is I can tell you from my own experience that as soon as someone absolutely embraces me in the weirdness and deviance and stuckness that I am, I change. I'm less defensive. I change. I feel accepted and loved and I get less rigid and twiglike. I get much more flowing and bending. It's a weird paradox to say, "Accept me as I am as a defensive, closed down, scared, angry whatever." As soon as I get that, I'm okay that way, I'm not that way as much. It's not like I do a personality transformation, but I soften just a bit.

Lynn: I see that in my relationship with my husband. When I'm most needy, he's least available. When I'm strong, he's there, and that reaction doesn't make sense. So my way of having him react the way I'd like him to is when I become distant.

Bill: Which isn't a great pattern either. There's something between being so independent and strong and on you own, and being clingy, needy and being frustrated. I'm talking about that middle place where you can absolutely appreciate him as he is, as limited as he is, as stuck as he is, and as scared as he is, as angry or whatever. That he has a contribution to the art at this moment, the art or the salad that you're making in your family. That would be one way to shift that.

As you would do that, what do you think would happen with the shoplifting impulses? Would that make a difference with those?

Lynn: It would in the sense that I would be putting my needs way down and being comfortable with that so that I don't need too much.

Bill: No, no, no. That's not it. That's not it at all. Its much more an active process of including your needs but not having them have to dominate the show like when you get clingy or needy or whatever it may be. No, if you leave your need behind it ain't gonna work because you're leaving your part of the salad out. I know that seems perplexing to you, but I'm saying not particularly to change him. It's sort of like to choose him the way he is and to bring you the way you are there at that moment. But somehow, when you say judgmental. . . .

Lynn: I sometimes wish I wasn't so aware of the energetic level between us so that I could just be myself. I fall into the pattern of sensing this anger or this frustration or whatever this power is coming from James and reacting to it in the way that I know how. That's the place that I need to change.

Bill: That's the ticket. Somehow, the energy just doesn't let his energy go. . . .

Lynn: I'm very good when he walks in and there's the nasty, overwhelming aggressive energy coming toward me. If I can deflect and pass through it, I'm fine. But that does take a lot of consciousness and a lot of effort. I guess I would get better at that if I keep doing it and keep doing it, it would become natural.

Bill: Somehow, put your energy out there rather that have it be overwhelmed by his. I think if you give away your needs it's that, "I'll go make myself busy other places; you're not gonna meet my needs. I'll be over here or I'm just gonna be frustrated and angry with you because you're not meeting my needs when I'm needy." I don't mean either of those. I'm talking about some place in the middle.

I have a friend who says that's your Obiwan Kenobei warrior energy. You need your warrior energy at that moment to say, "This is me. I'm not giving up me. I'm not going to shut down my needs and have the laser sword go down. My laser sword is out here. I'm right here." And I'm not going to be judgmental about you. I'm just going to be right here with you. I can see that energy is coming here and that's just what you're doing at this point. Somehow, actually, then, opening yourself energetically, having your warrior woman energy out there. Here are my needs; I'm real clear. I'm not giving them away. I'm not giving up on this and I'm going to be more compassionate toward you as you are.

There was a couple here yesterday. I was telling this story and I think it's worth repeating. Sometimes when I work with couples I say, "Okay, imagine right now that you're angry, pissed off spouse is a little four year old or three year old who's absolutely terrified. It comes out like anger and aggression and hostility, and like they were throwing a tantrum or just getting weird and you know they're absolutely terrified, scared, and hurt." So to have that kind of energy around James as your warrior woman energy like, "I've got my needs. I'm not giving them up, you're not gonna shut me down, and I'm gonna up my energy out there. You're in a tough place. I don't know why you're in a tough place; this is how you are right now, and I can include that."

Lynn: I keep seeing a tennis court image. I think it was Jennifer that brought that imagery to me. The idea of the partnership being a tennis court. I love tennis. It was the only sport that I felt aggressive in but not really aggressive.

Bill: Hostile . . .

Lynn: No, I could field my court. I knew what my territory was, very clearly it was defined and that's where I knew I had to work.

Bill: Oh, I see.

Lynn: I was playing tennis with James recently and I had that warrior woman feeling, that feeling of complete confidence. Not aggressiveness—I had no kill motive, nothing on that side of the net that I needed to do in a harmful sense, but I was doing what I needed to do in a very strong way on my side. So I understand the feeling, but I don't know how to maintain that.

Bill: Yes.

Lynn: And that's the next question.

Bill: So I have to ask that question back to you. How did you do it on the tennis court?

Lynn: Just stay conscious moment to moment. The tennis court was very metaphoric in terms of my struggle with James. I wasn't doing it as a game, I was keeping that other intention as the primary . . .

Bill: . . . Mmm. That's hard to do every second.

Lynn: But I'm good at it when I focus. It's a fireball but then as Jennifer pointed out I tend to put a lot of energy out in what I do whether it's the teaching process or whether it's my life or James, I put a lot into it and then I'm drained. It's at that low energy point that I don't have the wherewithal to summon that same direction.

Bill: Okay. So the other thing that comes to mind is when I work with people, almost always I look to the pattern—what repeats again and again, what variation can you get—for two reasons: one is you get out of the rut and something different can happen. The second thing is it wakes you up a little. You know, a great way to go into runner's trance, when you go out, or tennis trance is if you play the same way all the time, it's the same game. You just go into the rhythm of it and you go into trance—sort of a more narrow focus of attention; you wouldn't have that expanded consciousness. So, breaking the pattern. If I were going to learn from you, okay, I'm James you're you, teach me what the pattern would be. I come and I'm all aggressive and I've got that energy going out there. How do you respond to me when you're at the lowest energy and it's not going well.

Lynn: I don't want to deal. I will circumvent. I will walk away.

Bill: You would walk into a different room. When you're in the same room, would you make eye contact?

Lynn: Only initially to sense the whole background of the energy I'm feeling and then I'd divert. I want to be out of his presence, out of his level.

Bill: All right. So that's one part of the pattern. If there's communication or conversation between the two of you, how does it go?

Lynn: When we finally can sit down on the communication level, I feel more relaxed. To me, communication is when the words allow me to feel reconnected.

Bill: Okay, so a little conversation between the two of you goes a long way toward reestablishing that context, connection, and inclusion and all that stuff.

Lynn: Yes.

Bill: Okay. But usually, that conversation doesn't happen for awhile?

Lynn: It usually doesn't, because if I'm low energy I don't want to deal with the negative, the picking. He does a lot of what I feel as a lot of picking and derogatory statements. I don't want to deal with that. I don't want to say anything back like that. I don't want to become or be near that. I need to take time to digest and come back with a more useful way of talking. So I might go quite a period of time. James doesn't understand that there's anything wrong. What I see is he is oblivious, that there's a lack of communication.

Bill: He thinks everything's going fine as long as he's not hearing any complaints from you, huh? And then later he's a little shocked when you say, I was a little bothered by that or I'm feeling really disconnected'' or whatever. So I'm just thinking of what other options would there be at that moment besides that kind of knee-jerk reaction of, ''I have to get out of here, I have to get away.''

Lynn: I could try just pinpointing what I see. That sometimes works. ''James, I don't know what's going on, what happened to you.'' I don't say it like I don't know this person that just walked in. ''I don't know what brought you to where you are. You're not the same person that left this morning.''

Bill: Really? ''Go out the door, bring James back!''

Lynn: Right. That's a good one.

Bill: A little humor sometimes. ''I want my husband back. Who are you?''

Lynn: I think the humor is probably the best way to do that. I found that that works with my kids.

Bill: Okay. Sometimes humor. I'm thinking you could turn on a tape recorder and say, ''I'll listen to it later. It's really hard to listen to that now. You just put it all on here and I'll listen to it when you're done with the critiques and the jabs; then I'll be back.'' I've used that with a bunch of clients.

Lynn: I don't think that would elicit humor in him. That's a little too sarcastic.

Bill: Too sharp. Okay. How about hiding under the table?

Lynn: That'd be good. Maybe I could just take out a moose mask or something—something that I have to protect me.

Bill: There you go. Yeah, that's good. I know it's probably the opposite of what your impulse is, but how about going up and giving him a hug and saying, "Rough day?"

Lynn: I've done all those things, but sometimes I don't have quite the right amount of energy to get the tonality right so it's very subtle how that would be taken. I've tried it, but sometimes it works, sometimes it doesn't.

Bill: Or just go up and hug, forget the tonality, forget the conversation.

Lynn: Yeah, that's a good one.

Bill: Anything to blow the pattern. I used to study with Milton Erickson, this psychiatrist. He was a very weird guy. One of the things that disconcerted me about studying with him is that as soon as you walked into his context, you lived in his reality. He would pull the reality rug out from under you and you lived under his rules, his reality. He would define it however he wanted and I thought, since then, that I really don't like that.

Lynn: That's how I feel with James. I don't like living within that reality.

Bill: Right. When someone else's reality defines what my world is about. I'd rather it be a collaborative reality, or I'd just rather stick with mine; thank you. Somehow, some way, you get invited to a certain kind of reality when you react in that, "I've gotta get outta here or else I'm gonna be dominated by this." To actually come forward, even if you're low energetically, you can actually do that action. Even if it's not entirely heartfelt, "I'm not gonna live in this reality. I'm gonna give in a different reality. I live in the reality of love and connection, and he's living in the reality of something else. He can live there, but I'm not getting on his bus. I'm traveling on my bus."

Lynn: That feels correct for what's been working for me lately.

Bill: I suggested to a couple yesterday that they both just get squirt guns and go out and go nonverbal with the squirt guns. I saw a book once. This guy had this theory that couples got into trouble when they talked and all they had to do was go primate. You just growl at each other or pick things out of the other person's hair—whatever you do that's just modeling primates whenever you get in trouble. Then you'll get out of trouble one way or another. I saw the movie *Tarzan* and the ape just takes the person's hand and puts it on their head when they want to be forgiven or loved. I've done that in my relationships.

What could you do that would be creative so that you don't live in that reality or just have to react to that reality, you can bring your reality as a collaborative piece to that? There's still something about your art. Tossed salad is good, but there's something about your art and I'm just not sure. Maybe you two could follow up on that. There's something about the honoring of each twig and each person's contribution, but you can set the whole context, as the artist, so that each piece is a contribution rather than a detriment.

Lynn: In low energy, I think in a relationship I dishonor or can't see very subtle gifts to the relationship. James's gifts are very subtle, so I need to honor those on whatever level.

Bill: Yeah. I suspect that that kind of shift would invite him into a different relationship with himself and with you and with the family.

About the shoplifting directly—again, I would say there are two things that come to mind about it that I've learned from other people.

Lynn: I would like to know anything about it. It frightens me.

Bill: Sure. It's scary stuff. I know what you mean. The first thing is that I read a diet book years ago and it said, "When you want a piece of chocolate cake, ten thousand carrot sticks won't do it."

Lynn: You got that right.

Bill: So that when anybody has compulsions, I think somehow it's not that, like going back and checking doors. I don't know what it is that you're afraid of or concerned about, but it isn't that. Whatever it is, at that moment if you actually had the consciousness of it, the impulse to shoplift, when you feel the impulse, stop in one way or another and ask what it is that I actually need at this moment, rather than that, and figure one small thing you can do toward that. If it's, "I need some love," what's one thing I actually have in my power that I can do to move toward it. Take a note of it if you can't do anything about it at that point, so that your energy is starting to go into solving the actual problem.

Lynn: Instead of going around it.

Bill: That's right. The cake problem rather than the carrot stick thing. The story I heard was a little kid gets upset one day; bored, upset, and angry. Then that little kid can't figure out what to do about that problem, doesn't have the resources, the wherewithal. The kid wanders into the kitchen, sees some food, eats it, and all of a sudden for a little while doesn't feel lonely, scared, or angry or whatever and then that becomes a solution to lonely, angry, or scared, but it develops a whole different set of problems—weight, self-esteem, impulsivity—and years later this person has this struggle with food and has never handled the first problem, which is when you're lonely, what do you do? So if that truly were the problem, that you're lonely, instead of eating when you're not hungry, you take one step toward being less lonely, whatever that might be: write down one thing you could do to be less lonely, call a friend, whatever it may be that solves the lonely problem rather than get you into these other attempted solutions that don't really work. That's the first thing.

The second thing is patterns. I was working with a woman who was doing bingeing. I said, "Any time you didn't binge when you thought you would've?" She said, "No, once I start, I do and I do it every night." As we continued in the conversation she said, "Oh yeah, there was a time. A friend dropped in unexpectedly, and I never invite anyone over. I live alone because I know I'm gonna binge. She dropped over. I quickly put away the food I was bingeing on and let her in. We had a conversation, and she only stayed for about half an hour. She left and I didn't binge that night." I thought, "Whoa! That's interesting! You told me you always binged; it was on automatic pilot, once you started you could never stop. But that wasn't exactly true." So we talked about it. I said, "What do you think it was about that?" She said, "I don't know. Maybe I was hungry for friendship or contact with somebody and I eat instead and it isolates me from people, so it gets me further away from my goal." I said, "Okay, from now on, when you feel the impulse to binge, call a friend. You may still binge after your conversation with the friend, but call a friend or go out with a friend." She tried that and it cut back the bingeing by about sixty percent. It didn't totally solve it, but it really interfered with the pattern. Can you, at the beginning of the impulse to do the pattern or the beginning of the compulsive pattern, channel it in a different direction ten percent of the time, twenty percent of the time, fifty percent of the time? You've probably done some things like that before because you seem to have contained it and constrained it, although the impulse hasn't gone away or the feeling hasn't gone away.

Lynn: That gets into a matter of making good or bad choices. When I'm lonely or had those points it's been because of lack of attention, lack of support, or lack of interaction with my husband.

Bill: Right.

Lynn: And a bad choice would be calling a friend, the wrong kind of friend. When I have been at that point of lowness it's like which is the lesser of the two evils, so I've been developing safe friendships, women that I'm able to call up. I'm trying to break it, but at one point I think it was . . .

Bill: . . . That was part of the problem. I guess I'm saying when you have a train that only goes on one track, you have to have multiple tracks. It's not like you have to make good choices. There are just so many choices, there are a lot more options. I came across this quote, "There's nothing as dangerous as an idea when it's the only one you have." When you feel on that track and you come to a junction, you can make multiple choices. You and Jennifer can come up with multiple pathways that are options—not that you have to make that choice every time; that's perfection and we're not always available for that. I used to do crisis counseling with suicidal people. I came to a very simple understanding of why people kill themselves. They come to a place where their vision narrows and they only see two choices—being miserable or dying. If I could give them one more choice, I used to joke with people, "You could hop a banana boat to

Brazil; then you have to worry about how are you going to live on bananas, what are you going to do when you get to Brazil; and you don't have a passport, what if they catch you as a stowaway?" We were joking and I'd say, "Okay, maybe that's not a good one. How about you could reapply to school, talk to your roommate or whatever." As soon as they actually felt one more choice, they didn't get so desperate. So that's what I'm saying about multiple tracks leaving from the same station. If there are multiple choices, usually you'll choose those. If there's only one choice usually you'll choose that. If you feel the husband choice is blocked and those are the only two choices, why not shoplift, of course.

Lynn: Thank you. You've given me a lot to work with.

Bill: Any other things you think would be important for us to talk about or ask about or say, given the time?

Lynn: No. I came in here most concerned about feeling blocked about choices. I know I've got to create some new tracks or options if I make the decision to stay within this family situation. How could I best work with that? I think you've given me some good answers for that.

Bill: Okay, good.

Would it be okay with you if we had the peanut gallery ask us questions or make comments? They may have technical questions for me, which I'd be happy to answer in front of you because I'm pretty open about this stuff. They may have experiential questions for you, or they may have ideas for either one of us or both of us.

Group Observations, Reflections, and Feedback

Jennifer: I have a question. Can you tell us a time when you wanted to shoplift and you didn't?

Lynn: Yeah. I just went home and played with the boys. I diverted attention to thinking about the consequences and went back to do something that meant something to me.

Bill: Great. That was a good question, huh? I do think about that, but I was on a different track. I assume there were many more times than that, actually, that she's thought about it or felt the impulse to do it and hasn't done it that aren't even as blatant as going home and playing with the kids. Many, many times.

Jennifer: You moved toward it but then didn't ask it.

Bill: Yeah. I didn't ask it.

Jennifer: It arose in me. I followed where you went, but I also wanted to know when were the exceptions. You had said break the pattern and . . .

Bill: . . . Those are the natural ecological ways out of the pattern that we should probably have gone for and not tried to create any new ones. They're already there.

Lynn: Sometimes I replaced in a bad way by going to have a hot fudge sundae.

Bill: The food was one trap. There were other ones when maybe the impulse came or the frustration with the marriage was there. There were two answers with that one question. I hope you made the distinction between the two of them. One is she said I projected myself into the future and the possible consequences and the other was I went home and played with the kids. Those are two things she did. One was a mental projection, and one was a physical activity.

Alice: I've got a couple questions. First, I want to say how impressed I am with the energetic sensitivity that you have. My question is, if you feel it outside, can you also turn it inside and get a sense of where your energies are and when they're lower?

Lynn: Yes, and what I've found is that when I'm very low I sometimes don't take the time to check the fuel gauge. It might be in a hectic frame of mind if you've gone into one of those like ten things on a list and they start to spin instead of you just knocking them off. That snafu's a logical progression. I think you end up on a snowball field—that you're not aware or not in control.

Alice: I've been having trouble with a shopping addiction. In pinpointing it to Friday afternoons, I realized it has to do with my energies.

Lynn: Yes, and the expectations for the weekend. Just in case I'm not going to have a nice weekend, I'll take care of myself on Friday.

Bill: So there are certain vulnerable times that you sort of build in to check in with yourself Friday morning—meditate or take ten minutes and build it into your schedule—that kind of stuff.

Lynn: I'm getting better with personal celebrations: anniversaries, birthdays, all those things that I place such great stars and stripes around and they should be celebrated to no end. Before those dates come, I'm trying very hard to slow down and get simple.

Katy: When you talked about going home to your boys, and when you, Bill, were talking with her about doing different pathways, I was thinking about a book by Yvonne Dolan, *Resolving Sexual Abuse*,[96] and I've also been thinking about tactile and sensory things. I was wondering if there was a symbol that you could have with you all the time. Like, she talks about having them keep something in their pocket—a letter or something, and they don't have to take it out and read it, they can put their hand in their pocket.

[96] See Dolan, Y. M. (1991).

Lynn: I do that sometimes. I can think of five or six right now. A friend just wrote me a very caring letter that I've been carrying around in my purse for a while. I am a fetish person in that sense. But I haven't done it consistently. I don't know if any of you use word plays or are aware of them or can feel them or see them as they come. One thing I kept seeing for the longest time is my kids were into money and having change. There were these little piles of change everywhere on the floor. At first it was kind of cute and I understood the part about counting and all that. After a while it started to really irritate me because I was really tired of just picking up pile after pile of change. One day, it seemed like I had that splatter vision and I looked at the words to see what it was the spirits were trying to tell me or what it was that I was supposed to hear. I saw change. I started laughing. It's like, will you change, will you just plain change? Pick up the change and change. It became so clear to me that I started laughing and then the change disappeared, and I didn't see piles of money everywhere anymore. Whatever your belief in how the universe responds or doesn't respond, I look at word plays and imagery like that often in the fetish sense. I take them as signs and symbols. Maybe somewhat like the Native Americans do, I don't know.

Bill: There's this thing called a grace file that I heard about from this woman who came to a workshop. Her husband was a minister and he would get criticized and pulled in all directions in the congregation—couldn't satisfy anybody. He just couldn't be all things to all people. He was working eighty hours a week trying to meet everybody's needs. He just started to save in a file letters and notes people had written to him thanking him for the wonderful sermon he'd given or the time that he spent counseling them, he was the best minister they ever knew, or whatever, and he called it his grace file. He would sit down when he was at low tide and read these and say, "I'm not such a bad guy. I'm all right." Then he'd close it and go back to his eighty hour week. I immediately went home and started a grace file. I had just entered a very difficult time in my life and it was like I need that grace file right now to think I'm not a terrible person.

Lynn: I've found myself doing that recently in some of the traumatizing I've been bringing to myself. I've pulled together five years worth of thank you notes and inspirational notes from different residency sites. So I have my grace file, too, but I never heard it labeled that way. Another thing is I hate working with money, and when I sit down at the end of the year to do my taxes for my business, I have this quilt that's up in front of me and each portion of the quilt was made by a friend and I have that in front of me to help in doing this task I hate doing.

Jennifer: I've noticed how everyone wants to give solutions to Lynn. That was something else! I'm feeling rather validated because I always feel like I've nothing else to offer. One thing I've learned is she's done a lot of the things that we could possibly think of and I wonder what it is that we want to give them and also I want to celebrate that you invite that, Bill, and evoke that and make space for people to do that.

Bill: It's that collaborative thing.

Lynn: It's that eating up information thing: getting and reading books and getting different perspectives to help—to pick and choose. It's finding myself options, finding myself many possibilities, and then sifting out to find what works for me.

Lisa: It is fascinating. You have all these collaborators except for your husband.

Lynn: I think that too.

Lisa: But he must collaborate in some way.

Lynn: He collaborates in very subtle ways. Being facetious right now I'll say what his words are, he goes to work everyday and brings home a paycheck.

Lisa: And he's not an artist in the way that you are an artist.

Lynn: There are ways that he can collaborate, but there's a sense of what I consider withholding. What I deserve, what I don't deserve, in *his* perspective, which is again something I have to be careful not to take on as truth. He can be very helpful. I'm doing a cover for a new book right now, and my writer friend has another book coming out and I'm doing that in a complete generative way. I started with a photograph of what I want to work with and I'm working to manipulate it on a computer. He can help with that and he does have good intentions here and there. He'll put out some good information, but sometimes he will withhold the product of it. Like, there's a special program that I'd really like to get and I know that he would prefer I get it through him because he can get it cheaply because he deals with computer imagery and computer products all the time. But I need it right now and I'm in a Catch-22. If I say I really need that right now, he will be less apt to act on getting it than if I just allow him to do it on his own time. So I'm still trying to learn how to work with that in a nice way, in a clear way, to put out that I really need this thing. I'm not doing it to manipulate you, I'm not doing it for any other motive except I'd really like to use this right now and I know that you're the person who can get it. So it's hard for me. He does collaborate in that sense, but I have to really be clear, specific, and focused on what it is that I need from him and put it out there with plenty of time for him to follow through if he should decide to.

Continuing Conversations. . .

Bill: What did you hear in that session—because your awareness of metaphors has been raised and your awareness of language has been raised and your awareness of the solution process and possibility process has been raised can you highlight some things that stood out for you that you took notes about?

Beth: Your librarian story.

Bill: What stood out for you?

Beth: That really seemed to touch her. It touched a lot of people in this room.

Bill: Yeah, it did. She was tearful a couple of times and I was as well.

Beth: That story is very endearing. I think it can draw a lot of people in on very deep levels.

Bill: Yeah. How do I come up with that story? How does that emerge? That's a question, but I don't know if there's an answer to it. What's you idea about that? How do I come up with that story at that moment?

Alice: We'll turn the question to you.

Bill: I associated to it somehow. I don't know, exactly. That's the answer. I don't know exactly.

Alice: One of the things I notice is that you're telling stories when I would be doing explanations.

Bill: Yeah.

Alice: I would be putting out my understanding of something, finding a model.

Bill: Yes, that's how I do, I tell stories. But sometimes I do an explanatory piece. Like I tell this story about the librarian and I say, "So it seems to me that you had your sister and this woman that you ran to and maybe other people." She said countless names and faces. That seemed to contribute. So then I add a little summary explanation piece, "And how do you think that that serves you now?"—and then I move on to something else. I do a little explanation, but mostly I introduce themes and explanatory ideas through stories. I think they're more experiential.

Alice: That's what dawned on me.

Bill: It really did. She teared. I teared. We're in the experience of it, and it also has an explanation with it. It's not just a pointless story. And it's not just tell a story to tell a story. It clearly is woven into the fabric of the interview. That was something, actually, that she introduced in some ways. Her sister loved her and this woman took care of her, and the countless other people. I heard it as a theme, and by association I thought, "Oh, that's like that Patrick Carnes story; he's in a terribly abusive situation, and he had someone to love him." That's how I got it. How did I remember the Patrick Carnes story? For me, that's the file folder thing. I seem to have them in file folders in my head by class of solutions. I open up the file folder and the Carnes story is there; there's another story and a saying. Then there's another file folder that says, "If you haven't got any choices, you're screwed, you're gonna be suicidal or stuck or whatever," and in there are not only stories, but quotations, anecdotes, analogies, and full blown metaphors and stories.

Laurie: Your file folder is an explanation for what I'm seeing as your creative process.

Bill: That's right. It's not entirely run on the creativity that emerges. It seems to have categorizations of associations of classes of things. Within that class I might choose one for a particular client and another one would be absolutely inappropriate, or it doesn't even occur to me. It just isn't a good enough fit. I'm going belly/mind, but there is a certain kind of categorization. It isn't just total creativity. You've heard me tell the same story a couple of times, with slightly different points and slightly different emphases.

Megan: That, to me, is amazing. In the stories, you can find different parts in the story or even a completely different character than you identified with the time before. They're just so useful!

Bill: Flexibility. And the clients may respond to some part of them or they may not. She laughed when I said hiding under the table. I don't think she's gonna do that.

Katy: You never know. She's pretty creative.

Bill: The squirt gun, no. I think she'll do something, but it probably won't be that.

Laurie: You probably freed her up, and that was pretty exciting.

Bill: That was the point. And that's part of why I say, "So many possibilities." I say here's something in this class, here's something in this class, here's something in this class, you come up with this one. I want A, B, C, D, and you come up with E, because I know it'll be something you can do. But I've now set the pattern here of what kind of things you want to look for.

Laurie: Pattern and permission.

Bill: There you go.

Laurie: The use of the story is the teaching parable. That's what you're really doing. You're teaching the parable.

Bill: I am.

Paul: Have you ever had anybody ask you, "'why are you telling me that story? Let's get down to business, or be upset with you?

Bill: Not in recent years. I used to when I first started, but not in recent years.

Paul: They stay with you for quite a long time while you're telling a story.

Bill: Yeah, they do. It didn't seem descriptive or domineering. They don't complain about that. Therapists in workshops sometimes say, "Don't your clients get sick of you? You're talking a lot.'' Yep. I am. The clients do not complain about that. I've been critiqued by people saying I talk too much.

Paul: I showed your tape on depression to a group of people, and that's what they said. One person said, ''Well, he does hypnosis, so that's just the confusion technique he's going through.''

Bill: I don't think so, and that client absolutely found great vale and got over her depression from it, so you can't argue with results. I talked a lot. I listened for a great deal of time at the very beginning of that session. I didn't talk. She wanted to tell her story and I was willing to listen to her story. With some clients, I barely talk at all. With most clients, I talk a fair amount. There's a certain part of the session when I'm talking a lot and it's partly because I want to create a certain weave of a reality possibility, and I'm working a lot to do that at that particular point. I do it with words, with stories, a lot. It's my preferred mode. Other people do it with the wilderness stuff, some people do it with expressive arts. That's just their preferred mode. I do it with words and stories.

Laurie: The group process after the session with everybody and the client is very much a symbolic metaphor for group safety—the team concept, who's on your team, who're your resources. We act and react like resources, so it's kind of a parallel.

Bill: Social resources that you can see, that these could be supportive new ideas in a community of caring people. That's nice. What else?

Megan: In the beginning, she used collaborative to describe something, and you seemed to carry that and use that throughout the session.

Bill: Collaborative, community, conversational . . . yeah

Denise: Do you think she had heard that from Jennifer? I was amazed when she used that word.

Bill: Could be, but she's an artist.

Denise: She was talking about her artwork.

Bill: I think it's not a new idea. It's in various fields, but maybe Jennifer introduced it as the crystallized concept from what she was doing.

Laurie: What was it like for you when she picked up and elaborated so quickly on the metaphor of the tennis match?

Bill: I thought it was nice in some way, but I thought she had it too figured out in some areas. I thought the salad metaphor was obviously her, and she's gonna use that one. I would've predicted the art one would've been much more resonant with her, but the salad seemed to have spoken to her much more powerfully. The salad of her family. So there are new metaphors in that area.

Megan: I was surprised that she didn't go with what you were trying with the painting the picture of her husband and all that, but it was so interesting for me that I was kind of lost for a minute in how you dropped that one and looked for another one and just kept feeling those out.

Bill: That's it. Off course, off course, off course, and then she came up with the tennis metaphor, which was also a powerful one which she and Jennifer obviously had worked on before. I think tennis and salad were the most powerful metaphors for her for some reason.

Megan: You started out with the three aspects that didn't fit in her picture. Do you do that as mostly a joining?

Bill: It's a highlighting of things. Those are the resources, exceptions, and strengths, and competencies that I wanted to highlight, to give back to her and say, "I heard this in your story. Is that right?" And then get her to elaborate on and notice it. But it didn't matter what she said in response, as long as she noticed that I was holding it up saying, "See this? Is that right?" and then, "How can you use this to change that?" She didn't make the translation to how she was going to use it to stop shoplifting quite as readily as I had hoped.

Chapter 9

Stories, Stories, Stories

This chapter focuses on the power of stories in therapy and the use of teaching and therapy stories— narrative therapy—which uses a method for transforming identity stories. Finally, we take up the use and bypassing of stories in couples therapy and how to evoke solutions from clients.

The Room of a Thousand Demons[97]

There used to be an enlightenment ceremony in Tibet that would happen once every hundred years. All the students would get together with the lamas, the Tibetan priests, and the Dalai Lama, and in this big cavern they would have this room of a thousand demons ceremony. The room of a thousand demons ceremony was a ceremony in which you could get instant enlightenment. You could go through the ceremony, be enlightened, get off the wheel of karma, and that would be it. Reach nirvana. Most of the time in order to get enlightened you have to go through many lifetimes and do a lot of study and work. But this was microwave enlightenment. Anyway, everyone would line up and they'd announce the ceremony and say all you have to do to be enlightened is walk through the room of a thousand demons and come out the other side. It's not too easy. Each person has his or her own room, it's custom designed for each, and there are one thousand demons in there that take the form of your worst fears as soon as you walk in the room. Whatever you're most afraid of, heights, abandonment or whatever, and it seems very real because these demons have the ability to reach into your mind, get the images, and show you what you're most afraid of. We can't come in and get you; that's part of the rules. You just have to deal with your own one thousand demons yourself. When you walk in,

[97] For more information contact Bill's website http://www.brieftherapy.com.

the door closes behind you and there's no knob on the inside. You have to walk to the other side, find the doorknob and find your way out. Once you're in there, that's it. Some people stay in the room of one thousand demons tortured by their fears and they die. Some people make it out the other side. Some people decide not to go in. Those that make it out have told that two things were helpful, so there are two hints if you want to make it through. The first one was helpful for a small percentage of people, and it was remember that what the demons show you isn't real. It's illusion. The second thing, more helpful for more people, is no matter what you see, what you hear, what you feel, what you think, keep your feet moving because if you keep your feet moving you'll eventually get to the other side, find the doorknob, and get out. It doesn't matter what's going on in terms of your stories, interpretations or fears, as long as you keep moving toward that goal and going through to make it to your destination. I've had people come back to me after I've told that story and say, "Ugh, I had a really bad week but I kept my feet moving." It's designed to peg a certain kind of courage that people have or a certain kind of persistency people have in the face of fear, in the face of difficulties.

Hitting the Brick Wall[98]

Another one people quote back to me quite a bit, I got before my father died in the late 70s. He would come down to Arizona where I lived at the time and he would just tell stories about him growing up and the family, the uncles, aunts, grandparents, and things like that. He knew I was going into the family therapy field and he said, "Well, I've learned one thing from raising eight kids. One thing I learned that each of my kids has to hit a brick wall and that's how they learn about life." He said it's like your kids are riding a motorcycle and you can see they're heading in the wrong direction, they're going to get in trouble: they're hanging out with the wrong crowd, bad grades, drinking and driving, or just drinking. They're getting into some sort of legal, financial, or relationship trouble. One thing or another, be it a small thing or a big thing. He said you, the parent, see that they're heading for trouble and you want to kind of warn them and it usually doesn't work, but you still want to warn them anyway. And he said it's like they're riding a motorcycle toward a brick wall, and for your first two—those were my older brothers who rebelled a lot, broke all the rules and paved the way for the rest of us—he said "I would give them a lecture and yell at them while they were heading for the brick wall, 'Look out, stupid, you're heading for a brick wall, you're really making a big mistake, stop!' They'd speed up the motorcycle, give me a rude gesture, and then BOOM they'd hit the brick wall." And he said, "I was really stupid for the first two because I stood in front of the brick wall and they'd hit me with the motorcycle and we'd both go down and then we'd pick ourselves up and limp back into life. Luckily,

[98] See footnote #97.

none of it was fatal for them, but it could have been, easily. After the first two,'' he said, ''I got a little smarter. I moved away from the brick wall so they wouldn't hit me before they hurt themselves, and I still gave them the lecture and yelled at them and I got the rude gesture and they speeded up. After six, I got a lot smarter. I would sit back and say, 'Look, I'm an old man, been around for awhile. I think there's a brick wall, I think you're heading for the brick wall. I really recommend you go another direction, but I already learned from the rest of my kids that you probably won't listen to me. You think I'm full of it, but as a parent, I feel the need to say something as if my wisdom might actually speak to you. You probably don't think it's wisdom, and that's okay. I learned that all my kids have to learn for themselves. He said when you say it that way, the motorcyclists slow down a little bit, sometimes. The rude gesture dropped out. And they'd still hit the brick wall. (*laughter*) That's just the way kids learn (it's even the way some adults learn).

The first time I ever told that story, a woman came in and she had eighteen- and nineteen-year-old daughters. They both dropped out of high school and were really wild. Pregnancies, abortions, heavy drug use, heavy drinking, the worst kind of friends and boyfriends. They kept hitting their mother up for money. The mother was remarried and both had regular jobs and good money but couldn't afford to subsidize these kids forever. But they kept getting hit up to be rescued. They would get really frustrated with the daughters. At times, the daughters would move back in and then leave. At that time, the daughters were both living with them. The presenting problem that brought the mother in was that her work had put her on probation due to being off too many days with unexcused absences and she said it was because of spastic colitis, but they said it was because she was irresponsible. The doctor wouldn't write her an excuse because he thought it was related to her emotional issues. She was very close to being fired. I asked her what the spastic colitis was about and she said, ''I think there's a lot of stress with my daughters.'' I told her the brick wall story and said, ''You know, sometimes I think that parents think they're giving love when actually they're giving mushy kind of love when what they really need is brick wall love.'' She said, ''You know, that's right.'' So I said, ''Why don't you come back and we'll do some hypnosis and see if we can get the colon to stop the spasing. Then you can at least stay at work until you can find another job.'' It was a pretty stressful situation at work as well. She came back the next time and said, ''We don't need to do hypnosis.'' I asked her why not and she said, ''The spastic colon is gone. I went home that night and talked to my husband. We decided to give each of the girls $500, told them they had to move out tonight, they could never move back, and they would get no more money from us.'' The girls had hugged her and said to her, ''We wondered when you were finally going to come to your senses.'' She said her spastic colon settled right down and she talked to her boss and they made a plan for getting off probation and that was that. The brick wall story seems to be pretty memorable.

So sometimes you have stories like that. The room of a thousand demons was more of a fairy kind of story, a myth story from a religious tradition. The brick wall story comes right from my father's experience. One of my weirdest experiences was to hear somebody tell me the brick wall story that they had heard and never had met me. It obviously has been going around, somewhere, somehow. I like that, to hear it back as if it's this cultural story! Both of those seem to speak to people.

Narrative Therapy

Here's another territory that I think is very interesting. I was in New Zealand, 1986 or 1987, to do some workshops and this guy showed up. His name was David Epston. I'd known a little about him because I'd read an article by him. He showed up at an evening presentation I did on Milton Erickson. I showed some videos, talked about my experiences with Erickson, and talked about how solution-oriented approaches came out of Erickson's idea that people had the resources and abilities within and you can evoke them often with hypnosis. He introduced himself and said to me, "You said the reason you use hypnosis sometimes is because people sometimes don't know *how* they've solved a problem, but they have solved it. Every kid I've ever worked with knows how they solved the problem, and I can always get them to tell me how they did it." He ends up talking to me while I'm walking out to meet my family so I invite him into the hotel room at about 9:45 that evening. We're sitting around the room and the next thing I know it's 1:45 in the morning! David is so fascinating, telling me about all these kids he's worked with and how they've solved their problems: night terrors, bedwetting, and so on. I was totally mesmerized, and he reminded me of a guy I had just written a book with, Jim Wilk, who lives in England. They both had total enthusiasm and total creativity about how they solved problems in therapy and it was amazing to me.

The next day, David brings over a sheath of his papers which had never been published. I read them on the way home. One of them I read made me cry. I just cried and cried. You know, I've been doing therapy a lot of years and I've seen some moving things. So reading an article usually doesn't move me to cry about a clinical technique. But it was so touching. It was about this woman who had been raised in Italy as one of thirteen or eighteen kids—an amazingly large family. She was the last one, and basically she was like the Cinderella. They all abused her, she did all of the work, she was treated as the maid and sexually abused by her brother-in-law and never knew her father. There was only one guy in the whole town, an older man, who was nice to her. She later found out that was her father who had had an affair with the mother and that's why they treated her so terribly. She was exported to England where she didn't know a word of English, and that's when the brother-in-law sexually abused her for years and they wouldn't let her go to school. Finally, an English social worker got involved and got her in school and somehow she escaped to New Zealand, eventually. So she's in New Zealand, married and totally messed up, fearful and down on herself, having anxiety attacks and feeling like her life isn't worth living. David sees her for one session and her life entirely turns around in that one session. He writes a letter afterward which summarizes the treatment and the charges made about how she stood up to this and changed that and kept going through this and that when they had treated her like a slave and like an object. She became the author of her own life. She learned to write English afterward and things turned out very good. So, I'm crying and thinking there's something to this approach that does something that I don't do, but it's very much in the spirit of what I'm talking about—possibilities, orienting to people's competencies—but it's a whole different way of doing it.

So I just paid attention to it peripherally over the years. Some years later, after I kept reading and learning about it, I made another trip to New Zealand and met *Michael White,*[99] and I met David Epston again and I started to know more and more about what they were calling, at that time, a literary approach to psychotherapy. Now its called narrative. They had come out with a book, *Narrative Means to Therapeutic Ends*, which is sort of a summary of their method. I started to get some of the ideas, but I still didn't know them exactly. I was very intrigued.

So all of a sudden there was this stream of narrative therapists that began to come in. They had a whole different tradition than the Ericksonian therapists but similar sensibilities about people. In the Ericksonian tradition, what you've seen in hypnotic work, you try to include everything and value everything. In this tradition, it was called externalizing. Basically, they were using a technique that was throwing out the symptom and saying *the symptom is bad* and tries to undermine you. Now, my tradition was always that the symptom can be utilized to heal you. It was really a challenge to me. I could see that they were getting these profoundly moving results in therapy; people's lives were transforming in one or two sessions sometimes. What they were doing was antithetical to what I learned to do, so that makes it extra interesting to me. If I think it's the wrong stuff to do and it's working, that must mean there's something in it for me and I vowed I would figure out what it was and that's why I wrote that *Third Wave*[100] article.

In the Ericksonian tradition we value everything and include it and incorporate it and kind of dissolve it that way. In this tradition, you're putting things out and sort of saying that they're bad. This symptom, this bad thing, is trying to undermine you in your life and tell you you're a terrible person and restrict you, and they have this technique of *externalization*. I was on a five- or six-year quest to try to figure out what the heck they were doing and why it was so opposite of Ericksonian stuff, but it seemed to work.

[99] Michael White (along with David Epston from New Zealand) is known as a co-creator of the narrative approach to pscyhotherapy. He lives and practices in Adelaide, South Australia.

[100] See O'Hanlon, B. (1994).

Externalization: Four Problematic Stories[101]

So, here's the quick results of that research. When people are in symptom-land, they really feel stuck. They usually feel pretty bad about themselves. They go into a devalued sense of selfstate. They feel really stuck, and they feel like they've been repeating the same experience over and over again. The same damn thing over and over again kind of experience. The process of externalization is to move that symptom out there and develop a different relationship to it so the person doesn't feel so dominated by or defined by the symptom. What I've come to is that what that's about is that they never try to externalize experience. Experience is primary to a person, and there's no problem with experience. There's only a problem in two realms—the *viewing* and the *doing* as I've talked about before. In the viewing, there are four problematic stories that people get hung up with, along with the symptoms or the problems.

The first kind of story is the story of *impossibility*. Things can't change. The person gets stuck with that, their family members get stuck with that. Somehow the message is, "This situation is unchangeable or this family is unchangeable." Those stories can come from the clients themselves, the culture at large ("once a codependent, always a codependent; once an alcoholic, always an alcoholic"). They can be from the clients about other family members or intimates, or they can be by treaters or assessors about clients: impossibility stories.

The second kind of story that's problematic are *blaming* stories. Blaming stories are treating bad intentions or bad traits as people. Bad intentions are that this person doesn't really want to get better, they're playing games. You may have heard that once or twice during a staffing. They are trying to control, hurt, defeat or whatever it may be. Bad traits are, "this person *is* bad in one way or another. This kid *is* devious." These stories of blaming can come from the clients themselves about themselves (I'm sick, I'm crazy, I'm bad) or attributed by clients to family members, or therapists, treaters, or assessors can attribute that to the client.

The third kind of problematic story, then, is a story of *invalidation*. "I must be making this up—that I was sexually abused"—you invalidate your own experience. How often have you heard that? "I must be crazy to want to have sex with someone of the same gender. I'm a pervert." People struggle to try to come to terms with that and it invalidates their own experience. They try not to experience it or they think it's bad or wrong or they don't trust their own experience. Again, it comes from clients, family members or treaters or assessors. Psychotherapy, psychiatry, and medicine have a long history of invalidating people: The Freudian idea that women who had to have clitoral stimulation were having immature orgasms. Masters and Johnson came along and said, "They're all clitoral orgasms." A woman who feels she has a vaginal orgasm now? Oops, sorry! Masters and Johnson said there's no such thing. Expert's knowledge

[101] See Figure 9.1, *Problematic Stories*.

PROBLEMATIC STORIES

❖ **Challenge or cast doubt on four kinds of stories about clients or their problems:**

❑ **Impossibility ideas**

Clients or therapists hold ideas that suggest that change in the situation or with a person is impossible.

Example: This is an Axis II, so don't even bother staffing the case.

Example: She'll never change.

Example: Once a bulimic, always a bulimic.

❑ **Blaming ideas**

Clients or therapists blame clients for bad intentions or bad traits.

Example: This client is playing games and doesn't really want to change.

Example: I guess I must cut myself to get attention.

Example: This patient is a narcissist and can't handle any confrontation.

❑ **Invalidation ideas**

Ideas that lead to clients' personal experiences or knowledge being undermined by others (therapists or people in their personal lives).

Example: You mean, you never cried after your father's death?

Example: You're too sensitive.

Example: Just let it go and move on.

❑ **Nonchoice/deterministic ideas**

Ideas that suggest that someone has no choices about what he or she does with his or her body (voluntary actions) or no ability to make any difference in what happens in his or her life.

Example: My other personality cut me.

Example: I was raised in a home where violence was the only way to express anger, so when I get angry, I hit.

Example: If she didn't nag me, I wouldn't hit her.

❖ **Challenge or cast doubt in three ways:**

✱ Transform the story by acknowledging and softening or adding possibility

Validate the current or past problematic points of view but add a twist that softens a bit or adds a sense of possibility.

✱ Find counterevidence

Get the client/family or others to tell you something that doesn't fit with the problematic story.

✱ Find alternative stories or frames to fit the same evidence or facts

Give the facts a more benevolent interpretation.

Figure 9.1

sometimes undermines people's trust in their own perceptions or invalidates their own perceptions and experience.

The fourth problematic story is of *determinism* or *nonaccountability* or non-choice. "You can't help it because you're determined by your genes, your childhood, your developmental process"—whatever it may be. Your other personality makes you do it, somebody else makes you do it, your biochemistry, whatever. It's a story saying, "I'm not accountable for what my body does, *it* gets done to me, *it* gets controlled by the puppet strings of genetics, another person's input, biochemistry. I *have* to shoplift," etc.

In addition to the problematic stories, sometimes people have problematic behaviors, like shoplifting or cutting themselves. My idea about externalization is you externalize a problem or symptom when it involves one of the four kinds of problematic stories or problematic patterns of experience. And you internalize experience and perception, sensory perception, feelings.

Debbie: Can you explain that more?

Bill: Yeah. If a person was cutting themselves, you might externalize cutting but you wouldn't externalize sadness. Sadness is a legitimate internal experience. There's no problem with sadness. There's only a problem when the person gets sad and then says, "I can't stand it. I've got to get rid of this. I'm bad if I feel sad" or "I'm sick or crazy or I'll lose control and fall apart." That's an invalidation or a story of nonaccountability. "I don't have any choice, I have to cut myself." So you might externalize cutting or the stories of intolerability of sadness. And then say, "So, what is cutting telling you when you get sad?" "It tells me that it'll take me away from and save me from feeling sad." "So does it always tell you sadness is intolerable?" You start to investigate the person's relationship with their experiences or when those relationships are troublesome with the problem stories or acting-out or acting-in behavior, then you can externalize that. Externalization just means you talk about the symptom or problem almost as if it's a person or entity, and then that has a relationship with the client. Initially, when you talk to them, typically, their relationship is domineering or undermining. Cutting convinces that you're a bad person, you can't trust yourself. Cutting tells you that you will always have to obey it. It's a domineering or undermining relationship—a deterministic relationship.

So we start this process mimetic where we introduce the crystal seed of, "Guess what, you're not the problem. The problem is out there and you're over here and you have a relationship with the problem." The difficulty that this is trying to deal with is what's sometimes call the "totalizing effect" or the "defining effect." Instead of, "I have bulimia," it's, "I am bulimic." Instead of, "I suffer from schizophrenia," it's "I am schizophrenic." Obviously the person is more than schizophrenic, but sometimes other people forget and they forget that there are any choices outside of what's given to them by schizophrenia. We're just trying to shift the relationship from the person to the problem and free the person from defining themselves or other people experiencing them or defining them as the problem. The motto here is, "The person is never the problem, the problem is the problem." Now in my method and manner I've made a seven-step process for externalizing problems.[102] This is the way I understand things. I think Michael White and David Epston don't appreciate this sort of formulaic simplifying of their rather deep and complex ideas, but that is the way I learn things.

Externalizing Problems

The first step in externalizing problems is to start to talk about it. This is the mimetic and virus part. You're introducing a virus of an idea saying, "You're not the problem, the problem is separate from you." You personify it, you name it, maybe a metaphoric name like "Grizzly Bear" for the temper of a little kid. Start to use the language of externalization. At first the person still uses internalized language, "I am the problem," or "The problem is in me and that part of me really comes out." This isn't a parts model. The problem is over there and you're whole and complete and over here. When Grizzly Bear comes to visit, how do you feel, what do you do, what's it like?

That brings us to the second part, which is to investigate the effects or the influence of the problem on the person or their intimate's life—their family member's life. When the problem comes to visit, how does it effect you? There are several areas to investigate and there are other things you can do. You can bring in sociopolitical ideas—how men have been taught to be men. Most men are living under the influence of that, but some, myself included, have chosen not to live entirely under the influence of it. Sometimes those are unarticulated influences. This step may be used to start to articulate, "How is it that you think that culture has invited you to this problem?" You can introduce cultural and the sociopolitical influences that make them very personal and specific to the symptom or the problem that they have. The secondary effect of this step is you will be using externalized language again and again. Instead of saying, "When you get depressed, how does that affect your self-esteem," you're gonna say, "When depression comes to visit and sit on your back or your lap." That's a different way to talk about it. You're introducing the virus of externalization and as you do that more, at a certain point during the session the person is going to say, "Yeah, last time depression came to visit . . .," and you'll know that the virus has started to crystallize in their experience. They'll start to talk about it as if it's separate from them, and that's when you've got a little opening and in that opening there are possibilities. So the third step, then, is the influence the moments when the person feels power and choice in relationship to the problem. Those are like exceptions in solution-based therapy. When did it go differently?

[102] See Figure 9.2, *Externalizing Problems.*

EXTERNALIZING PROBLEMS

Externalize symptoms and problems and ideas about blame, determinism, and "unchangeable" problem identity ideas. *Motto: The person is never the problem; the problem is the problem.*

Name/personify: Talking to the person or family as if the problem was another person with an identity, will, tactics, and intentions which often have the effect of oppressing, undermining, or dominating the person or the family.
Example: "When Paranoia whispers in your ears, do you always listen?"
Example: "So Depression has moved in with you for the last month?"
Example: "How long has Anorexia been lying to you?"

Find out how the problem has affected the person and others: Finding out how the person has felt dominated or forced by the problem to do or experience things he or she didn't like. Be careful about using causal statements ("makes," "causes," "gets").

Investigate areas of (1) experience, feelings arising from the influence of the problem; (2) tactics or messages the problem uses to convince people of limitations or to discourage people; (3) what actions or habits the problem invites or encourages the person or the family to do; (4) speculations about the intentions of the problem in regard to the person or relationships; (5) preferences or differences in points of view the person has with the problem.
Example: "When has jealousy invited you to do something you regretted later?"
Example: "What kinds of foods does Anorexia try to get you to avoid?"

Find moments when things went better or different in regard to the problem: Finding out about moments of choice or success the person has had in not being dominated or forced by the problem to do or experience things he or she didn't like. Inquire about differences the person has with the problem.
Example: "Tell me about some times when you haven't believed the lies Anorexia has told you."
Example: "How have you stood up to the Temper Tantrum Monster?"

Use these moments of choice or success as a gateway to alternate (hero/valued) stories of identity: Encourage the person or his/her intimates to explain what kind or person they are such that they had those moments of choice or success.
Example: "How do you explain that you are the kind of person who would lodge such a protest against Anorexia's plans for you?"
Example: "What qualities do you think you possess that give you the wherewithal to oppose Depression in that way?"

Find evidence from the person's or family's past that supports the valued story: Finding historical evidence explaining how the person was able to stand up to, defeat or escape from the dominance or oppression of the problem.
Example: "What can you tell me about your past that would help me understand how you've been able to take these steps to stand up to Anorexia so well?"
Example: "Who is a person that knew you as a child who wouldn't be surprised that you've been able to reject Violence as the dominant force in your relationship?"

(continued on next page)

EXTERNALIZING PROBLEMS (continued)

Get them to speculate about a future that comes out of the valued story: Get the person or the family to speculate on what kinds of future developments will result if the path of resisting the problem is continued or expanded.
Example: "As you continue to stand up to Anorexia, what do you think will be different about your future than the future Anorexia had planned for you?"
Example: "As Jan continues to disbelieve the lies that delusions are telling her, how do you think that will affect her relationship with her friends?"

Develop a social sense of the valued story: Find a real or imagined audience for the changes you have been discussing. Enroll the person as an expert consultant on solving/defeating the problem.
Example: "Who could you tell about your development as a member of the Anti-Diet League that could help celebrate your freedom from Unreal Body Images?"
Example: "Are there people who have known you when you are not depressed who could remind you of your accomplishments and that your life is worth living?"

Figure 9.2

They call these *unique outcomes*[103] in their jargon. Erving Goffman[104] was just talking about, "How about a time when it doesn't really fit with the general story about who you are?" That's a unique outcome. Instead of in solution-based therapy when once you got a solution you'd say, "Wow, how did you do that? Do more of that." The solution approach is an action approach saying, do more of what worked and next time you're pulled toward this thing, do more of that. In the externalization approach it's much more of an identity story that we're trying to shift. Once we get that moment of exception or moment of choice or times when it went differently, the door to a new story is opened. A story of identity.

So the question is, "Who are you such that you can take that step? Who are you such that it went differently? What quality do you possess?" Sometimes people can't answer these questions, so you can ask them, "If your best friend were here right now, what would she say about what that says about you as a person?" "She would say that was pretty courageous and I've always been courageous." So you get hero qualities, good qualities, or competence qualities. That's what you're looking for in this step. Then you expand the quality by what they call thickening the story—the alternative story. Thicken the strands of the story to make it have more evidence and it's not just a therapist's clever reframe, because otherwise it doesn't have any credibility for the person or the family. What you need to do is reach back in history and say, "Give me some more examples of that quality showing up in you life." As you get more and more

[103] See White, M., & Epston, D. (1990).

[104] Erving Goffman was an anthropologist who was once described as "the most original anthropologist of his generation." Most of his efforts focused on North American culture as opposed to traditional studies involving remote cultures. He died in 1982.

evidence of that quality being who the person actually is, and this symptomatic stuff being peripheral to the person's identity, even though it may have been domineering for the last thirty years, you really are unearthing or digging out from the rubble their hero or value qualities, and you're finding more evidence that it's always been there. So you historicize it by asking for historical evidence and getting them to tell you about their hero qualities. If they can't do it themselves, ask family members to give you evidence or get them to imagine what the family members might offer that would show hero qualities. And the client starts to think, "That's who I've always been. How'd I get away from that?"

Then you futurize it. Say, "Go into the future and tell me if you continue to act this way what will happen? If you continue to realize this is who you are, what will happen?" Then you socialize it. Spread it in the current social context and maybe imagine a future social context. "Who else could you imagine knowing this story about you, or could you actually bring family members in and have them witness the unfolding of the new story?" Or just have them do an imagination; "What do you thing that your third grade teacher would say if she could hear you talking about the courage that you showed that day?" Or "Your best friend and coworkers—what would they say? Do you think they would be surprised or not to know that about you?" You're starting to have them imagine that the story, if you will, gets into the social context so that other people start to see them in that way. That's how we develop identities both with self-stories and with social stories. People tell us who we are, what kind of people we are. When I was growing up they told me I was the shy, quiet one and it worked until my late twenties. Then I developed a different story, and it took a while for my family members to actually shift their stories. They still saw me as the shy, quiet one. I still have a story about myself that I'm lazy. I do. I occasionally tell that to people and they go, "You're so crazy, you're not lazy!" But it's my story about myself. There's other evidence, but I still have that idea.

So those are the steps to externalization. In order to teach it to myself, I had to learn the metaphors. The first metaphors I learned were violent metaphors, "Kill the fear monster," or "Defeat the fear monster." I didn't like those violent metaphors, so I searched for a bunch of different metaphorical frames in order to talk about this. "When depression gives you misinformation about who you are, that's the spy metaphor," or "When you discovered the truth about who you are." And there's the prison camp one: "Anorexia's put you in a prison camp and sentenced you to die—how did you escape from the prison camp at that moment? How'd you recognize the prison?"

To a certain extent, you could say this is problematic—you're giving so much power to the problem and almost talking as if the person's determined by the problem, so you don't want to get into a story of determinism, so I usually say that the problem suggests to you, tries to fool you, tries to convince you, rather than makes you. I hear the narrative folks use the metaphors of "make" and "caused" quite a bit, but I wouldn't use those metaphors. It's more like suggests, tries to convince you of—more like a verbally abusive spouse is the way I think about it, not physically abusive, verbally coercive. I heard Michael White use one: "How did depression take out a life membership in the club that you belong to?" And "Is there a way to decertify that membership?" There's also, "How did depression recruit you into a depressive lifestyle?" Recruiting, suggesting, coercing, intimidating—those types of words.

Let's do a little practice. Somebody should role play your own stuff or your client's stuff, and I'll interview you using externalization so we can show a little example of this.

Beth: I'll do one of my clients.

Bill: Okay, good.

Beth: I just keep thinking about it and thinking about it. These thoughts jump into my head and they won't go away. They won't stop. They never stop.

Bill: Uh huh.

Beth: Sometimes somebody will say something to me and I just can't stop thinking about it. Then I've got to call them and find out and I worry if they get mad at me. I'm thinking about it for weeks. I'm not sleeping. I'm not eating.

Bill: So the broken-record thoughts keep going around and around. When something happens it's like the record just skips and goes over and over?

Beth: Yeah.

Bill: So in the broken-record, thoughts are with you. What else happens to you—like to your relationships?

Beth: I can't work. I go to work and I can't think about anything but that. I can't sleep.

Bill: So the broken-record thoughts distract you and they call your attention to them rather than work or people you love or are close to or whatever it may be. You're not attending so much when the broken record is on.

Beth: Yeah. I start to think I must be crazy. There must be something wrong with me. Why can't I just stop thinking about this.

Bill: So the broken-record also tells you or invites you to conclude that you're crazy and sick and you won't get over this maybe, too? Okay, and that there's something really wrong with you.

Beth: There's definitely something wrong with me. None of my friends do this, why can't I get over it?

Bill: Right. So the broken-record stuff invites you to compare yourself to other people and say "Ooh, I'm much crazier than they are, I'm weird." That kind of stuff?

Beth: Exactly.

Bill: Okay. What else happens in terms of your daily life that you think that the broken-record starts to play over and over again, that you think is not so great for you.

Beth: When I go to work I like to be able to think about work and I can't because all I think about is call that person, do this, do that. I start thinking about it and I don't do anything else.

Bill: When the volume goes down on the broken-record or it stops skipping, what happens then?

Beth: The volume never goes down.

Bill: The volume never goes down. Sometime, somehow, after a while something's happened with a friend or in some situation and it's replayed over and over in your mind, over and over it comes to visit again. The broken-record. And then either a new broken-record starts, a new tune starts to play, or somehow that one goes away because you're not still thinking of the one eight years ago, you're thinking of the one . . .

Beth: Some of them, I do. They come and go.

Bill: Some of them you do, but some have gone away. You may visit a greatest hits collection from the past—oldies but baddies. There are some that are pretty familiar by now and some that have diminished and gone away. How does that happen?

Beth: Sometimes I can get things to go away if it's something somebody said and I think they don't like me or something; then maybe if I ask them and talk about it it'll go away sometimes.

Bill: Okay. So sometimes checking it out, getting it out of the broken-record in your head and putting it in the actual world and saying, "Is this right?" or, "Are you mad at me?" or whatever it may be. I'm really curious because the broken-record at that point is saying to you, "You're bad, you're crazy. This is your problem, there's something wrong with you." How in the face of that have you been able to find the courage and confidence to go? Some people might give up on themselves and say, "Well it's just my problem and I'm not going to get it to stop. I'm crazy. I give up." Somehow you haven't given up on yourself and you've gotten yourself out of the house and to work even though it's very difficult. It's an annoying situation to go to work and not be able to concentrate. I guess the question is at your clearest moments what would you call that quality that you are able to persist through the really scary or unconfident part to go check that out or to get yourself out of the house? What would you call that quality that you have that keeps you moving through that stuff?

Beth: Some people think I'm stubborn.

Bill: Stubborn. Okay, so this certain stubbornness of not giving up and would you say also a commitment to stopping the broken-record, too? You seem pretty committed to that.

Beth: I want to stop it, the broken-record. Yeah.

Bill: So would you call that a commitment to yourself and feeling good or feeling better? Or would that be too big of a stretch?

Beth: I don't know if I'd do that or not.

Bill: Okay. So it's hard to say at this point. Somehow there's a commitment to, "I've got to get over this, I've got to get through it," but stubbornness comes to your aid at that point. That's when stubbornness can be really, really helpful.

Beth: Right, sometimes it helps me.

Bill: So when you bring stubbornness with you, to get you out of the house or go check it out with somebody, that can sometimes be really helpful.

Beth: Yep.

Bill: When the broken-record just stays with you and tells you what to do, you'd probably stay in bed all day and not go out.

Beth: That's right. That's what I do sometimes. I just stay in bed and I sleep eighteen hours.

Bill: Right. Okay, that's good enough. So you get that sense? There's the exceptions, the moments when it goes differently. And when we're trying to get qualities, valued qualities or a self-report that says, yeah, I do have some wherewithal, some competencies, even if it's stubbornness, it's some competence. I can *do* things and I *do* do things and here's my explanation about why I do those, or other people's explanations. Some people say I'm stubborn." So that's a quality.

Beth: As you were doing that, it felt good to have you bring that to me.

Bill: As a value quality. Sometimes it's helpful and sometimes it's not, and that's fine. Sometimes the metaphor I've heard Michael White use is, "So sometimes you want to have it closer to you and sometimes you want to have stubbornness farther away, because sometimes you want to externalize stubbornness." So I say, "When you bring stubbornness along with you," so it's always *you. You* are the central piece of this. They don't say, "The part of you that's stubborn or the part of you that's the broken-record." It's always *you*—whole and complete. And you can have that quality with you and have it farther away from you. Dominate you or you can get out from under domination.

Beth: Because you make choices about that relationship.

Bill: Make choices. That's exactly, for me, the point of this. As soon as that space happens, there are choices and possibilities that come into that space. If you believe you *are* stubbornness, if you believe you *are* the broken-record, anorexia, schizophrenia, there's no space. No options. You're just dominated by or determined by or controlled by or defined by that. That was the valuable aspect to this approach.

Alice: Is that changing the boundaries? There are inside boundaries and outside boundaries. Instead of the problem being on top of you, you are separating it out, so you have a boundary there.

Bill: You change the spatial relationship and the boundaries. It's almost like there's a roommate that's living with you and he keeps coming into your room and saying, "You jerk, you asshole," and you say, "I'm closing the door." So it is sort of internal-boundary-making in some ways in saying, "You can't do that anymore," and you find the lock for the door or you tell them to stay out and knock first. It is a bit like that, I think. So it isn't like you're throwing it out. That's what I first thought. It was like they're throwing these parts of people out. But it's not like they're throwing parts of people out. The experience is always valued and validated. It's just the stories that sometimes become difficult. Those are like, as Steve Gilligan says, the aliens that come to live with you. You can't get rid of the aliens entirely, although sometimes they diminish.

Beth: The way I learned to talk about it was, "What's your relationship with this externalized thing?" I also learned that they asked you if there was anything positive or good about it. Has the externalized thing helped you? Is it your friend or your foe?

Bill: Right. When would you like to bring it closer to you and when do you need it farther away and when has it dominated you?

Woman: Because if you try to sort of throw it out there they're not gonna throw it out if they need it.

Bill: Exactly! I think that's right. That's what I had some difficulty with at first with the externalization, because it seemed to me that they were suggesting that it had no positive benefit or qualities and that it always had to be thrown out and basically defeated and killed. I think they've modulated that a bit.

Beth: When I learned it they didn't necessarily follow just steps.

Bill: Yeah, they had their own tradition which was nice and they were taking some of that thread and using it but, yeah, when I first heard from Michael White and David Epston, it was much more evil empire.

Paul: One extreme is the throwing it out but what about embracing it? I've sort of used the idea of embracing from Viktor Frankl.[105]

[105] Viktor E. Frankl (1905-1997) was a psychiatrist whose work has been described as the Third Vienna School of Psychotherapy after that of Sigmund Freud and Alfred Adler. He was the developer of Logotherapy, an existential approach to psychotherapy. In part, due to his experience as a survivor of the Holocaust, Frankl wrote extensively on the subject of human beings' searches for meaning.

Bill: Well again, here's the distinction I'm making: embrace the experience and the bodily perception—the physiological perception—the seeing, hearing, smelling, tasting, the feeling of it. Don't necessarily embrace the actions of it or the story of it. The story of it may not be what's right for you or it may not be who you are. It's an externally imposed story. You could say, "Embrace your John Wayne part." Maybe, but perhaps that's a story that doesn't fit for you. It was externally imposed. It's not right for you. You're going to have to live with it, it's an alien presence, it's a roommate that's there. If you live in this culture you're going to hear the voices of what a man is supposed to be like, but is that something you should embrace? Maybe not.

Beth: Or you might want to ask if there are times when you might want to embrace it.

Bill: Exactly. There are times when you want to have it close to you but maybe not take it in as your identity. But is it really part of your identity story? That's the question. If you take it in and embrace it, it's probably going to become part of who you are. Is that what you want or is that not what you want?

Paul: That's why I asked the question. Embracing it is taking the power out of it. If you embrace it you're not fighting it and your energy can be put in other directions.

Bill: To use a different analogy, it's like holding a snake by the back of its head. You may not want to embrace it, but you may want to have a certain kind of relationship with it. Then, when it's time, you may want to get it farther from you. What I'm suggesting is always if it's an experience, embrace it, allow it. If it's a story, it may be like the snake. You may just want to make sure it doesn't bite you; then get a little farther away from it. I think stories can be absolutely undermining in a sense. Like David Whyte said, "Experiences are like you allow it, dissolve it, and it becomes who are." Stories are a different thing. What that experience means is something different.

Lisa: One thing I noticed that you did and I kind of thought about was externalizing the metaphor. You externalized the metaphor of the broken-record versus the thoughts. When I do this, I sometimes have a hard time figuring out what I need to externalize, what would be helpful to externalize. So that's helpful to include that in my thinking about it, that I could do that.

Bill: Yeah, you can do the actual thought or you can do the metaphor.

Lisa: Which was more helpful, it seemed like, because it wasn't so close.

Beth: With this particular client we used obsessions.

Bill: And maybe obsessions would be the word and that would be fine. But broken-record is a more common everyday thing and it depathologizes it a little and doesn't make it quite so heady and heavy. I often use metaphorical work, but it's got to resonate with the person. If it doesn't resonate with the person, I go right back to "obsession" or the particular thought, the "didn't lock the door" thought or the "people don't like me" thought.

There's a lot in this approach. I think it's written in very jargon-filled ways, which is too bad; it's off-putting. The questions I've given you, some of them are a bit complex. What I'd say is if you read some of the original material it's good in some ways and challenging in other ways. The most recent book that's out about it that I know about is called *Narrative Therapy* by *Jill Freedman* and *Gene Combs,*[106] which is a lot more accessible. There are a couple more coming out. *Vicky Dickerson* and *Jeff Zimmerman* also have a book called *If Problems Talked.*[107] That's basically the same set of ideas. There are a few other books about narrative stuff: *Story Revisions*[108] by *Parry* and *Doan* and another one called *Narrative Solutions in Brief Therapy*[109] by *Eron* and *Lund* from upstate New York in the Catskills. They've been doing this work for a long time and have combined MRI, solution-based, and narrative stuff in their work, mostly with children. Again, a lot more accessible, a lot less jargon-filled—a broader definition of narrative.

I think narrative will have a big influence on the field—the idea of narrative and the methods. I'm excited and I'm weary. I'm weary of the jargon and the popular nature, the pop psychology of it. It's going to get popular and overused and also there's something about the shadow stuff. There's something in the black bag for the narrative folks. There's something that's bothersome about it. I've been talking to *Sara Wright,*[110] one of the supervisees, about this. She's saying there is a Jungian thing with throwing out certain things. And I find the political carefulness to be a little too precious for my tastes. I'm a little more irreverent, I guess. It's like being at early feminist meeting—watch what you say because you're in deep shit if you say the wrong thing. Even if your intentions are good, if your language goes slightly off—BOOM—somebody will jam you, and I think in that environment, everyone tenses up a bit. I really recommend that you investigate this stuff. I represent it only in a generalized way and probably not as well as it could be represented because I can't get with any dogma. It just doesn't appeal to me, and this will become dogmatic.

[106] Jill Freedman and Gene Combs are innovators of the narrative approach to psychotherapy. They reside near Chicago, Illinois. See Freedman, J., & Combs, G. (1996).

[107] Vicky Dickerson and Jeff Zimmerman are innovators of the narrative approach to psychotherapy. They practice in Cupertino, California. See Zimmerman, J. L., & Dickerson, V. C. (1996).

[108] Alan Parry and Robert Doan are psychologists in Alberta, Canada, and Edmond, Oklahoma, respectively. They are innovators of the narrative approach to psychotherapy. See Parry, A., & Doan, R. E. (1994).

[109] Joseph Eron and Thomas Lund are directors of the Catskill Family Institute (CFI) in Kingston, New York. Their writings reflect an integrative approach based on ideas of MRI, narrative, solution-focused, collaborative language systems, and reflecting team apporaches. See Eron, J. B., & Lund, T. W. (1996).

[110] Sara Wright, Ph.D. is a psychologist in Minnesota.

Couples Therapy

Megan: I wanted to ask for your thoughts on working with really angry couples or families, but I'm thinking more of a couple of couples that I've had that had an argument just before getting there, just before "getting there." That, to me, is a scary thing.

Bill: I saw Virginia Satir early on in my career and it was really helpful. The most helpful thing was seeing her in person and seeing how big she was. She was a large person and what she did with this couple was she stood up between them (stands up and demonstrates) and would not let them speak to one another. And I thought, "Oh, I thought you were supposed to get them to talk." It was very clear that she was a commanding presence, both emotionally and physically. She was large and she just got so much in the way that they couldn't talk to one another. Then she'd talk to one of them and get them in a different place. She'd talk to the other and get them in a different place; then she'd step aside and facilitate the communication between the two of them. If they started to get into it again, she'd be right in there working with one or the other. I think that's the first model that I had—do not be a bridge until you know they're not going to blame, invalidate, tell stories of impossibility, or stories of nonaccountability. You step in there and you're a filter for those stories. I have more of the spoke model. I'm the hub and I have spokes out there to each of them. They do not communicate with each other right at first, especially if they're volatile. I don't let them use "I" messages with one another. If they talk about him doing this or her doing that, I'll filter it. If she says, "He's just selfish," I'll say, "So you've seen a lot of stuff that gives you the sense that he's just selfish and doesn't care for you." That's acknowledgment with a little possibility in there. "What gives you that sense? Can you give me some descriptions of some things that have happened recently? You said that on the way over here you had an argument. What gave you the sense that he was selfish? What things did he say or do?" To the guy I say, "Just wait a minute, I'm not going to say you're a selfish guy who's incorrigible. I'm just going to hear from her now and I'll give you a chance to say what you think about it in a minute." Then I find it out and elicit from one of the partners a complaint—something they don't like—which is usually mixed with one of those stories that I've talked about: blaming, impossibility, nonaccountability, or invalidation. What I want to do first is work with the one person. Acknowledge their perception and story and feeling in the situation, but filter out the story part and just get a description of it. Keep validating and acknowledging the story part but filter out so I can get a description of what actually happened. "So when he rolled his eyes, you saw that as really putting you down." Rolling the eyes is the description and putting you down is the story—interpretation. I'll quickly move from the complaint to a descriptive, or action complaint. Then I'll quickly move to the future because the solution cannot be in the past for this. Sometimes they don't even agree what happened in the past. Then I'll say in the present and the future what would look like him caring for you and not putting you down? How could he show you that? What language, gestures, voice tones, and the like could he use that would do that, and I ask for a request.

Megan: "But he's told me he'd do that before and he doesn't. I've heard that before."

Bill: "So far he hasn't even done that and you're skeptical that he would even do it. I'm not sure he's heard it in the same way that I'm going to get it across to him. I'm gonna make sure that he hears it and then if he doesn't do it, I'll be here as a witness and handle it the next time he comes in. I'll make sure that he's held accountable for that. If he agrees to do it and doesn't follow through, then I'll make sure that he pays the price. Right now, you wouldn't believe that he would do that, and I'm telling you I'm not so sure he's had the opportunity to do it in a way that invites him compellingly to do it, so I'm gonna work on that now." I get a description from her about what she wants that looks like kindness and not putting down and I turn to him and say, "Okay, she says you did this and this, and she has this idea of why you did it. My guess is you were just upset or hurt or whatever it may be and it's different from her idea that you want to control her, you hate her, or whatever. My guess is you were frustrated at that moment. What she'd like to hear when you're frustrated or hurt is this instead of that. She'd also like you to do this and this—that seems more kind and caring to her." I move from one person and their complaint that's vague, blaming, and unhelpful generally to a specific complaint that one can change and do something about. Acknowledge, acknowledge, acknowledge while I'm doing that and keep opening possibilities. Then move to the other person and negotiate with them, sort of like mediation at that point, "Would you be willing to do this, does this make sense?" If not and he would be willing to do something else, I'd check it out with the other person by asking, "Is that loving and caring and not putting you down?" If not, go back and forth until I find something he's willing to do that would blow her story abut him and would be more of what she wants. Do this same thing with him. The next level is to disrupt the pattern. Solution patterns disrupt problem patterns. Squirt guns, recording things on audio, approaching each other in a different way. When people come in really angry, it's okay as long as you don't get them to communicate with one another, I think that would be a mistake, even though that's how most models of couple's therapy would do it. People want to feel heard and understood at that moment, and they want change to happen. Usually, even if it's facilitated, that's not going to happen when they're left to their own devices. I'm the hub at first and then say, "Now you can turn to each other," or I'll let them go outside of the office and turn to each other. I give them the parameters so they don't blow it.

Alice: I have a couple whom I work with in that manner. They'll be fine until the end of the session, and then they'll start sniping at each other.

Bill: I'd just preempt and predict. "Oh, now we're gonna do the sniping part of the session, huh?"

Alice: I just comment, "Gee, you just can't stand it when things go well."

Bill: I wouldn't say that. That's a story about what it's about. I'd just comment on it, "I noticed this." I don't go beyond that because it gives them this idea like, "Yeah, I guess we can't be too intimate, we need to distance." There may be evidence for that story, it's just not a story I'd inculcate into the context. I'd just note it, acknowledge it, and preempt it. Then say, "What do we need to do to make sure this doesn't happen?" Use a little humor, maybe, to disrupt the session.

So, anything else about those angry couples?

Megan: Once we do this and decide on what's going to be different and decided upon, and they come back and the wife says, "That makes it even worse when he says he's gonna do something and when we come back he hasn't done it."

Bill: I'd say, "What happened? It sounded pretty good in here last time, you said you'd do it, it made sense to you and seemed doable. What happened? How come you didn't do it?" We'll talk from there, "Was it too much to do? Were you too busy? Didn't feel right at the time because you got too pissed off?" I make multiple choices if he doesn't have a clue, which do not include negative choices like, "you don't want this marriage to work." Nothing like that, but choices about common, everyday concerns that might happen. "Do you need to write it down to make sure you do it?" I'll go into other contexts, "If you were at work and you had agreed to do something and didn't do it, how would you get yourself to follow through? What would your coworkers think after a few times of not following through? They probably wouldn't trust you. How would you regain their trust?" I don't assume that they're resistant or don't want to change or are trying to be controlling. I assume common everyday difficulties of misunderstanding, not enough time, and so on.

Somebody asked me a few years ago, "Do you think change happens from what happens in the session or outside the session?" I said, "Yes." (*laughter*) I want to see change in the session, and I want to find out that change happens outside the session as well. I'll make sure that he does something in the session that shows her he is willing to make a change.

Evoking Solutions

Bill: Let's refer to the evoking solutions handout.[111] There are five places to search for solutions. One of them is to ask what happens when the problem ends or starts to end. Ask what happens when they feel the impulse to do the problem but it didn't happen. Ask what happens when the problem gets interrupted or is not as bad. Search for other contexts of competence. The last one is to externalize. You could add, "How come it's not worse," but, it's sort of implied in some of those. "How come it's limited?"

[111] See Figure 9.3, *Evoking Client Solutions and Competence.*

EVOKING CLIENT SOLUTIONS AND COMPETENCE

The idea is not to convince clients that they have solutions and competence but to ask questions and gather information in a way that convinces you and highlights for them that they do.

Ask clients to detail times when they haven't experienced their problems when they expected they would.

❖ Exceptions to the rule of the problem

❖ Interruptions to the pattern

❖ Contexts in which the problem would not occur (e.g., work, in a restaurant, etc.)

Find out what happens as the problem ends or starts to end.

❖ What is the first sign the client can tell the problem is going away or subsiding?

❖ What have the person's friends/family/coworkers, etc., noticed when the problem has subsided or started to subside?

❖ What will the person be doing when their problem has ended or subsided different from what he or she is doing when the problem is happening or present?

❖ Is there anything the person or significant others has noticed that helps the problem subside more quickly?

Find evidence of choice in regard to the problem.

❖ Determine variations in the person's reactions or handling of the problem when it arises. Are there times when he or she is less dominated by it or has a different/better reaction to it or way of handling it than at other times?

❖ Have the person teach you about moments of choice within the problem pattern.

Resurrect or highlight alternate identity stories that don't fit with the view that the person *is* the problem.

❖ Find out from the person (or from his or her intimates) about times when the person has acted in a way that pleasantly surprised them and didn't generally fit with the view that the person is the problem.

❖ Get the person (or intimates) to trace back some evidence from the past that would explain how or why the person has been able to act in a way that doesn't fit with the problem identity.

Search for other contexts of competence.

❖ Find out about areas in the person's life that he or she feels good about, including hobbies, areas of specialized knowledge, or well-developed skills, and what other people would say are the person's best points.

❖ Find out about times when the person or someone he or she knows has faced a similar problem and resolved it in a way that he or she liked.

Ask why the problem isn't worse.

❖ Compared with the worst possible state people or this person could get in, how do they explain that it isn't that severe? This normalizes and gets things in perspective.

❖ Compare this situation with the worst incident and find out if it is less severe. Then track why or how.

Figure 9.3

Debbie: We use "out of control" so much, but I don't know what out of control means.

Bill: I don't orient to out of control. Again, Erickson oriented to people's abilities. He'd note inabilities, but orient to abilities. He'd search for abilities, even dissociative abilities. "You have an ability to dissociate. You have an ability to go into denial." He would think of it as an ability. It's not being used in a way that serves you well now, but it's an ability. So I only orient to people's abilities, solutions, strengths, and possibilities. I notice their limitations and difficulties and orient to abilities. That's where my attention goes.

Sometimes people think you're just supposed to be positive and convince people that they're filled with strengths. That stuff seems like cheerleading and Pollyanna to me. What I want to do is say, "You did that?" They're giving me the evidence. I'm just reporting it back to them saying, "You did that. I didn't just give to you as a clever therapist idea. You did that and I want you to note it." I'm going to give it back to them and it's going to be highlighted and amplified and suggested that they notice it in a particular way. But it's the evidence that they bring from their lives, not the evidence that I'm trying to convince them about. That's the stuff that's most powerful and that's the evocation piece. It's like hypnosis. You're not going to add the therapist's new ideas from the outside. You're going to evoke from the inside. It comes from them and then you give it back in a way that's useful.

Debbie: I had a supervisor who used to say that her approach was to act like Columbo. That was a wonderful image for me that she would just scratch her head and say the words you're saying.

Bill: Right. "I'm wondering about this." "I'm curious about this." "I noticed this and how do you explain that?" You knew he had an idea, but he was so clever about how he approached it.

Chapter 10

Exploring Doorways

This chapter gives a sampling of the individual consultations that are an integral part of the group. All participants had such a consultation, but we haven't included them due to space limitations. After the seminar, many participants report that these consultation experiences were pivotal to coalescing the experience of the seminar.

Individual Consultations

Bill: What I want to do is, one person at a time, do a consultation consisting of, one, three or four things—a hypnotic experience—you can put in that something specific that you would like to resolve or dissolve or examine—so that you can know from the inside what this is like. You could do a nonhypnotic and say, "Here's a personal or professional issue that is the door for me." We could consult about that. We could also do that in terms of certain kinds of cases that maybe you have trouble with—it could also be specific and you may want to talk about a particular case. The point of doing this all together is to not lose the group energy but to keep that going. The second thing is you can observe and notice what the moves are within the supervision process—if we're doing that—and this consultation process. I consider this a one-time consultation that is part of the learning process.

"Paul"

Paul: If I didn't speak up, I probably would be the last one and you'd have to say, "Paul, you haven't gone yet." This morning you talked about David Whyte and going across that bridge. That's kind of what this is all about. This isn't an easy thing for me to do, and I think I have a problem with trust—trusting myself and trusting others. I tend to be kind of an introvert. I've had a lot of training where I work and we did a live supervision. I was panicked up until the time.

When I did the live supervision, it went well, but there doesn't seem to be a carryover effect on that, so the self-doubt can filter in on a regular basis. But I do feel I have the strength. I go to work every day, I keep my feet moving. I do things. Usually by the end of the day I'm quite satisfied with what I've done. But in the morning there's that kind of, "Oh, God!"

Bill: Anticipatory self-doubt.

Paul: Anticipatory self doubt, yeah.

Bill: When you're actually in the experience or afterward, you say, "Hey, this is going okay, I'm doing fine," and looking back it's like, "I did all right."

Paul: I sort of think I hold myself back. When I warm up, and that can take a long time, I have some really good times when I feel quite loose, but there's always that thick passageway to walk through first.

Bill: You'd like to either reduce that distance or the intensity of it or eliminate it altogether.

Paul: Yeah.

Bill: Just be able to move into the experience.

Paul: I've done some trancework. I went to a workshop with Michael Yapko.[112] He did some trancework. He did it for the group and then we did it with one another. It worked and I was able to go into that. But I am somewhat oppositional to it at the same time.

Bill: No you're not.

Paul: Yes I am. (*laughter*)

Bill: Just checking. Okay, you are and you aren't. I'll get you with inclusion! You better watch out!

Paul: Even thinking about this or saying I wanted to do this right away, it's like I'm being spontaneous because I'm thinking what I'm gonna say and making sure I'm saying everything I want to say before I say it. There's a little bit of what Katy was talking about. My mind wanders. I really think I have that splatter vision. Everything like goes out at once and I can lose track, disconnect.

Bill: Okay. I think of one story, maybe more, but probably one story and then we'll do some trance. Or not. You've probably read this, but I think it may come alive in a different way. Audrey Berlin, who worked at my clinic, the Hudson Center, came in as a master's level counseling student. She was pretty bright. She would sit in the staff meetings and after a few weeks or months she would be talking about using hypnosis and doing paradoxical interventions and family

[112]Michael Yapko, Ph.D., has written and taught extensively on the applications of clinical hypnosis, particularly in the area of depression. He resides in Solana, California.

therapy. It was stuff they weren't teaching in her graduate program. She was getting great results and I was thinking, "How did Audrey learn this stuff in two months when it took me two years to even try my first trance?" So I started paying attention to her and asking her about it and asking, "How did you do this?" The story that I heard and the observation that I made is that she would sit in a staffing or read a book that we suggested as part of her training and she would go right from the staff meeting into the next session and say to a client, "I just heard this new technique. EMDR. You want to try it? I just learned it. I don't know what I'm doing," or "I just learned this new technique—hypnosis. I really don't know what I'm doing, but I read a book on it and I heard what to do about your kind of problem because I talked to them in staffing." She would just jump in and do it and I would think, "This is so weird. That is so different from the way I would do it. I would obsess about it, read books about it, go to workshops about it, think about it, self-doubt. I would think I had all these books to read before I could even try it because I didn't know what I was doing. And the books would sit by the side of my bed and I wouldn't get to them because I actually have a life and I'm busy. Then I'd go to more workshops and find out what's in those books I was supposed to be reading because it's easier to get it from workshops for me. Finally, I would someday take the plunge and go for it. Of course, I would learn a whole lot and it would go okay. I wouldn't always succeed, but I'd learn a lot. The client would usually appreciate it and it would go well. That's the Bill O'Hanlon method, the obsess, self-doubt, worry about it, take a long time and then finally try it, maybe. Or maybe just not try it and think I just don't know enough about it yet. After I learned the Audrey Berlin method, I thought, "That one seems to work a little better. Why don't I do the Audrey Berlin way of learning things and just walk over the cable bridge. Just go for it." The fears were so out of proportion to the actual experience that I just thought, "Yeah, of course I've got these fears, worries, and self-doubt and probably the best way to get myself through them is to plunge into it," as you've found. The anticipation is almost always worse than the experience—more anxiety provoking than actually going through it, even when it was something I didn't know well, even when it was a tough situation. Anticipating or avoiding it costs much more energy, time, and anxiety. So I think that you've done the Audrey Berlin method except for the beginning part. You're saying you have some torture beforehand. That's what we'll do something about in this trance, or invite you to do, because you're an oppositional type of guy, so we wouldn't want to say we're gonna DO IT actually. That would be a bad mistake.

Okay, good. You can go into that Michael Yapko kind of place that you go to or have been to and maybe even recall that place, that space, that experience. That's right. And just let yourself be where you are, and, again, not have to do it right. And notice again what changes in your pattern that you've been making this week, that you decided to plunge into experience rather than spend the whole time anticipating and worrying about it—what you were going to say and how you were going to do it. So you can just acknowledge that and note that . . .shift . . . and also be curious how you made that shift, because as you've learned again and again, when you know you need to do something, probably the best way to do it is to go right into action and experience-land rather than anticipation. So you somehow took care of yourself in that way and did that and maybe being away from your usual patterns for a week, it was easier to shift the patterns. And now while you're here I suggest that your body, not just your head, memorizes what that was like and how you did that. How you do that. That moving into experience, out of anticipation. That speaking up rather than holding back. And of course you know what I would say: that you better bring your oppositionality with you all through your life; that it's part of what protects you and balances you; that there's nothing wrong with it or no difficulty with it. You'd better bring your distractions with you into trance. The difficulties. Letting go. Holding on. Whatever that may be. That's part and parcel of the experience. You're already showing some of the behaviors that we talked about that a good trance subject shows. But you don't *have* to show those behaviors, you don't *have* to go into trance. The immobility of the hands. Perhaps you've already noticed some shifts in the experience of your hands. The change in the angle of your head. I can even see the heartbeat moving your head slightly with each beat. Maybe from the carotid artery, maybe from the veins in the back of your neck, maybe in your skull. Shifts in your facial muscles, shifts in your breathing. Other kinds of shifts as you go into your own experience and find your own way into trance perhaps you could have that experience that maybe you had in the Yapko workshop or in other settings, of the little change that can lead to a bigger change. Maybe around those hands and arms. Maybe a slight movement of the thumb or the finger that can lead to a lifting. Hand levitation. Hand lifting. Arm lifting. That kind of movement. And usually when the hands are together, they feel like they're glued together in trance. Not always. And then it's a really interesting process, either watching them go up together, noticing them go up together *or* starting to pull apart a little at a time in that stepwise, autonomic movement, jerky kind of movement way. That's right. A little thumb movement here. A little finger movement there. Maybe you can notice the changes in the hands already. Maybe you haven't noticed the changes in the hands. And for me, it's little spasmodic movements in the upper arm, in the forearm, in the wrist, and the palm, in addition to the finger movements. And which one will lift up first? Or will they have a race since you're an oppositional kind of guy? As you say it. I'm a little skeptical. Sometimes people's hands have a race to see which one goes to the face first, and I always think that's nice because if you're gonna have a race you might as well win either way.

Which one lifts up . . . more? Are they going to continue to move apart? Or move up together? Will only one lift up? As it's lifting, will it lift all the way to your face or just lift a little off your thigh? Will it be floating in midair? And what will you be learning and resolving? What will you be experiencing as it does that? That kind of movement shows to me that you're cooperating with yourself and that you've plunged into experience in a way that you can let that movement happen, that you can really get involved in the experience. Could you have that experience of anticipating the movement and have it be excited anticipation? Or witnessing the movement and have it be excited witnessing rather than anxious anticipation? How much will it go up? Kind of an anxious anticipation. "Hmm. I wonder what this experience will be like." As it continues to unfold, as the hand and arm continue, or hands and arms continue to do what it or they will. So I think it'd be nice to have a curiosity, anticipation. A kind of a not-knowing anticipation, instead of a "I really don't know what's gonna happen," it's "I really don't know what's going to happen." "I wonder what's gonna happen" instead of "I wonder what's gonna happen."

Continuing to lift only as far as it's supposed to lift. Continuing to move only in the way that's right for you. And I think you expressed that oppositionality just perfectly; that one hand has stayed really still and one hand's moving. It's nice to have some resistance and some cooperation; some oppositionality and some compliance at the same time, to integrate all the aspects of your experience and value all the aspects of your experience. It's sort of a compliant oppositionality. Compliant defiance. In control out of control. Heady body. Your body thinking. And how did you make that change when you lived in New York City? You must have trusted yourself so deeply that you were willing to risk it all. I'm sure you had some anticipatory anxiety and you plunged into experience. It seems to have worked out. And when you have a reverence for your intuition and you trust you intuition . . . more and more . . .and deeper and deeper. As your unconscious mind comes up with ways to resolve what you'd like to resolve. Hand lifting even more, or not. Arm lifting even more, or not. Actually it's one of the things that I tell people is one of the few indicators of trance; otherwise trance could be just sort of a role play. But to me, if you tried to hold your hand in such a position deliberately, after a while it would start to be pretty uncomfortable. For some reason, in trance, it just seems to float there in its own way. It'd be very difficult to hold your thumb in that position and not move it much. And that seems to be very characteristic of trance, as well as the stepwise movement, that autonomic, automatic movement. Something shifted for you this week, as you said. And how could you take that shift and really contribute it not only professionally but personally to your life? To find, as Denise said, the circles and the spirals rather than just the angles, right angles, and straight lines. The inclusiveness, rather than have to do it a particular way. How you've done your trance is just right and unique as your fingerprints. Absolutely unique as your fingerprints.

And I hope the experience has been affirming for you and has led to a new level of comfort with yourself.

Now, I think much more could develop over time. I don't know which way the development will turn, how it will unfold. I'd like to invite you to either deliberately or automatically, whatever's right for you, let the hand come to rest on your thigh and complete the process of movement for now, to just come down to rest on your thigh and as that happens, to use that as the cue to complete this particular trance experience. Now you have as much internal subjective time and about a minute or so of external clock time, given the time constraints that we have, to do that. That's right. And when you're ready, the hand can go down on the thigh. That's right. And you can start to re-orient to the present time, present place and when you're ready to come all the way out, you can open your eyes and come all the way back. That's right. Leaving behind in trance what's for trance and bringing out what's for your conscious mind to consider. . . .

All right. Tell me about that.

Paul: The first thing I was feeling, when you were talking at the beginning, was kind of a funny sensation in the back of my head. I could really feel my heart kind of like pounding and I thought I was going to drool. It was very emotional for me because when you talked about that New York thing, I can't talk about that too easily without tearing up a little bit. I could feel my arms going up, but it was like I know it was just happening and I wasn't making it happen.

Bill: Ever had that happen before?

Paul: No. I'm curious. Where was it?

Bill: I'd say right about here. Still touching your thigh a little.

Paul: There were a couple of times when I thought maybe I would come out of the trance or something. I know I didn't know what to do with my hands sometimes. I heard everything you said, I think. I'm not sure. It didn't seem like a long time, maybe five or seven minutes.

Bill: It was a little longer than that. How long would some of you say the trance part was?

Denise: Fifteen.

Bill: Fifteen or twenty? Yeah.

Paul: I just feel real relaxed.

Bill: Uh huh. All right. What questions, comments, observations do all of you have for Paul or for me?

Paul: One other thing. I had pins and needles.

Laurie: Going in or during or . . .?

Paul: Going in I felt a funny feeling in my head like I was floating.

Bill: All right. What else? What'd you see? What'd you hear?

Denise: The hand part was very cool. That's the first time I've seen that. That was very cool to see.

Bill: Why, did it look automatic? How do we know he wasn't just lifting it up?

Denise: You had described that it's more of a jerky sensation. At first I couldn't see very well and I didn't want to move the chair because it squeaks, but then it was like, "Wow! It's out there, it really is moving!" but not quickly.

Beth: It was in sort of a strange position.

Denise: And the twitching in the upper arm prior to the hand moving—you commented about that.

Megan: I was watching your breathing and it seemed fast.

Bill: Yeah, it was fast. You don't have to slow down your breathing to go into trance. Clearly.

Laurie: The first day, when Cindy was here, her breathing was very slow.

Bill: I think it generally is, even when she's not in trance, but I may be wrong about that.

Debbie: Did it feel like a nervous rest trance?

Paul: In the beginning, I could feel my heart beating and it was like when I used to run track. Like anticipation before the race. I think there was some sense of anxiety. After a while, I didn't experience the heart stuff.

You had said something, I think, about the idea of just doing it. It's like once you push the start button you can't turn it off, you don't need to turn it off, but it's a lot of energy wondering whether you should push it or not.

Bill: Yep. That's what you used to do.

All right, what else did you observe? What do all the sessions this week have in common?—the consultations we did, the consultations with clients—what do they have in common so far?

Katy: I think the whole experience is included. That has been more apparent through mine and by watching his. You took everything from the whole week and included that in the experience. That's a lot about inclusion.

Paul: I thought I was really tough at this. I had this saying, "Nobody tells me what to do, not even myself."

Bill: Yeah, Paul, you were a really tough subject. I really struggled. I was wrestling you to the ground to get you into trance.

Alice: You did a lot of permission and including the oppositionality and "that's fine." And a lot of "how will this happen?"

Bill: Yeah, those posthypnotic suggestion kinds of things. How will, when will, what will happen when . . .

Megan: . . . You were weaving the really meaningful stuff into a new direction.

Bill: It is that weaving and that's how it's like poetry to me. It seems to come together in sort of a poetic and organic whole. It seems right and it seems like beyond what my mind is capable of remembering. I couldn't remember it all. If you ask me to recite it, I couldn't, but when I'm in that state, clearly it registers at some level or it's just coming through.

Katy: It's really incredible to watch.

Laurie: That's probably why you have to risk to try because you have to be able to let go and risk that the script will be there.

Bill: That's right. Exactly. You can know some things beforehand, but you can't know everything beforehand or else it will be kind of dry and mundane. It's very sacred. Extremely sacred. It's a sacred space to enter.

"Megan"
Megan: I have to get rid of this anxiety.

Bill: Get rid of it?! No. Embrace it and transform. Well, tell me about it.

Megan: I've been struggling with knowing what to talk about and then I kind of just said well maybe that's what I need to talk about.

Bill: Yes.

Megan: The fear that I don't have something really deep and what it takes.

Bill: What it takes to . . .

Megan: . . . To really do what I love. I don't separate this from life. It is just a part of it and I love it. It's the self-doubt of whether I really have what it takes as a complete person. I know that I'm a great listener. I can listen until those damn cows come home and I love it. I really love that. But then I think, "Well, what do I really have to give back?" The techniques and stuff that I learned can't be it. That's not it. I can do that stuff. Not long ago, somebody said something that was really powerful for me in that it has to go together, I have to have those life experiences. I've got to take care of myself to really be able to give to others. Does that make sense?

Bill: Sure.

Megan: Sometimes I also struggle with I don't have major life stuff. I am a stable person and have always been very stable. Sometimes I think my shit's really not that important and that's why I let myself go to the end of the line. And it's not that I think my life is perfect or great. I deal with that stuff and it's never something that seems that important.

Bill: All right.

Megan: I value other people's little things and I see it in them, but then when it's me I'm like, "Oh, I don't want to talk about myself," you know. I have an emptiness that I get afraid if it's there, even though I know deep down.

Bill: Yeah. Okay.

The first thing is Werner Erhard[113] said something one time that I really liked. He said that there are three layers to people. The top layer is your presentation and what you're putting forth to other people, how you want them to perceive you. The next layer is what the Jungians might call the shadow stuff. It's the antipresentation. Like if I'm full here, I'm empty in the next layer. The layer between. Steve Gilligan was telling this story one time about this guy, a minister, he was treating who has molested a kid and is sent to therapy. He's acknowledged that he's molested a kid and wants to change. He's talking to Steve in this very reasonable way about how could he have done this and he feels so terrible for the family of the child, for his congregation, and he wants to do whatever he can to get over this. Steve's sitting there and just not connecting with him. He's looking at the guy and he's saying to himself, "This guy's so nice and reasonable." And he told me, "I just kept wondering about the ax murderer behind his eyes." That's the antipresentation layer. It's not necessarily what's there, it's what you're afraid is there. There's another layer. What I would say is what's in that other layer is the place from which emptiness and fullness spring. It's the place from which the ax murderer and the kind, gentle minister spring. It's the place that generates all that stuff. Inclusive Self. It's not a place at all, it's more generative space or something like that. That's what I was relating when you were saying, "I'm afraid there's an emptiness there." Tell me more about that because I don't exactly get it. I was trying to make sense of it in that way.

Megan: Maybe I don't exactly get it either.

Bill: So what are you worried about? I can't quite get the worry yet.

Megan: What I'm aware of now is that I worry that there's not something there that I can really pull from that can be used.

Bill: And what's supposed to be there, again?

Megan: I don't know. A deep spirit. I don't know.

Bill: Do you have a shallow spirit?

Megan: Not under there.

Bill: Right. But that's the fear?

Megan: Maybe.

Bill: So, when you were getting emotional, how do you make sense of that?

Megan: It was probably true.

Bill: That that's the fear and that's the experience.

[113] Werner Erhard was the founder of Est. Due in part to massive scrutiny and criticism surrounding his beliefs and teachings, today Erhard remains in hiding.

Megan: Or that I put a lid on that.

Bill: On which?

Megan: When I touch on that deeper part, I put a lid on it, and I don't know quite why I do that.

Bill: Why do you do that? Why would a person do that?

Megan: Because of maybe the doubt that what's in there is important.

Bill: Yeah. It's that word important that seems to keep coming up. In one sense I can get that. I was thinking about myself during one of the breaks and what I want and what's going on in my life is not really all that interesting and important. On another level, it's absolutely fascinating and important and it's my tool for what I do and things like that. At another level, it's profoundly uninteresting. One time Erhard said, "What you want isn't important." I thought, "Well, what is then?" There was something there for me and I thought that's really, really profound, I'm sure, but I don't quite get it; I have a sense there is something there. After all these years, I still am getting only glimpses of it. It seems profound and deep and spiritual and Buddhist to me to know that that's true, that what I want isn't important and I don't quite get it because what else is there? How else would you steer your ship if you didn't know what you wanted in this life? How else would you steer your ship if you didn't attend to what was going on with you and what you were feeling and use that as your rudder and your sensing equipment to make it through life? There was something really important in what he was saying about what you want really isn't important.

Megan: Because you'll be taken there anyway?

Bill: No, it wasn't really that. For me, the glimpse I got was sort of that Mother Teresa, Buddhist sense of, it's all an illusion anyway, so why are you getting wrapped up in what you want; not that you'll be taken there anyway, although that's probably true as well. But that's a different story. It's just more like my friend saying, "You're fucked either way." There's something profoundly liberating if what you want isn't important. There's something profoundly liberating if what's in there isn't really important. It doesn't feel liberating, I understand. I got that. This is great. I love this. So, tell me why it needs to be important.

Megan: It won't be useful to others if it's not.

Bill: Okay.

Megan: I don't like the word mediocre. In fact, I hate that word.

Bill: Excellence or nothing for you, huh?

Megan: And that's hard because on the other hand I fly by the seat of my pants, and those don't go together always. I'm not sure what else to say, just that it's very important to me so I want it to be something significant and useful and I have that fear.

Bill: Yeah, and what if it's not significant? Really, that's what I'm pushing against, a little. What if it's not significant and useful? What would that mean?

Megan: I can barely even go there.

Bill: That's where the juice is, then. That's where the juice is, for me. I don't even know why, but it is. It's quite curious to me.

Megan: Well, that makes me think of a friend of mine who was in the same direction as I, but to me she was very intelligent and she really had it together. I don't see myself like her in that way. She was really doing well. She finished her degree, her profession was very important to her, and then she got married, had a kid and all of that just completely went by the wayside, none of that was important, so she shifted, did a right angle and said, "I was supposed to be a mother. Motherhood is my calling. That is what I have to be good at." I was like, "How did *that* happen?"

Bill: That what she thought was important could change just like that?

Megan: Right, and years later she still hasn't picked it back up.

Bill: So what'd you make of that?

Megan: I contradict myself frequently.

Bill: That's okay. It's inclusive therapy here, so it's okay to contradict yourself. Go for it.

Megan: I feel like I just don't want that to happen. It's such a scam for me but on the other hand life for me is very much about changing my mind when I see something new.

Bill: So what's important about doing the work of a therapist?

Megan: Loving myself first or I won't be of help to anyone else. What's important about it?

Bill: Why do it?

Megan: Because I love it.

Bill: Why bother?

Megan: I can't not. People can get so much change in their lives.

Bill: What's important about changing in their lives?

Megan: That they're looking for it and I'm able to, with them, help them with that.

Bill: And why is that useful and important?

Megan: Because they're searching for it, and if I can help with that it's an amazing thing.

Bill: All right. Let's do trance.

I'd like you to keep your eyes open, if you would. Just start to breathe into it a bit. Let yourself be as comfortable as possible. Tune in or tune out, either way. Let yourself feel your way into trance while you're looking out here. So, it's really something about maintaining a connection with the world and with someone else as well as a connection with yourself at the same time, really inviting you into what Steve Gilligan calls three-point attention where you can attend to what's going on with you, put your attention out in the world and connect with me and be in this context all at the same time. Maybe that's a fourth point of attention in some ways—that's analyzing and thinking about, or maybe that's not there. So, just including all that and the contradictions and the fears and the three layers of who you are; the presentation, the antipresentation and the inclusive self or generative self that comes up with all the self-doubts and fears, the experience or fear of emptiness, that's really the mantra for me: What's important and what's not important. There's a scene in Mel Brooks' movie *''Blazing Saddles''* in which they're about to have a battle. The bad guys are about to swoop down on the town and kill the good guys. They have a preacher with them. The bad guys ask the preacher to bless the battle. The preacher refuses and says that he can't bless the battle, because they're about to go down there and kill people. They put a gun to his head and he agrees to bless the battle. He's a skinny little character actor sitting on a horse. His hands go together and he's shaking because of the gun to his head and says, ''Dear Lord, is what we're about to do here today really important or are we just jerking off?'' I always ask myself that question. ''Is this work that I'm doing really important?'' When I'm doing a counseling session, am I really in there and am I really committed to it? Is it really important work or am I just putting in my time? Is it gonna make a difference for this person or is it just in one ear and out the other ear?'' I just remind myself to go into the place where it is important. Why is it important? Because I say it's important. That's it. In this existential universe, I just choose it to be important and I can imbue it with importance and then it seems to be important. Is it really important? If one looks at it with the ashen eyes of a Buddhist, no and yes. What you do is absolutely unimportant in the large scheme of things and it's absolutely essential in the large scheme of things. Those Buddhists monks learn to look at things with eyes of ash, dispassionate. But their smile is always there, so they're compassionate. So, is what you're doing really important or are you just jerking off? That's the question. It's not necessarily the answer that's important, although you may come to answers. It's really living in that question. And letting that question really inform what you do.

Another thing is sort of harkening back to that. I remember Werner Erhard once talking about the transformation of the organization because it had come to a crisis point. He was going through a lot of worry and angst and doubt about the whole thing and he happened to talk to the lawyer that represented him who wasn't an Est graduate or anything. The lawyer was kind of a cut-through-the-bullshit kind of guy. He said, "The question is, Werner, are you gonna be your petty little self about this or are you gonna rise above it and handle it?" I always think of that when I get worries and doubts. That's like what I was talking to Karen about. You don't get to indulge that when you're doing this work. It doesn't mean you can't feel it, you just don't get to indulge it. To indulge yourself in that. Does Mother Teresa indulge herself in her worries as she's tending to those kids? I would think not. I bet she has worries. I bet she has doubts. There's just no indulgence from what I can see from the outside. So you can live in that question. Is what you're doing really important or are you just jerking off? That's gonna be my mantra question for you. And remember it's gonna be asked with those ashen eyes with the Irish twinkle around them.

Anything else before we complete this particular part of the experience?

Megan: Just that I know that it is important.

Bill: All right. Let's reorient. A little more of that scatter vision rather than focus vision.

Paul: Why did you ask her to keep her eyes open?

Bill: It just seemed intuitively right to me. She was willing.

Megan: I would have gone far away had I not.

Bill: That's the ticket—that's why.

Megan: I wasn't feeling in a trance at all, but my chin was numb.

Bill: Oh, you were in a trance, girl.

Megan: I couldn't even see anybody else.

Bill: They were there. You were in a trance. What else?

Debbie: I wasn't completely sure what you were saying about yourself in the whole exercise but what I thought you were saying was you hadn't had difficult experiences in your life to draw from.

Megan: That's part of it.

Debbie: And I was thinking that throughout this workshop, you have been someone who has enriched the experience for me the most by your comments. Your comments really pull things together and they're very rich. What a contrast that you don't think there's that richness or depth, if that's what you were saying.

Denise: I don't want to call it an existential crisis because it doesn't sound critical, but I really liked that conversation about that there is no answer to it and staying in the question. That really touched me.

Beth: I connected with that, too.

Denise: And *"Blazing Saddles"* is one of my favorite movies.

Megan: For me, this week is much more than the things that you've taught us. It's looking at myself and the spiritual side. That's not something that I usually do. I have gone to things that were a lot of meditation, way over what I can handle and I just cannot relate to that. But this is just where I can feel it.

Bill: The spiritual aspects of Mel Brooks. That's where you can enter, huh? Same here. Every time I try to talk about spirituality it sounds so mundane and pedantic and New Age and it seems to be between the lines here. I think that's right. It's a very spiritual and sacred experience for me and partly why I was behind the idea of this being recorded and studied. I want to know what that is that gets created, what happens for people and how it happens. I'm very curious about it.

Megan: It's not just the sharing, because I've been in those groups before where we share and that is strengthening in itself, but that's not it. That's a wonderful piece of it, but it's something along with that.

Karen: I can completely relate to what you're saying, and it started in the beginning of the week before a lot of the sharing came out. I can't explain it either, but I feel exactly the same way.

"Lisa"

Lisa: It's possible that people admire and respect my work, but that's a new way of thinking for me. It impacts me a lot in my profession and in my relationships. I can't believe my husband still loves me. It's been three years and. . . .

Bill: He hasn't discovered the truth yet?

Lisa: No, he hasn't found out who I really am. I'm just a really good actress. I guess I've convinced everybody. Because I have that thinking or that story about myself, it's hard for me to find my voice a lot of times. I lose it and I don't.

Bill: You know it, but you don't let it out.

Lisa: In fact I'll be sitting here ready to say something and I'll go, "Oh, it's not important. It's not worthwhile, it's not important, it's not useful."

Bill: Like, "Don't say that, don't take up the time."

Lisa: It's like everybody else should have a chance. It's hard for me to make space for me, in this setting and in other settings like my family.

Bill: I've got a couple of questions, though it sounds like you might have more to say.

I agree with what Jennifer said, and I would say it in a slightly different way. How do you think that you came to be in denial about your competence and lovability? How do you explain that that developed? I've just got to stop and say that I'm appointed as spokesman for this group at this particular point. We're all a little surprised to hear that you have this story about yourself, because you don't come across like that and it's a little saddening for me and it's a little upsetting and we want to shake you.

Lisa: I'm being a good actor. I convinced you already.

Bill: All right. I understand about that except be careful, we're all professionals here and we've actually been trained to see beyond the surface of people. We've seen beyond the surface of you, and what we've seen is not what you have as a story about yourself. Yeah, we don't know you as well as we could. We could get in and see all the crap and the stuff, but we already know that. As appointed spokesperson for the group, we're kind of pissed at you for having that view about yourself. We think it's, as Jennifer said, delusional. We think you're in denial about your lovability, likeability, and the contributions that you have to make and it doesn't surprise us one bit that they want you to be associated with this practice, not one bit. It doesn't surprise us that your husband is still in love with you after this many years. It doesn't. Not at all. It's a bit upsetting to hear that that's been the idea that you've had about yourself. Very upsetting, actually. And we won't tolerate it!

Lisa: Is this the Est workshop you were talking about?

Bill: Yeah, this is that.

Lisa: Maybe I needed a kick in the ass. Okay.

Bill: Yeah. It's enough already. It's enough. Enough already.

Lisa: So, what was your question?

Bill: The question was how did the truth about you get obscured for you? It's like there's this wonderful pool there and then there's like metal plates that come and close over the pool so you forget the pool is there and you think, "gosh, I'm in this little room and this dumb person here doesn't have much going and there's this pool, this wonderful grotto" and you think that if people saw this space they'd know that there's all that yucky water down there. But you'd actually open up this space and people would say, "My God, what a wonderful place this is." What's your explanation for how that got obscured or those plates came in there, that you felt you had to hide that wonderfulness?

Lisa: I think it was safer. It was really unsafe.

Bill: Why? What was so scary about it? People might see who you are and say, "Okay, we thought you were okay, but . . .?"

Lisa: It's safer to stay in that place.

Bill: It doesn't look too safe, but . . . safe and not safe. I understand.

Lisa: It feels safer. I don't want to be there, but I am.

Bill: Right, yeah. The second question I have is how do you wrap your mind around things like Jennifer saying they'd like you to be part of this practice? In one way you're a really good actress, but also you know they're very intuitive, smart, sharp people who've had a fair amount of contact with you and heard and seen some of this from you, yet they still seem to want to have you in the practice. How do you explain that? Does that make a dent in that story? You called it a story which I thought was hopeful, that you could actually see that it might not be the truth.

Lisa: I know it's not the truth. It's hard for me to say that. It's the story about me and it's a really unhelpful story. It keeps me very, very stuck.

Bill: Yeah.

Lisa: It really stunts my creativity and all kinds of things.

Bill: Yeah.

Lisa: I keep losing your questions.

Bill: That's fine. You answered it pretty well. I liked that. The third question is, you got your degree, you got married, you had a child, you've pushed through and do this work sometimes in the face of opposition and criticism at your job. This doesn't fit with the picture of the person who would think she's incompetent and not worthwhile in all those ways we were talking about. Let me tell you a story and then you can answer it. Maybe it'll help you remember the question. I had a woman who came to see me who'd been in a very verbally abusive marriage for many years. She came with her husband a couple times. He was a pain in the butt generally and really mean, I thought. I calmed it down a little and they were able to get along a little better, but I didn't really make a difference. A couple of years later he had an affair and left. He'd had affairs before, but this time he left. She was pretty devastated. They'd been married for many years and had several kids together. All her friends got together and gave her a party. She starts to think maybe she was a little delusional about the relationship. She goes on and recovers but is not really excited that it happened that way. All the time in the marriage her husband would say to her, "if your phony feminist friends know how phony you were they wouldn't respect you." He was doing that constantly. So, he's gone, she's moving on with her life. She has to get another job because he's left her with the youngest child who's now twenty but profoundly developmentally and physically disabled and needs full-time care. She loved her old job advocating for women and she gotten a new one as a more general public advocate position which has more salary and better insurance for her child. But this job is much more political and there's more criticism. She does all right for awhile, but then she doesn't really know the politics and people start doing shady maneuvers behind her back and pulling the rug out from under her and she starts to hear the voice of self-doubt. "I really don't know what I'm doing. I'm in over my head here." She starts to make bad decisions, get real shrill and defensive. Things are not working. She comes to see me again and says, "I remember you really helped me when we were here before. You need to help me now. I'm gonna lose my job. My child needs to have insurance. I can't lose my job, plus I'm doing something important. I can really make a difference in this area for a lot of people. Help me!" She goes into trance and says, "I have these negative tapes—I got them from my father when I was growing up—about what it is to be a woman. I got them from society and I got them from my husband. Before, I could keep them." I say, "But now they're full blown." "I'm undermined all the time by these." I said, "Yeah, but you must have had some other tapes, because you went out there and advocated for women even when you were hearing this terrible stuff at home, and you were quite admired and successful in that endeavor. There must be some alternate tapes that pull you through as well as the ones that pull you down." So she smiles, comes out of trance and says, "Yep, I got them." "Well, turn up the volume on those, turn down the volume on the others. What are they?" She said, "Eleanor Roosevelt and Margaret Mead."[114] This was in the 1980s, she was in her late fifties and those were her role models. Margaret Mead was married and divorced three times, got a Ph.D., talked about sex on American television in the 1960s, wrote about sex, and was widely admired and respected as a very expert spokesperson. She was very different from our models of what was allowed for women in those days. Eleanor Roosevelt, in the face of severe criticism, just did what she thought she could do and she had the famous quotation, "No one can make you feel bad without your permission." She was a strong woman who was called ugly, stupid, and manipulative—like Hillary Clinton, but worse. She was hated by a lot of people, admired by others.

So she had these alternative tapes. What're the alternative tapes for you that carry you through, or the alternative story or view?

Lisa: A couple people come to mind in my life that believed in me. My parents believe in me.

Bill: What do you get from that, and what do they say and how come they haven't seen through you yet or seen down into the terrible depths of you? I'm joking with you, of course, because I don't believe that shit, but what do they say to you? What messages did you and do you get from them that are counter to the "I'm not okay" messages?

Lisa: "You have things to offer people. You have things to say that I want to hear. What's your opinion? I'm interested in what you think and what you feel." I feel noticed. And valued.

[114] Margaret Mead (1901–1978) was an American anthropologist who was one of the most famous women of her generation. She was particularly well-known for her views on educational and social issues. She authored or coauthored numerous academic and popular books.

Bill: Who else and what else have you taken in?

Lisa: It was really hard for me to go to graduate school. It was scary. I got accepted to some really good schools and couldn't believe it. I had a professor that cried from a story that I told the first semester about an interaction that I had with a client. I was such a blank slate that all I had was my humanness, my ability to sit with people.

Bill: No tricks or techniques.

Lisa: I had to just fall back on being me, and I told this story about an encounter with a client and it brought this professor that I really admired, who was really real, to tears. That blew my mind! I've held on to that. That's a gem that I keep, a gift that I keep.

Bill: It's in your grace file.

Lisa: He wanted to know what I had to say. That amazed me. It was a special thing for me.

Bill: How come you can let that stuff in, given that story that you've carried around? How do you explain that?

Lisa: Maybe I was able to turn up the volume on a different story. I think I have a different story about me.

Bill: I know it might be a little embarrassing for you today, but can you tell us what you think that different story might be if the other story moved to the side and you were able to have a different story or experience of your life? I know it'll sound to you like bragging and false.

Lisa: Well, that what I have to say is worthwhile and that it's important, creative, and beautiful. That I'm beautiful. That's hard for me to say, but sometimes I have that story. Turn up the volume on that one, I guess.

Bill: You know, it'd be interesting if you discovered that was the truth and not even a story.

Lisa: That'd be quite a gift I could give myself, huh? I'd have to be pretty worthwhile to give myself that gift, wouldn't I?

Bill: No, I think you can do it before you're worthwhile.

Lisa: You do?

Bill: How come you thought you were worthy to be in this group?

Lisa: That's a good question. I wondered about that. I wondered about it all week. I feel so blessed, really, to have been in this group and I learned so much from other people's experiences. I don't know. I'm not sure. Jennifer has been important to me. She said, "Think of the Nike ad: Just do it."

Bill: Yeah.

Lisa: Sometimes, when I can't stop the story, I can say, ''Just do it,'' and that's what helps me to speak in groups, to take risks and say what I think.

Bill: You don't let the story stop you from keeping your feet moving and just doing it.

Lisa: The ''keep your feet moving'' story was really important for me to hear.

Bill: That's one thing. I think it's a really important thing and I think it's what you've done. Then there's the other thing which is if you could remind yourself, at those moments when the story tries to obscure you, undermine you, or tell you something about yourself which I think isn't the truth, of other people who seem to know you pretty well and what they think about you. I'd like you to hold those experiences, not even the story, but those experiences closer to you at those moments when you come up to stepping over the line as we were talking about with Karen. To not only have to force yourself through it despite the fact that you're not worthwhile, incompetent, and bad, terrible and evil and all that stuff but to actually bring that stuff closer to you so that the stepping over the line isn't such a have-to-do-it-despite-the-story. Not the volume on a different story. I'm really talking something different here. I'm talking about experience and trusting your feelings, inner voice, and perceptions. Creativity, as you'd call it. If you could be okay even when you weren't okay, you'd be okay, wouldn't you? It's a bit like that. That's the point. If you could speak about not being okay and be okay with that, it sort of diminishes the not-okayness in some ways. And you did that just now.

Lisa: Thanks. Yeah, just now I was doing that.

Bill: The only trap, and you sort of spoke about it, is to get down on yourself for getting down on yourself. Be careful about that one. It's the only one I worry about in our conversation. I'll get down on you for getting down on yourself, but don't you do that. It's my job. It's our job. You can just be compassionate with yourself even when you're getting down on yourself. All right?

Lisa: Yeah, thank you very much.

Bill: Great! Let's hear what other people have to say, because I was sort of speaking for them. I thought I did on okay job, but they may actually think you're terrible and I may have misrepresented them! (*laughter*)

Alice: I'm just surprised you took such a strong stand.

Bill: Me?

Alice: Yeah.

Bill: Uh huh. She pissed me off. She pissed me right off.

Alice: Well, it wasn't totally inclusive though.

Bill: No. Remember, it's inclusive, except when it's not.

Lisa: At first, I had a shame attack. I literally sat here and had a shame attack. Like, "Oh, God. I've been bad. I'm a bad little girl." Then I snapped myself out of that and said, "I'm getting what the point is." I needed to hear it. I needed it. It kind of shocked me.

Bill: Shock therapy! (*laughter*) Yeah, I thought a little shock therapy was needed.

Beth: It was also tempered with really becoming emotional with her and really feeling with her, at least that's what I saw—that the shock therapy was tempered with being right there with her in it.

Bill: Yeah, we both teared up a few times. Yeah, I didn't want to hold it as story, I wanted to hold it as truth. I didn't say "Well, let's make up a new story about you." That didn't seem right, exactly.

Denise: That feels inclusive. That is inclusive, isn't it?

Bill: Or not, right? I know, it felt inclusive. It felt right to me. I wasn't worried about inclusive therapy at that time, I was with Lisa. Inclusive therapy had to wait in the waiting room.

Carl Jung said, "Learn your theories, learn your techniques and methods, then go into the session, leave them behind and marvel at the unique human being before you." That's what I was doing, what I'm interested in.

Alice: I think that's what you've demonstrated well this week. The flexibility—sometimes trancework is there and sometimes it isn't. Sometimes you include everything and sometimes you say, "No, don't give me that bullshit."

Bill: Yeah. That's what I hope was the cumulative effect of what we did with the clients who came in for consultations and with all of you. It's like it's different each time, but there are threads that run through the whole thing, clearly—values that run through, methods that run through, theory that runs through. It's great. I love it.

Alice: It comes across more here today.

Bill: That's right. That's why I put this at the end of the week because I learned that. First I just said, "Well, the people want to do this, and there are ten people signed up. It's gonna take awhile. We can't get to the rest of the material in the group." Then I realized that this *is* the group, it's the end of the group. It's what we need to do to finish it in some ways, to bring it together. It was such power to go again and again and again through this process. Really powerful.

Paul: The thing that was very powerful for me was that everybody had a different story here but in a lot of ways they were the same story. We're all alike in a lot of ways.

Katy: I noticed that Lisa has really nice language. Like, when she said, "This is the story I have about myself and I recognize it's an unhelpful story." I just really liked that. I'm sure that that's language that you know how to use with clients, too. When it starts coming through when you're not with clients, you know that it's really there.

Debbie: I was in a workshop once where we had to label ourselves with whatever our story was and live with it in the group and introduce ourselves that way. I remember that the leader helped me find this label which was "little lost orphan child," and every time I spoke in the group, I had to use that. That was my story for awhile, and then at some point I was ready to discard it and I had an opportunity at a campfire ritual to do that. Now I feel that the story's integrated, that it's there, a part of me, but it's not the dominant me.

Bill: I've got one for Lisa: "Shameful imposter."

Lisa: I liked what you said about not throwing it away. That's really important to me. I think that's what I struggle with sometimes. Actually, your sister told me to just let it be there and then do something else. You don't have to do that. It's there, but you don't have to do that. You can just let it be there. I was like, "Hmm. That's a choice or a possibility that I hadn't thought of."

Debbie: You can't force change.

Bill: Actually, I think it's part of your charm, to tell you the truth, a certain friendliness, taking care of others. I'm sorry to say that. But it's part of your charm. The self-doubt is part of the charm. It hooks me in a friendly, likable way. It's not great if it's the only story and it dominates one's internal experience. Now you'll have the habits of a lifetime that are really friendly, really nice—nice person habits, as well as your own voice and confidence.

When I was going through my divorce one of my clients said to me, "Wow, this must be really difficult for you." I said, "I'm so unremittingly a nice guy and I feel like not a nice guy. I want to be perceived as a nice guy even if I'm not a nice guy. It's really horrible not to be perceived as a nice guy." She said, "Never doubt that you're a nice guy. It's so clear; you are a nice guy." I was clearly not knowing that I was a nice guy at that time. And I thought, "That's right. I really am. I know that. It's not that I have to have people believe that I'm a nice guy, because I actually *am* a nice guy. Even if they don't see me as that. It's not my true nature that I'm not a nice guy."

Chapter 11

Continuing Possibilities

A final checking in with participants and a sendoff.

What Did You Experience?

Bill: All right. We've got time to go around and find out from people: What was this group about for you? Remember when you thought in the beginning of the week what it was about and what you were here for?

Debbie: I just thought I was gonna learn about your solution-oriented therapy, and I would walk away with an outline and a formula and that didn't happen. I guess what has happened is that I feel it's been more transformative for me. It's been creative stew for me. That's what you offer. And now I'm trying to figure out how I can go forward with the part of me that is my passion and not drag the ball and chain, which is the negative two on the scale of the job. I have to get licensed, but I am afraid I'll lose my spirit if I continue in this job.

Bill: All right, so you really have to find a way to balance that.

I really appreciated it when you brought up that you were in analysis and this woman was sitting with you. I take great pride that you told me that because I think if you went to a solution-focused supervision for a week, the space wouldn't be there for you to say that and feel okay. The space wouldn't have been there for you to say that you were in analysis for this many years and such and such is what the person was doing. That would not be okay. It would be judged and criticized in some way. It seemed perfectly appropriate and okay and wasn't going to be a problem here. That's my critique of formulaic, closed-down ideas and approaches.

Debbie: You had me in this inclusive place.

Bill: I feel great pride in that and greatly critical of the other people who do it wrong! (*laughter*)

Paul: I thought this would be like the next step in learning more about this stuff.

Bill: Advanced solution-based therapy.

Paul: Right. But it was a transformative experience. It was so much more than just the next step and the idea of inclusiveness and not being so caught up on one way of doing things. It was wonderful for me. The other thing for me was, when Lisa was speaking, I wrote down in my pad about how the line between strength and weakness is kind of blurred now. They're both, in a sense, the same. Even though I've gone to the seminary and I'm not a person that goes out and tries to convince people to believe, I thought of a Bible passage which I've never understood. It goes "my strength is made perfect in weakness." In other words, strengths and weaknesses are part of the same thing.

Bill: That's nice. Nice Bible quote, I like it.

Beth: It's going into his file folder. (*laughter*)

Paul: So, it's been wonderful.

Bill: Thanks. Great.

Katy: I remember that I said where I thought I may be stuck was in ending with clients—not ending with clients and kind of hanging on.

Bill: Right.

Katy: I guess I'm not really worried about that anymore. I don't feel like I've gotten the answers to it, but I'm not worried about it. I'm not really worried about anything. So it's sort of been more of an experience than a cognitive thing. Hopefully, over time it will be able to get out of here.

Bill: Maybe a little cognition!

Katy: I know that when I came in, the agency stuff was taking up a lot of my energy and I think I've sort of decided that I can make a choice about how much energy that's gonna take up and I'm gonna decide about that. I think that it's helped me to not close down possibilities like that this job can't be okay because I have this garbage to deal with. I think it's helped in that area and in other areas. Even before I came here I've been thinking about not saying, "Well, I can't do that, I'm not good at that." If I say that, that sets a limit. It's been very helpful. That's what I can say about the week.

Bill: Great. Thanks for making an effort to be here at the last minute.

Katy: I was more than happy.

Bill: Great.

Megan: I'm having a hard time putting your words to the visuals I have. When I got that call about what I expected, I remember I didn't really expect anything.

I just knew that I was pulled here and I wanted to be able to do it a little bit better. I didn't really know what that meant. But definitely what you said is true for me. It hasn't been just learning skills. I'm gonna remember splatter vision, definitely . . . just a very wide picture of more of what it's *all* about and not just about what I'm doing with a client. Much, much bigger picture for me. Another thing I'm thinking of is the movie *Phenomenon*. I don't feel more intelligent, but I feel like a lot of things have been stimulated and things are just more colorful. That's kind of how I'm seeing the world, I guess. One last thing. I feel like with that I'm gonna be a lot better reading a lot of those books, especially your books, because they'll have meaning and they'll have a depth.

Bill: Context. That's nice.

Alice: Um, what they said.

Bill: Ditto?

Alice: Yeah, ditto. For once, I'm speechless. (*laughter*)

Bill: Get me the heart pill! Get that nitroglycerine!

Alice: It's been nice.

Karen: I think I've said this before, but I thought I was getting a little bit more advanced stuff like I'd gotten at the three other brief therapy workshops I've attended. I thought this would be more intense, more advanced. I guess it's those steps and formulas that I expected. This was more of an experience than learning steps, and it's very refreshing and it seems like it's affected me both individually and professionally—the way I'm thinking and the way I'm thinking about working with patients is broader. It's more individualized. In the past few years where I work the focus is on the pathology. The brief therapy stuff is more focusing on strengths and change. This seems broader than that. It's more experience and things are okay and it just feels right. It's refreshing and it's been very enlightening. Reading the books now, it does have more meaning. And the language was a big thing that I'll focus on now a lot more. I think I've learned a lot and I feel good about things. Thank you all. My face is red, but it's okay. (*laughter*)

Bill: And it's okay!

Denise: Actually, it wasn't red before you said that, I don't think. (*laughter*)

Beth: For me, what I came in expecting was being able to put the possibility therapy together with the narrative therapy, and I still think the two can fit very nicely together. And I think I sort of expected it to be more structured than it was, given that I had only been to one of your workshops. But I'm glad that it wasn't. I think I probably learn better in this kind of a situation. The thing I got out of it that I didn't expect to get was I'm probably the only one in the world who didn't know about your books and the solution-oriented therapy, but I got that. It feels like that can fit right in there, too. It all goes right in there and it feels really good. It's giving me a really good direction to take my practice in. It's been wonderful. Thank you.

Denise: I thought I was getting a review. And I didn't realize it was going to be so experiential or I would have been here years ago. I had no clue that it was this experiential. My biggest expectation was that I'd have fun this week and I have! In addition to everything else. It's definitely more than I bargained for and I appreciate it.

Bill: All right.

Lisa: I think I'll know even more later—what I got out of it. But I feel like it's so much richer. I think richer is the word that comes to mind. Before, it was up here. It was really in my head and it was a technique and it felt like there were certain words to memorize and ways to ask questions. It doesn't feel that way to me anymore. It feels very rich and like there's a tremendous use of self in this model, like that's the key to it, use of self and being real. I really wanted that. That's what I believe to be true about being a good therapist—being real and human and with people. It feels more like I'm getting it and I can see the fit of all that. I'm hearing that that's the most important part of what you're saying. So that's really exciting to me. I'm excited to go out and use this more with a richer, deeper understanding of it and of myself.

Returning to the Obvious

Bill: Great. Well, I like these weeks. I don't like to work too much. I prefer to work a few hours a day these days. I worked really hard for twelve or thirteen years, from morning to really late at night. I really enjoyed it, but it was very taxing. I've decided I don't want to work so much, so these are really hard weeks for me because I have to work like forty hours! It's really insane *and* I love what goes on in these weeks. As I said before, I'm totally fascinated with it. I don't know how it happens, precisely. I do trust that it does happen. And I had to give up the structure, which was difficult for me at first. Then I just learned to trust it. I really love what you're saying and what happens. I'm feeling my way, stumbling my way toward this inclusive, possibility therapy. I don't precisely know what it is, and I'm stumbling my way through to that transformational training and clearly the universe has got me in mind for that. I don't know where that will lead. And this has been a really big part of that. What happened here will show up next August in part, my approach. And I really appreciate what you've all brought. I've said that before, and maybe you think I'm just being positive, but I've had some groups with some duds in them, people that were really troublesome and problematic. You all brought your uniqueness and individuality and were willing to take the time and the energy and the vulnerability that you showed. I know that the group and the week opens up, but you didn't have to do that. You didn't have to and you could've talked about something other than what you talked about, and I appreciate the willingness that you all showed. I had a good time this week, laughed a lot, and had fun. That's important, right? We had a really good sense of things in here.

I think you've been going through a transformational process and I think you'll continue to go through it. It's just like trance—you don't know what's gonna show up after this but as I said, many people go through personal transformations after this, personal, big shifts. Don't be surprised if that happens. It doesn't have to happen and obviously the point of the week was in large part to help create a professional transformation. Both of the transformations, I hope, will be in the direction of you valuing who you are and what you're doing much more and realizing who you are and what you're doing. So it's more of a return to the obvious, rather that a going someplace else. Once you return to the obvious, obviously you'll go somewhere else, but I'm really talking about returning to the obvious of who you are.

I hope this week has been a returning to the obvious, a validation of where you are, a strong opening of new possibilities and a broadening, like with the circles and the spirals, rather than the right angles and sharp corners and straight lines; that you've included more than you thought you would, as many people have said. And I suspect that that process continues on in a way that hopefully will be delightful and surprising to you as you go along but will certainly be interesting, I think.

Bill: Okay, let's say good-bye.

All: Good-bye.

Afterword

I've been teaching workshops since 1977 and I've gotten pretty good at them, if I do say so myself. But there has always been something that has bothered me about them. In workshops, due to the limited time available and the general nature of the material, the richness of therapy is diminished in some way, I think. One has to tie things into a neat, well-organized package, whereas therapy itself is more like spilled paint. It doesn't lend itself to neatness or packaging.

One time, early in my career, I almost stopped teaching. I did a workshop in Syracuse, New York. About 125 people attended. Before I left for the airport after the workshop, the sponsor gave me a chance to look at the feedback forms participants had filled out. As I looked through them, most gave me good ratings and positive comments. There was one participant, however, who clearly hadn't liked what I had taught. "Bill O'Hanlon is glib, articulate and shallow," his form had read. (It's amazing what a memory I have for that fifteen years later, isn't it? I certainly couldn't give you any quotes from a positive feedback form from fifteen years ago, let alone three months ago.) I blushed with embarrassment and shame, which on the plane home turned to hurt and anger. "I'm not going to do this anymore," I told myself. "Here I am traveling all over the country, making myself vulnerable, and this is what I get. I can't take it. I quit." By the time I got off the plane, I had gotten a grip on myself and realized that 124 of the participants had not shared the harsh assessment of my teaching or myself. I decided that my passionate mission of spreading these ideas was worth the risk of getting hurt or criticized.

The problem was that I agreed (in part) with my critic. The workshops were shallow. This book goes some distance to correcting that, I think. Due to the nature of books and space limitations, of course, some of the depth of this experience is missing from the book as well. But it's closer to my experience of what therapy is about: the richness, humanity, humor, and messiness of it. I hope the book has communicated this sense of the complexity and flexibility that a phrase like solution-oriented therapy or possibility therapy can't convey.

Bill O'Hanlon
Santa Fe
November 1997

Bibliography of Bill O'Hanlon

Books

(1987). *Shifting contexts: The generation of effective psychotherapy.* New York: Guilford. (Coauthored with Jim Wilk.)

(1987). *Taproots: Underlying principles of Milton Erickson's therapy and hypnosis.* New York: Norton.

(1989). *In search of solutions: A new direction in psychotherapy.* New York: Norton. (Coauthored with Michele Weiner-Davis.)

(1990). *An uncommon casebook: The complete clinical work of Milton H. Erickson.* New York: (Coauthored with Angela Hexum.)

(1992). *Rewriting love stories: Brief marital therapy.* New York: Norton. (Coauthored with Pat Hudson.)

(1992). *Solution-oriented hypnosis: An Ericksonian approach to inner healing.* New York: Norton. (Coauthored with Michael Martin.)

(1993). *A brief guide to brief therapy.* New York: Norton. (Coauthored with Brian Cade.)

(1994). *A field guide to possibility-land: Possibility therapy methods.* Omaha, NE: Possibilities Press. (Coauthored with Sandy Beadle.)

(1995). *Love is a verb: Stop analyzing your relationship and start making it great! [Stop blaming, start loving*—paperback title] New York: Norton. (Coauthored with Pat Hudson.)

(1996). *The handout book: Complete workshop handouts of Bill O'Hanlon, M.S.* Omaha, NE: Possibilities Press. (In Press.)

(1998). *Solution-oriented therapy for chronic and severe mental illness.* New York: Wiley. (Coauthored with Tim Rowan.)

(1998). *Even from a broken web: Brief, respectful solution-oriented therapy for sexual abuse and trauma.* New York: Wiley. (Coauthored with Bob Bertolino.)

(In press). *Evolving possibilities: The Selected papers of Bill O'Hanlon.* Philadelphia, PA: Brunner/Mazel. (Coedited by Steffanie O'Hanlon and Bob Bertolino.)

(In press). *You can't make me!: Successfully parenting the strong-willed child.* Golden, CO: The Love and Logic Press. (Coauthored with Ray Levy.)

Journal Articles

(1982). Splitting and linking: Two generic patterns in Ericksonian therapy. *The Journal of Strategic and Systemic Therapies*, 1, 21—25.

(1982). Strategic pattern intervention: An integration of individual and family systems therapies

based on the work of Milton H. Erickson, M.D. *The Journal of Strategic and Systemic Therapies*, 1, 26–33.
(1983). An annotated Erickson bibliography. *Family Therapy Networker,* 7, 39.
(1983). Paradox reduced: Reply to Jim Warner. *The Underground Railroad*, 4, 3–4.
(1984). Framing interventions in therapy: Deframing and reframing. *The Journal of Strategic and Systemic Therapies*, 3, 1 4.
(1984). Is lying possible in therapy? *The Underground Railroad,* 5, 4–5.
(1984). Permissive vs. authoritarian induction approaches. *The Milton H. Erickson Foundation Newsletter*, 5, 7.
(1984). Uncommon sense in therapy: Milton H. Erickson and Ericksonian therapy. *Assert,* 55, 3– 4.
(1986). Custom reframing: The use of analogies for a change. *The Underground Railroad, 5,* 5–7. (Simultaneously published in Finnish in the *Finnish Journal of Family Therapy.*)
(1990). Debriefing myself: When a brief therapist does long-term work. *Family Therapy Networker,* 14, 48.
(1992). The limits of setting limits on mental health services. *Medical Interface*, *5,* 33–40. (Coauthored with Mark Hubble and Kathy Revell.)
(1992). Theory countertransference. *Dulwich Centre Newsletter*, Spring, 25–30.
(1993). Rewriting love stories. *Family Therapy News*, 9–10. (Coauthored with Pat Hudson.)
(1994). The third wave: The promise of narrative. *Family Therapy Networker.* 18, 18–26, 28–29.
(1996). Case commentary I. Family Therapy Networker. 20, 84–85.

Articles or Chapters in Books

(1985). Frameworks of Milton Erickson's hypnosis and therapy. In J. K. Zeig (Ed.), *Ericksonian psychotherapy: Vol. 1: Structures.* New York: Brunner/Mazel.
(1986). Fragments for a therapeutic autobiography. In D. Efron (Ed.), *Journeys: Expansions of strategic and systemic therapies.* New York: Brunner/Mazel.
(1986). The use of metaphor to treat somatic complaints in therapy. In S. de Shazer (Ed.), *Indirect approaches to therapy.* Rockville, MD: Aspen.
(1988). Psychotherapie Ericksonienne. In J. C. Benoit & J. A. Malarewicz (Eds.), *Dictionnaire clinique des therapies familiales systemiques.* Paris: ESF.
(1988). Solution-oriented therapy: A megatrend in psychotherapy. In J. K. Zeig & S. Lankton (Eds.), *Developing Ericksonian psychotherapy: State of the art.* New York: Brunner/Mazel.
(1989). Solution-oriented hypnosis. In S. Lankton & J. K. Zeig (Eds.), *Extrapolations: Demonstrations of Ericksonian therapy.* New York: Brunner/Mazel.
(1990). A grand unified theory for brief therapy. In J. K. Zeig & S. Gilligan (Eds.), *Brief therapy: Myths, methods and metaphors.* New York: Brunner/Mazel.
(1992). History becomes her story: Collaborative solution-oriented therapy of the aftereffects of sexual abuse. In S. McNamee & K. J. Gergen (Eds.), *Therapy as social construction: Inquiries in social construction.* Newbury Park, CA: Sage.
(1993). Frozen in time: Possibility therapy with adults who were sexually abused as children. In L. VandeCreek, S. Knapp, & T. L. Jackson (Eds.), *Innovations in clinical practice: A source book* (Vol. 12). Sarasota: FL: Professional Resource Press.
(1993). Possibility Therapy: From iatrogenic injury to iatrogenic healing. In S. Gilligan & R. Price (Eds.), *Therapeutic conversations.* New York: Norton.
(1993). Take two people and call them in the morning: Brief solution-oriented treatment of depression. S. Friedman (Ed.), *The new language of change: Constructive collaboration in psychotherapy.* New York: Guilford.
(1994). Co-authoring a love story: Solution-oriented marital therapy. In M. Hoyt (Ed.), *Constructive therapies.* New York: Guilford. (Coauthored with Pat Hudson.)
(In press). Love is a noun (except when it's a verb): A solution-oriented approach to intimacy. In J. Carlson & L. Sperry (Eds.), *The intimate couple.* New York: Brunner/Mazel. (Coauthored with Steffanie O'Hanlon.)

(In press). Possibility therapy: An inclusive, solution-based, collaborative therapy. In M. Hoyt (Ed.), *The handbook of constructive therapies*. New York: Guilford.

Audiotapes

(1991). *Love is a verb: The relationship class*. Omaha, NE: The Hudson Center. (Four audiotapes) (With Pat Hudson)

(1992). *Keep your feet moving: Favorite teaching stories from Bill O'Hanlon*. Omaha, NE: The Hudson Center. (One audiotape)

(1994). *Moving on: Two healing trances for resolving sexual abuse*. Omaha, NE: Possibility Productions. (One audiotape)

(1995). *Frozen in time: Briefer and goal-oriented therapy of sexual abuse*. Omaha, NE: Possibility Productions.

(1996). *Calm beneath the waves: A tape for panic, anxiety, desperation, and hopelessness*. Santa Fe, NM: Possibility Productions.

(1996). *ADHD and solution-oriented therapy: An interview with Dr. Ray Levy by Bill O'Hanlon, M.S.* Santa Fe, NM: Possibility Productions.

(1997). *Beside yourself with comfort: Solution-oriented hypnotic help for pain relief.* Santa Fe, NM: Possibility Productions.

Videotapes

(1994). *Escape from depressoland: Brief therapy with depression*. Omaha, NE: Possibility Productions.

(1998). *I'm not leaving you, just going out for awhile: Solution-oriented therapy with a same sex couple*. Los Angeles, CA: MastersWork.

References

Andersen, T. (Ed.). (1991). *The reflecting team: Dialogues and dialogues about the dialogues.* New York: Norton.

Bandler, R., & Grinder, J. (1975a). *The structure of magic: A book about language and therapy.* Palo Alto, CA: Science and Behavior Books.

Bandler, R., & Grinder, J. (1975b). *Patterns of the hypnotic techniques of Milton H. Erickson, M.D., Volume I.* Capitola, CA: Meta Publications.

Bateson, G., Jackson, D. D., Haley, J., & Weakland, J. (1956). Toward a theory of schizophrenia. *Behavioral Science,* 1, 251–264.

Berman, E. (1996). Letters: Mr. Spock goes to therapy. *Family Therapy Networker,* 20, 7.

Bertolino, R. (1998). *An exploration of change: Investigating the experiences of psychotherapy trainees.* Unpublished doctoral dissertation. St. Louis University.

Chomsky, N. (1957). *Syntactic structures.* The Hague: Mouton.

Chomsky, N. (1965). *Aspects of the theory of syntax.* Cambridge, MA: MIT Press.

Chomsky, N. (1968). *Language and mind.* New York: Harcourt Brace Jovanovich.

de Shazer, S. (1988). *Clues: Investigating solutions in brief therapy.* New York: Norton.

Dolan, Y. M. (1991). *Resolving sexual abuse: Solution-focused therapy and Ericksonian hypnosis for sexual abuse survivors.* New York: Norton.

Freedman, J., & Combs, G. (1996). *Narrative therapy: The social construction of preferred realities.* New York: Norton.

Gergen, K. J. (1991). *The saturated self: Dilemmas of identity on everyday life.* New York: Basic Books.

Gergen, K. J. (1994). *Realities and relationships: Soundings in social construction.* Cambridge, MA: Harvard University Press.

Gilligan, S. (1997). *The courage to love: Principles and practices of self-relations psychotherapy.* New York: Norton.

Grinder, J., & Bandler, R. (1976). *The structure of magic II: A book about communication and change.* Palo Alto, CA: Science and Behavior Books.

Grinder, J., & Bandler, R. (1981). *Trance-formations: Neuro-linguistic programming and the structure of hypnosis.* Moab, UT: Real People Press.

Grinder, J., DeLozier, J., & Bandler, R. (1977). *Patterns of the hypnotic techniques of Milton H. Erickson, M.D., Volume II.* Cupertino, CA: Meta Publications.

Haley, J. (1973). *Uncommon therapy: The psychiatric techniques of Milton H. Erickson, M.D.* New York: Norton.

Hastings, J. M., & Typpo, M. H. (1984). *An elephant in the living room: A reader's guide for helping children of alcoholics.* Minneapolis, MN: Compcare.

Heinlein, R. A. (1961). *Stranger in a strange land.* New York: Putnam.

Kaplan, S., & Kaplan, R. (1994). *The experience of nature: A psychological perspective.* New York: Cambridge University Press.
Korzybski, A. (1933). *Science and sanity* (4th ed.). Lakeville, CN: Non-Aristotelian Library Publishing Company.
Lakoff, G., & Johnson, M. (1980). *Metaphors we live by.* Chicago, IL: University of Illinois Press.
O'Hanlon, B. (1994). The third wave: The promise of narrative. *Family Therapy Networker,* 18, 19–26, 28, 29.
O'Hanlon, B. (1996). Case commentary I. *Family Therapy Networker,* 20, 8, 85.
O'Hanlon, B. (in press). The use of metaphor for treating somatic complaints in psychotherapy. In. S. O'Hanlon & B. Bertolino, (Eds.), Evolving possibilities: The selected papers of Bill O'Hanlon. Philadelphia, PA: Brunner/Mazel.
O'Hanlon, B., & Beadle, S. (1994). *A field guide to Possibility-land: Possibility therapy methods.* Omaha, NE.: Possibility Press.
O'Hanlon, B., & Bertolino, B. (in press). What constitutes an Ericksonian approach? In S. O'Hanlon & B. Bertolino (Eds.), *Evolving possibilities:* The selected papers of Bill O'Hanlon. Philadelphia, PA: Brunner/Mazel.
O'Hanlon, B., & Wilk, J. (1987). *Shifting contexts: The generation of effective psychotherapy.* New York: Guilford.
O'Hanlon, S., & Bertolino, B. (Eds.). (in press). *Evolving possibilities: The selected papers of Bill O'Hanlon.* Philadelphia, PA: Brunner/Mazel.
O'Hanlon, W. H. (1987). *Taproots: Underlying principles of Milton Erickson's therapy and hypnosis.* New York: Norton.
O'Hanlon, W. H. (1988). Solution-oriented therapy: A megatrend in psychotherapy. In J. K. Zeig & S. Lankton (Eds.), *Developing Ericksonian psychotherapy: State of the art.* New York: Brunner/Mazel.
O'Hanlon, W. H., & Martin, M. (1992). *Solution-oriented hypnosis: An Ericksonian approach.* New York: Norton.
O'Hanlon, W. H., & Weiner-Davis, M. (1989). *In search of solutions: A new direction in psychotherapy.* New York: Norton.
Parry, A., & Doan, R. E. (1994). *Story re-visions: Narrative therapy in the postmodern world.* New York: Guilford.
Perls, F. S. (1969). *Gestalt therapy verbatim.* Moab, UT: Real people Press.
Perls, F. S. (1973). *The gestalt approach.* Palo Alto, CA: Science and Behavior Books. (Paperback edition, New York: Bantam, 1976).
Rosen, S. (1982). *My voice will go with you: The teaching tales of Milton H. Erickson.* New York: Norton.
Rossi, E. L. (Ed.). (1980). *The collected papers of Milton H. Erickson on hypnosis* (Volumes I-IV). New York: Irvington.
Rossi, E. L., Ryan, M. O., & Sharp, F. A. (Eds.). (1983a). *Healing in hypnosis: The seminars, workshops, and lectures of Milton H. Erickson* (Volume I). New York: Irvington.
Rossi, E. L., Ryan, M. O., & Sharp, F. A. (Eds.). (1983b). *The seminars, workshops, and lectures of Milton H. Erickson* (Volumes I-IV). New York: Irvington.
Shapiro, F. (1995). *Eye movement desensitization and reprocessing: Basic principles, protocols, and procedures.* New York: Guilford.
von Glasersfeld, E. (1984). An introduction to radical constructivism. In P. Watzlawick (Ed.), *The invented reality: How do we know what we believe we know? Contributions to constructivism.* New York: Norton.
White, M. (1995). *Re-authoring lives: Interviews and essays.* Adelaide, South Australia: Dulwich Centre Publications.
White, M., & Epston, D. (1990). *Narrative means to therapeutic ends.* New York: Norton.
Zimmerman, J. L., & Dickerson, V. C. (1996). *If problems talked: Narrative therapy in action.* New York: Norton.

For Product Safety Concerns and Information please contact our EU representative GPSR@taylorandfrancis.com
Taylor & Francis Verlag GmbH, Kaufingerstraße 24, 80331 München, Germany

www.ingramcontent.com/pod-product-compliance
Ingram Content Group UK Ltd.
Pitfield, Milton Keynes, MK11 3LW, UK
UKHW022001180926
475701UK00003B/144

9781138005068